Meditation Case Studies

Concise Explanations of Phenomena
Encountered on the Spiritual Path

William Bodri

Top Shape Publishing LLC
1135 Terminal Way Suite 209
Reno, NV 89502

ISBN-10: 0-9980764-5-7
ISBN-13: 978-0-9980764-5-4
Library of Congress Control Number: 2017910666

DEDICATION

To aspirants of all spiritual paths who want to know what is happening to them, and why, due to the devoted practice of meditation and other spiritual exercises.

.

CONTENTS

ACKNOWLEDGMENTS

This book would not have been possible without the teachings of Nan Huai-Chin, Meher Baba, Vasubandhu, Swami Muktananda, Swami Vivekananda, Sri Ramana Maharshi, Sadguru Siddaharmeshwar Maharaj, the author of the *Vijnana Bhairava* and Shakyamuni Buddha.

CHAPTER 1
THE MIND-BODY ASPECTS OF MEDITATION PRACTICE

The most primary of spiritual practices is meditation. All over the world people practice meditation in order to calm their thoughts and increase their mental clarity. The clarity of your awareness means what you can notice within your mind. Because meditation improves your mental calmness and clarity, thus sharpening awareness, it is promoted in countless religions to help people police errant thoughts, cut off improper habit energies and purify their consciousness. Because it also improves the circulation of vital energy within your body it can also lead to a greater degree of health and longevity.

The road of spiritual progress ultimately entails tracing the mind (and body) back to its most fundamental energy source that birthed the universe, but in order to make this investigation your consciousness must first become clear. For instance, only after the disturbances upon the surface of a pond settle can you then see through the clear water to reach its very bottom. Meditation is a practice that can help you reach a similar clear mental state free of wandering thought disturbances, but the path to that crystal clarity will be filled with all sorts of disruptions and disturbances as your mind begins to settle. This book, on meditation case studies, will help you interpret these changes.

Because we are essentially mind-body creatures, there are two types of disruptions that will occur to you as you practice meditation.

1

The first type deals with suffering uncomfortable body sensations, and the second type deals with your mind experiencing unwanted thoughts or emotional disturbances. Hence, the disruptions dealing with the body involve sensations due to your nerves and internal energy movements while those dealing with your mind involve thoughts and emotions. On the road of spiritual practice you will experience changes in both of these mind-body aspects.

PHYSICAL EFFECTS

As your mind begins to settle and purify due to meditation practice, the inner vitality of your body will begin to arise, called Qi or prana, and start working its way through the Qi channels (*nadis*) of your body that interpenetrate every millimeter of flesh and bone. This movement of energy, aroused through meditation, will produce all sorts of purification or detoxification reactions. The movement of Qi within your body will start clearing the energy pathways in all of your flesh, thus "burning out obstructions" and "spiritualizing your body." This will produce phenomena such as warmth, itching, shaking, perspiration and so forth because the movement of internal energy inside you will open up Qi channel blockages and thus is actually a detoxification-purification process. This is typically called the "kundalini phenomenon."

The highest result possible from meditation practices is an independent spiritual body – called a subtle body, deva body, deity body, impure illusory body, *sthula deva*, astral body, etheric body, energy body double, will-born body, or *yin shen* - that can go in and out of your physical body at will. If you do not achieve this physical spiritual result, which is one of the first milestones on the pathway to enlightenment (called the "initial fruit"), at the very minimum the benefits of opening your Qi channels, which always happens due to meditation practice, will be greater health and longevity. Therefore meditation is beneficial to your health and longevity even if you don't attain the target of higher stage spiritual accomplishments. For better health and longevity you should always take up the practice of meditation.

Whenever anyone asks why they should meditate or what physical benefits it might bring, better health and longevity are two of the surefire physical benefits that commonly arise due to meditation practice. Meditation can actually help cure some cases of sickness or disease.

MENTAL EFFECTS

In terms of the mental benefits you gain due to meditation, over time the practice of sitting quietly and watching your thoughts will calm mental disturbances and teach you how to control your mind. The meditative practice of watching your thoughts will lead to the ability to ignore common mental disturbances and lay the groundwork for greater powers of concentration.

After undertaking meditation practice for some time, the stream of random thoughts that normally disturb your mind on a daily basis will begin to settle and your mental realm will become clearer as they subside. Over time as the energy pathways within your body tissues are cleared of obstructions due to meditation, your mind will develop a more pristine degree of awareness by which you will be able to move clearly observe and know all the thoughts running around in your mind as they arise.

Rather than get caught up with unhealthy thoughts or emotions and subsequently make errors in your life, you can then know them with detachment rather than entanglement. Therefore because of this independence you can more easily edit what you physically say and do rather than just blindly (and unthinkingly) follow mental or emotional impulses. In other words, a heightened sense of awareness allows you to constantly inspect your mind (be aware of your thoughts, emotions and compulsions) and with that new degree of awareness you can rise above your habit energies and predispositions to transform your behavior. This is how to become a better human being.

This is one of the ways for changing not just your personality but your astrological fortune and fortune, which is achieved by observing your thoughts to spot errant habit energies and cutting them off when they arise instead of following them down a path of wrongdoing without consideration. Everyone needs to create the habit of constantly cutting off mental errors and cultivating virtuous behavior instead. As you do this, not only will your personality and life change, but so will your Qi internal energy.

This is the path taken by Yuan Liao Fan, Benjamin Franklin,

John Climacus and Frank Bettger – as detailed in my book *Move Forward: Powerful Strategies for Creating Better Outcomes in Life* – for they all used mental introspection to change their life in a positive fashion and uplift it to the level of greatness.

THE ULTIMATE GOAL

At the highest level of results, meditation practice can ultimately lead you to what is called spiritual enlightenment, liberation, moksha or union with God. There are many alternative ways of saying this. Spiritual achievements like this entail both a mental result and physical result, namely (1) a highly purified consciousness – the enlightened mind - that is very clear and can know the minds of other beings and, (2) a beautified spiritual body, called a *sambhogakaya* or Reward body in Buddhism, that is progressively attained after the initial deva body is first achieved. To attain these two objectives you must cultivate both your mind and body, both your consciousness and internal Qi energy.

The deva (subtle) body attainment is the first major fruit of the spiritual trail along these lines. Spiritual masters of every tradition attain it, but they will never tell you that they have done so. Buddhism calls this is the "*Srotapanna*" stage of "entering the stream to enlightenment," and it is attained after much spiritual cultivation work. The deepest spiritual practices of religion are actually aimed at helping you attain this achievement. To attain the deva body you need to practice meditation.

Those who become the saints and sages of the world's various religions first practice meditation and other spiritual practices to calm their mind, purify their behavior, cultivate virtue, transform their physical body to rid it of energetic impurities and thereby attain the deva body. After attaining this "initial fruit" of the spiritual path they continue working hard at their spiritual practice until they finally attain complete enlightenment.

CHAPTER 2
MINDFULLY WATCHING THOUGHTS AND USING WISDOM ANALYSIS TO DISSOLVE MENTAL AFFLICTIONS

In our school systems, the sole purpose of education is not just that we acquire knowledge and skills so that we can live an independent life. The additional purpose is that we become *virtuous* people and good citizens. In order to become virtuous we must purify our lower human tendencies that impel us to act in unfortunate ways. Our actions start with our thoughts, so in order to purify our behavior we must first start by purifying thoughts, which means purifying our minds. Doing so means, among other things, getting rid of the mental afflictions that cause us to act improperly.

All societies have rules of proper conduct and behavior that channel how we think and act. Naturally this helps to peacefully regulate society by restricting errant behaviors to some degree. However, if we are totally honest we must admit that the rules of proper conduct in society merely suppress evil and wrongdoing rather than transform people into virtuous citizens.

For sure, moral principles should guide our thoughts and actions. They produce better lives and promote harmony in social interactions. They are necessary for helping us become virtuous human beings. However, to truly become virtuous we must not only refrain from evil thoughts and deeds, cutting them off when we find they have arisen, but must avoid giving birth to them in the first place. We must

5

also push ourselves to actively cultivate positive virtues. In other words, you must support virtue in being born or when it has already arisen and cut off non-virtuous ways after they have appeared. Furthermore, you should *not prevent* virtuous actions from being born and cultivated but should always prevent non-virtuous deeds from initially arising. This is the basic pathway of cultivating virtue.

The admonition to "cultivate virtue" lies at the very heart of religion. All the means you might adopt for becoming a virtuous person have the common ingredient that you must cultivate mental awareness because your deeds – whether virtuous or non-virtuous – are the outcome of your thoughts expressed. If you do not use awareness to police your thoughts, then non-virtuous behavior and eventually wrongdoings will proliferate for yourself and society.

All major religions therefore stipulate that you should follow the path of virtue and good behavior for your own good and society's good. Buddhism, for instance, says that the path of virtue is essentially that you should "do good, don't do evil, let all good arise that hasn't yet risen and don't let any evil arise that has not yet risen." Confucians follow the stipulation that you should not do to others what you would not choose yourself. Christians follow the Golden Rule of reciprocity to "do unto others as you would have them do unto you (treat others as you wish to be treated yourself)." These principles are various ways to codify virtuous behavior.

Christians and Jews also refer to the Ten Commandments for ethical guidance on virtuous conduct. Muslims follow a set of moral stipulations, similar to the Ten Commandments, which come from the 17th chapter, "Al-Israa" (The Night Journey) of the Koran. Islam, the Bahai Faith, Jainism, Sikhism and other religions all have strong codes of virtue, ethics and morality that adherents are urged to follow while the path of Yoga refers to virtuous behavior in terms of the injunctions of *yama* and *niyama*.

In order that we might cultivate virtuous thoughts and deeds, spiritual traditions commonly advise aspirants to take up the mindfulness practice of mental observation. Through the meditative practice of constantly watching your thoughts, called mindfulness or witnessing, we can all cultivate the ability to spot and then cut off non-virtuous tendencies whenever they arise so that they eventually lose their hold on us.

For instance, Christian contemplation instructions (which are similar to meditation teachings) teach people to constantly police their minds to spot various "sins" such as greed, lust and pride so that people don't get entangled in them. When Christians spot any moral infractions in themselves they are supposed to immediately cut them off however they can. Then they are immediately taught to repent and reform.

This practice of cutting off errant tendencies rather than succumbing to them through indulgence requires willpower, but it builds character. Mindfully watching your mind also builds powers of concentration. By doing this over time, every day, an individual can eventually start purifying their behavior because they will gradually abandon negative tendencies and cultivate a higher standard of behavior.

Hinduism talks about negative thoughts, bad behaviors and moral infractions as "karmic hindrances." It too teaches people to transform negative tendencies so as to cultivate better behavior.

The Confucian culture of Asia also strongly emphasizes the importance of self-introspection (mental watching or mindful witnessing practice) in order that people purify their minds and cultivate virtuous behavior. The overall idea is for people to police their mind, recognize errant thoughts when they arise, and use the principles of ethical guidance on whether or not to follow them.

Buddhism instructs that an individual should cultivate their mind, through meditation and other spiritual exercises, so that it is pure from moment to moment. This is not just because a pure mind gives birth to virtuous behavior that is beneficial for self and society, but because as one progresses up the spiritual ladder one's thoughts will become able to affect others. If your thoughts are not virtuous and pure (such as being free of arrogance, greed or ill will) then out of selfishness they might harm others. Additionally, you should also cultivate a pure mind that is free of harm because this is the only type of mentality that can ultimately achieve moksha, liberation, self-realization or enlightenment.

Therefore the major meditation practice in Buddhism is vipassana, which is watching one's mind to cut off evil, bad, non-virtuous or errant thoughts whenever they arise so that they do not turn into improper behavior. This path of always mindfully witnessing your mind and knowing your thoughts – so as to prevent behavioral wrongdoings - is the basic cultivation path of a superior human being.

NEGATIVE THOUGHTS

Normally your mind is continuously populated by chaotic thoughts and feelings as well as good and bad impulses and desires. During the course of an ordinary day thousands of thoughts and desires flit through your brain. Some of these thoughts and inclinations even clash with one another, such as the desire to rebuke someone harshly while you also desire to be kind and spare someone's feelings. This type of clash or mental conflict, as well as the very existence of unwholesome thoughts or tendencies, are a form of affliction that mentally bothers people.

Afflictions constantly defile our minds. They are unwholesome disturbances that cause us to mentally suffer. They are alternatively called *kleshas*, impure thoughts, mental disturbances, mind poisons, negative proclivities, *samskaras*, vices, evils, or bonds and compulsions. They are contrary tendencies, predispositions and habit energies, deeply embedded in our psyche, that do not easily die of themselves. If left unchecked and untamed they can externally manifest as wrongdoings that cause ourselves and others to suffer.

A life of extravagant money, power, status or fame provides fertile opportunity for the growth of indulgent afflictions that can destroy us. As the saying goes, "power corrupts people" so high living with power and money will typically surround people with negative temptations that may ruin lives. A person always must choose between following negative temptations or not, just as they must constantly choose between good and bad or virtue and vice in life. Only mental introspection helps you accomplish this self-restraint, and you can practice this skill through witnessing meditation practice.

Our thinking is always burdened by the presence of unwanted thoughts and desires. Everyone must fight a daily battle with lower impulses and negative intentions. The habit energies of these unwholesome thoughts and negative impulses interfere with our desire to be good and exercise virtue. If impure thoughts and negative intentions predominate in our minds then a person's character and behavior will decline and they will go from being a good human being to a bad one.

To practice virtuous behavior, we must rid ourselves of any errant thoughts that might negatively impel us or color our actions in an unwholesome way. We must transform habit energies and errant thought patterns. If we always let errant thoughts and impulses remain after they arise and become entangled in them because of playing with them, they will slowly take a foothold in our personality and eventually color all that we think, say and do.

For instance, the more we automatically follow negative habit energies the deeper our bad habits will become, so it is important to find some way to purify ourselves of unwholesome thoughts and desires. Neural studies show that every time you follow the same mental path a specific pre-existing pattern is activated that then becomes even more defined. It also becomes easier to activate that same mental circuit a subsequent time too. This means that you continually follow the same negative thought patterns, the bad habit neural pathway will become the unconscious default for your thinking and behavior. Your brain, which just wants to follow the most efficient route, will default to those negative patterns you build through regular entanglement.

Whether we continuously engage in virtue or vice, whether we pursue good or evil actions with intent, this type of ethical choice over time will also definitely produce a karma of happiness or misery. When an individual doesn't purify his mind of these tendencies, however, the negative thought patterns he builds (such as greed, anger, hate or conceit) will persist across several lives and express themselves in negative karma. Only by cleansing our minds and eliminating negative behavioral problems at their root can we avoid future bad destinies.

Our accumulation of thoughts, deeds and habit energies indeed determines our character, fate and destiny. You should therefore desire that your karmic accumulations are mostly positive rather than negative. If you continually follow a non-virtuous road of thought and behavior then your load of negative karma will go on increasing until you eventually find yourself helpless before an onslaught of a bad fortune that controls your destiny. Looking at it from another angle, if you don't correct unwholesome thinking and behavioral tendencies then you will become addicted to error that harms both yourself and others.

Only by practicing mental introspection can we check this progression toward inferior states of bad fortune. Only through spiritual practice, namely the meditation practice of watching our thoughts, can we become emancipated from the pressure of negative impulses and afflictions. Through meditation you can reach a state of mental calm where the volume of wandering thoughts, including negative tendencies, subsides. You can then cultivate a state of mental purity absent of mental afflictions, which are technically referred to as *kleshas* (Chinese: *fan-niao*).

Human psychology is polluted with all sorts of unwholesome mental states (*kleshas*) that have been extensively studied and catalogued by numerous religions. Christianity calls these sins or non-virtuous behaviors. Confucianism calls them desires. Hinduism also calls them *samskaras* (karmic impulses and mental dispositions) while Buddhism calls them afflictions. Buddhism in particular studies the *kleshas*, or afflictions, that commonly plague the mind. When you inspect your mind-stream and differentiate the afflictive thoughts and emotions that arise, Buddhism calls this Abhidharma analysis.

Enlightened Buddhist masters of the past have carefully observed and analyzed all the different types of thoughts and emotions that typically occupy consciousness. For instance, according to one schema in Abhidharma teachings there are fifty-one mental factors that commonly populate the mind. These fifty-one mental events can be partitioned into virtuous, neutral and non-virtuous mental factors, and are also referred to as bonds and compulsions.

Some of the non-virtuous mental factors are considered fundamental *root afflictions* while others are accompanying afflictions. For instance, the "six root unwholesome factors" include anger, desire, ignorance, pride/conceit, doubt and wrong views. There are also twenty "secondary unwholesome factors" afflicting consciousness that are built upon these six basic afflictions.

These various mental factors fully penetrate your consciousness and continuously affect how you think and react. An ignorant person – especially someone who does not meditate – usually cannot clearly see them in his mind-stream and therefore blindly follows them, whether for good or bad, as habitual impulses. The negative ones contaminate his mind and behavior while the positive ones tend to uplift him. Disentangling oneself from recurring negative mental states is therefore important for the spiritual path but they cannot be cut off within one stroke. They must be slowly dissolved away over time using effort, and the best or most efficient method usually involves meditation practice.

According to Abhidharma analysis of the mind-stream the secondary unwholesome factors that commonly afflict consciousness, and which be slowly cut-off or purified over time, include the following emotions or character traits:

- *krodha* - rage, fury, wrath
- *upanaha* - resentment, enmity, rancor, bitterness, refusing to let go of thoughts of anger/harm
- *mraksa* - concealment, fraudulence, deceit
- *pradasa* - spitefulness, spite (vindictiveness related to anger and resentment), maliciousness, animosity
- *irshya* - envy, jealousy
- *matsarya* - stinginess, miserliness
- *maya* - pretension, duplicity, fraudulence, deceitfulness, deception, faking, feigning good qualities one does not possess, dissimulation
- *sathya* - hypocrisy, deceitful demonstration of false virtues, concealment of shortcomings, hiding one's faults
- *mada* – haughtiness, excessive pride or vanity, smugness, a puffed up mind, mental inflation, conceit, arrogance
- *vihimsa* - maliciousness, harmfulness, hostility, cruelty
- *ahrikya* - shamelessness (non-shame), lack of self-respect (not to be ashamed in front of oneself to give rise to *kleshas* and do wrong)
- *anapatrapya* - absence of propriety, lack of respect for others (not ashamed-embarrassed to do harm when considering others), inconsiderateness (inconsideration for others), disregard, lack of dread of blame, lack of conscience
- *styana* - mental dullness, foggymindedness (fogginess), torpid-mindedness, muddle-headedness, mental lethargy
- *auddhatya* - restlessness, unpeacefulness of mind, mental excitedness, mental disquiet, agitation
- *asraddhya* - lack of faith (faithlessness) or trust, disbelief, non-conviction, lack of confidence in, non-wish for virtue
- *kausidya* - laziness, slothfulness
- *pramada* - carelessness, heedlessness, negligence, non-conscientiousness, not-guarding of the mind against afflictions
- *musitasmrtita* - forgetfulness, an unclear mind that is forgetful (often with respect to virtue), loss of mindfulness

- *asamprajanya* - non-introspection (unknowing engagement in activities), inattention, non-alertness, lack of discernment
- *viksepa* - distraction prone, mental wandering (so as to be unable to remain in one-pointedness), scatter-mindedness, a dispersed mind, desultoriness

These unwholesome mental factors are like constantly running meta-programs that sometimes grab a hold of your consciousness, so they need to be purified on the path of spiritual cultivation. If they become personality flaws, then they will affect all that you think, say and do. Because the spiritual path involves becoming a better person who cultivates virtue, in addition to purifying your mind, it is necessary to work on yourself to get rid of such faults and vexations.

Consider this. If you had a lousy personality that caused harm to yourself and others, but due to spiritual cultivation work obtained an immortal body with the power to affect other people's thoughts, would it be likely for you to always do good or would you possibly harm others at times with your powers? Whatever you choose to do with your powers would depend upon your thoughts and personality, namely your *kleshas*. You can perform evil/wrong deeds because you are bothered by *kleshas* or because you simply are an evil person. Therefore they must be eliminated.

The Buddhas will not help evil people become enlightened, where the first stage is attaining a subtle body that can live for hundreds of years (and affect people's thoughts), and therefore tell people to cultivate virtue. To do so they must rid themselves of *kleshas* and various mental afflictions that might cause them to go astray and cause harm. This is why these lists are useful, and why you need to cultivate your mind and behavior on the spiritual trail. The teachings of Yuan Liao Fan, Benjamin Franklin, and Frank Bettger show how to create a method of monitoring your thoughts so as to reduce or eliminate faults and become more virtuous.

Another Buddhist Abhidharma system identifies 108 mental defilements, afflictions or *kleshas*. This extended basic list, with the addition of several others, proceeds as follows:

abuse
aggression
ambition
anger
arrogance
baseness
blasphemy
calculation
callousness
capriciousness (unaccountable
changes of mood or behavior)
censoriousness (being severely
critical of others)
conceitedness
contempt
cruelty
cursing
debasement
deceit
deception
delusion
derision
desire for fame
dipsomania (alcoholism
characterized by intermittent
bouts of craving)
discord
disrespect
disrespectfulness
dissatisfaction
dogmatism
dominance
eagerness for power
effrontery (insolent or
impertinent behavior)
egoism
enviousness
envy
excessiveness

faithlessness
falseness
furtiveness
gambling
garrulity (tediously talking
about trivial matters)
gluttony
greed
greed for money
grudge
hardheartedness
hatred
haughtiness
high-handedness
hostility
humiliation
hurt
hypocrisy
ignorance
imperiousness (assuming
power or authority without
justification)
imposture (pretending to be
someone else in order to
deceive)
impudence
inattentiveness
indifference
ingratitude
insatiability
insidiousness
intolerance
intransigence (unwillingness to
change one's views or to agree
about something)
irresponsibility
jealousy
know-it-all
lack of comprehension

lecherousness
lying
malignancy
manipulation
masochism
mercilessness
negativity
obsession
obstinacy
oppression
ostentatious
pessimism
prejudice
presumption
pretense
pride
prodigality (spending money
or using resources freely and
recklessly)
quarrelsomeness
rage
rapacity (being aggressively
greedy or grasping)
ridicule
sadism
sarcasm
seduction
self-denial
self-hatred
sexual lust
shamelessness
stinginess
stubbornness
torment
tyranny
unkindness
unruliness
unyielding
vanity

vindictiveness
violence
violent temper
voluptuousness
wrath
belittlement
deviousness
discontent
laziness
lust for domination
lust for power
unfriendliness

This list exposes many different kinds of *klesha* mental troubles that are certainly annoying, definitely troublesome and even dangerous if they take hold of your psyche. You don't want these negative behaviors to solidify into regular patterns. They not only produce personal emotional distress but can end up hurting others and are a type of wrongdoing, even when unexpressed, that defile a clear mental state.

You should think of the *kleshas* as errant impulses that stain the purity of your mind and behavior. They should certainly be eliminated not just because they are a nuisance affliction but because they can entangle the mind in wrongdoing. If we don't attempt to purify them, another danger is that we can slowly become emotionally null to their existence, and a further development is that you become more corrupt, egotistical or evil over time.

Wrong always starts from a bit of affliction in the mind. Because our behavior is linked to our internal afflictions – because our actions are our thoughts expressed - *kleshas* can easily lead to temporal wrongdoing. The road of spirituality entails untangling your thought-stream and behavior from the grip of afflictions because of the polluting harm they can cause. Its purpose is to purify both your inward mind and outward behavior, and we can only do so by freeing ourselves of these afflictions. This is actually the fundamental basis of spiritual practice.

When people with great power have mental afflictions they can cause great harm to society. If someone were therefore to attain enlightenment, where they could affect the minds of millions of people with their own thoughts, and yet they still harbored afflictions as habitual mental patterns, they might cause immeasurable harm to society. This is another reason why you must purify afflictions.

In order to carry out great vows and aspirations, we must make the mental activities by which we carry them out pure. If we want to arrive at enlightenment, which is realizing the true nature of our mind, we can only do so by examining ourselves every moment, through mindfulness of thoughts, to see whether there is the slightest bit of affliction. By eliminating afflictions we can eventually create a pure mental realm that can eventually manifest the empty pure nature of consciousness.

In some spiritual traditions, afflictions in the mind are is considered a serious breach of spiritual discipline since they represent

15

internal (and possibly external) wrongdoing. We must find a way to eliminate afflictions from the mind-stream forever and thereby free ourselves of negative impulses that might motivate improper behavior. The good news is that even the most intractable of these one hundred plus *kleshas*, even though they are ingrained compulsions, can be eliminated through meditation practice. Supplemental assists can and should be used to help in this effort.

The key point is that meditation and other spiritual practices are not just about cultivating your body's Qi to attain higher spiritual bodies but about eliminating afflictions that plague the mind and behavior so that they can become pure with the highest intentions. You might achieve an independent spiritual body but if your thoughts and behavior are still bad then you will be nothing but an asshole who uses people or hurts them. However, even with the best of intentions we will still find errors in our behavior for there is no such thing as a sun without sunspots. Nevertheless we must cultivate the meditative mindfulness of inner watching (witnessing) to eliminate afflictions that might negatively color our thoughts and actions. This is a basic practice common to most spiritual traditions and is one of the main purposes of meditation practice.

This is why one must begin to practice witnessing-cessation meditation practice (which is also called *chih-guan*, calming-contemplation meditation practice or stopping-observation meditation) for this meditation practice will help eliminate afflictions over time. We should also use other methods, such as wise analysis of our thoughts, to also help undo these negative tendencies.

The goal of meditation is to create a mind-stream that is pure from moment to moment. Even if afflictions continue to arise, which they always will, the proper road of spiritual practice is that we loosen their hold on us and refuse to act on them when they do arise. We must learn how to ignore their impulses so that they don't give birth to further mental afflictions and improper behaviors that produce unfortunate consequences. Even if they do arise, you must know how to cut off their hold on your mind and behavior.

As a type of spiritual practice you must definitely go through this list of mental *kleshas* and first identify which of these problems commonly afflict you the most. After going through this list you should note the top ten or more *kleshas* that commonly afflict your mind.

Using the mindfulness monitoring strategies of Yuan Liao Fan, Benjamin Franklin and Frank Bettger as detailed in *Move Forward: Powerful Strategies for Creating Better Outcomes in Life*, one should thereafter, as a daily spiritual practice, continually shine awareness on your thoughts and actions in order to cut off the predominant habitual *kleshas* of your mind. Work on the most predominant or bothersome ones first. You should give special consideration to those on this list (or other negative habit energies and character traits) that you might particularly wish to change.

This is a superior type of mental practice for cleansing the mind and behavior that will even lead you to changing your fate and fortune. People actually want to transform their mind and behavior into a more perfect vehicle of purity.

You need only note that two of the most popular Bible verses looked up on the internet, derived after analyzing hundreds of millions of Biblical verse searches, to see that people are most interested in the right way to use their minds. These are (*Philippians 4:8*) "Finally, brothers and sisters, whatever is true, whatever is noble, whatever is right, whatever is pure, whatever is lovely, whatever is admirable—if anything is excellent or praiseworthy—think about such things" and (*Romans 12:2*) "Do not conform to the pattern of this world, but be transformed by the renewing of your mind. Then you will be able to test and approve what God's will is—his good, pleasing, and perfect will."

HOW TO ELIMINATE THE *KLESHAS*

The question now is how to deal with *kleshas, samskaras* or impure thoughts if we want a road for purifying our mind and behavior. How do you become free from the bondage of *kleshas*, impure thoughts, unwholesome karmic impulses, mental and emotional afflictions or negative tendencies and the bad behavior they produce?

Should we try to cut them off so that they are completely eliminated? Or, should we just wait until they pass away and refuse to act on them in the meantime? Should we try to uplift them by transforming them into their highest possible harmonic? Should we try to negate them without offering a more positive substitution? Should we try to transform negative thoughts into positive ones?

Should we analyze them in the attempt to disperse them through wisdom and understanding?

All these remedies have pros and cons. Along these lines, here are some principles you should consider.

REMEDIES

When impure thoughts appear one of the most powerful strategies for countering them is to give rise to feelings of remorse and repentance for those negative inclinations. This will serve as a type of antidote against their hold. You should also deliberately recall with disapproval past incidents of the afflicting *klesha* and reflect on those situations with a remorseful heart. By deliberately recalling, with intense remorse and disapproval, past unfortunate incidents that the *kleshas* caused (such as prior manifestations of greed, anger and lust) this can help you break free of their pull. This is a positive step toward purifying your mind and behavior.

This type of wisdom analysis is a powerful way to unravel the hold that non-virtuous tendencies have upon your mind. It is the path of eliminating *kleshas* by proper knowledge and discrimination, namely by analyzing why they are improper and what harm they might cause so that you create a strong motivation to abandon them.

If you mentally review any harm or wrong that you have previously caused due to your *kleshas*, this type of introspective awareness will help to consume those tendencies. The fire of wisdom analysis burns them away. Therefore, by mentally analyzing your *kleshas* using reason, wisdom, knowledge and understanding you can slowly cut off these mental knots and compulsions.

In Buddhism the sword of Manjushri symbolizes the practice of cutting through the afflictive bonds and compulsions of the mind. While the most typical form of meditation practice simply shines light on the mind until they die down (you observe thoughts without acting on them until the mind reaches quiet "cessation") and refuses entanglement with whatever thoughts arise, wisdom analysis uses discriminative reasoning to help unravel the knots of afflictions at their root. This analysis technique is more difficult than just watching thoughts passively because it involves more mental engagement, but it produces a better and more long-lasting result when successful.

Therefore, in terms of meditation techniques you have the

standard road of simply watching your thoughts with mindfulness and not acting on them. This is insight meditation practice, which is also called vipassana or mental observation practice. Sometimes it is called introspection, mental watching or witnessing.

You also have another road of mentally analyzing thought *kleshas* through meditative contemplation. The hope here is that your mental analysis can eventually lead to the destruction of their root causes so that they never arise again. This is "contemplation" or wisdom analysis rather than simply witnessing or observing thoughts.

Both of these roads can be used to help purify your mind-stream to eliminate *kleshas*. The road of wisdom ("prajna") analysis is to be considered the superior one of these two.

To purify your mind and behavior through meditation, the first rule is to never let the *kleshas* take hold of your mind in the first place and then manifest through your speech and action. Even if you cannot prevent *kleshas* from arising in your mind - such as thoughts of anger, greed or hatred - you can and should always prevent the *kleshas* from being translated into material actions such as words or actions. This will prevent the creation of unwholesome karma.

Therefore never let any *kleshas* sprout into overt speech or behavior. If they remain at the level of thought because you cannot banish them then so be it, but never act on them. Your actions are your thoughts expressed, so you must refrain from fulfilling negative *kleshas* and base inclinations through outward action. This is a positive step towards purifying your behavior.

Whenever *kleshas* arise in your mind but you deny them their expression, they will simply remain in the mind without the power to affect the world. If you take the further step of submitting them to the intensity of the fire of contemplation concerning why they arise and what harm they can cause, the seeds of those desires will be consumed.

Tendencies do not go away by themselves but you can help uproot them through the mental practice of repulsion, rules of behavior to break old habits, or by rational wise thinking. In addition to rational wisdom analysis (prajna discrimination), you should also work on developing countertendency strategies and use other types of assistance to resist their pull.

Contemplative analysis – analyzing negative *kleshas* that arise in the mind without acting on them – is the work of dissolving them through the power of discriminative analysis, or wisdom reasoning. You can call this wise reasoning, analysis, discrimination or prajna wisdom for short. It is a powerful form of spiritual practice that everyone should employ.

Another powerful method is the sublimation technique of replacing the *kleshas* of lower inclinations with higher values. This approach, which is similar to the "Swish Technique" of NLP (neurolinguistic programming) that replaces an unfavorable emotion or behavior with a more useful one, has the benefit of engaging your mind with an active interest in virtuous striving. This sort of active engagement helps with the struggle because it brings about a sense of fulfillment whenever you succeed at simply applying the technique. It gives you a positive feeling of doing something about your problem.

In order to rise above the *kleshas* we can try many methods to purify our mind and behavior. Impure thoughts will always occasionally arise in the mind for it is the nature of the mind that they naturally will appear. However, we must learn how to rise above any of the baser instincts that appear and renounce what is harmful or unwholesome for what is better.

The problem is that we are tightly bound to these tendencies, and they are strongly intertwined with our mind-stream. Some *kleshas* can be kept in check through the practice of proper living via standard rules of conduct. This is the general rule used for managing society: teach people rules of good behavior or societal norms and expect them to keep to these standards. The most intractable and ingrained *kleshas*, however, must be eliminated through the intensive practice of introspective meditation. If they have become habitual compulsions these deep-seated habit energies will be among the hardest *kleshas* to purify, and meditation is the means to help do so.

There are two principles you should remember regarding the struggle involved with defeating afflictions. First, you should never mortify yourself through the self-condemnation of physical punishment when *kleshas* arise, such as was the case with Medieval supplicants who would whip themselves for "sins," wrong doing or incorrect thinking. Abusing your body in any way (such as by misinterpreting the Biblical phrase that you should "pluck out an eye if it offends you" and doing so) is not the way to handle *kleshas* that turn into actions. After a deed is done you should work on changing yourself rather than berating or punishing yourself.

Kleshas are always arising within us, and we are not to be berated for any negative or impure thoughts that automatically, spontaneously arise. Their appearance is natural and following them into external behavior is the problem. The mind makes snap judgments on many things in life without our slightest effort. Not a day goes by where we don't act automatically in some way. It is therefore what we do when *kleshas* manifest that matters, for how we ultimately act is what we should be judged rather than what automatically arises in the mind. All sorts of crazy stuff naturally arises in your mind. You shouldn't be penalized for what automatically arises or how you think, but only for how you act in letting them control you.

Until the mind-stream becomes perfectly pure, the arising of afflictions is to be considered as something natural to be managed. What we should be criticized for is not that an affliction arises but that we keep dwelling in improper thoughts, never letting them go, or act on them with intent.

A second point is that some *kleshas* are influenced by the body's constitution, such as anger being a habitual problem because someone has a weak liver or is alcoholic (which affects the liver). Fear, as another example, is often a problem for people with kidney problems while excessive grief is often a problem for those with lung conditions.

Physical adjustments, such as herbal medicine interventions or chiropractic treatments, can help dissolve the arising of *kleshas* connected with the health of your internal organs. It is a different story when instead of imbalances we try to eradicate natural impulses, such as the desire for food and sex, because they are the product of evolution and come packaged with life. You might try to spiritualize them by somehow elevating them in some way, but you cannot totally eliminate them. We should put our energies into eliminating negative *kleshas* subject to free will that can be exterminated or sublimated into higher impulses.

Unfortunately, controlling your actions does not cleanse the root of negative impulses so that they never arise again in the future. Nonetheless, the admirable thing about self-restraint is that it does prevent problems. Nevertheless, negative *kleshas* (impure thoughts and inclinations) will usually arise periodically, and if you do not solve them at the root they will manifest throughout life and next again in a subsequent reincarnation, especially if they have been thwarted by severe self-restraint that never cleanses their roots. Deferring behavior without transforming it, by somehow damming it up or blocking it, seems to eliminate the problem on the surface, but all dams break in time and then the problem spills out. This is not a way to address a problem so that it is truly eliminated forever.

For instance, a man who subjects himself to severe dietary restrictions in one life may become a glutton in a subsequent life in order to express inclinations that were severely repressed. In a similar manner, those who try to dam up sexual desire will usually fail because their efforts are like putting a rock on top of weeds while they will continue to sprout up from beneath it. Since the sexual impulses cannot be eliminated they will continue to look for a free outlet unencumbered, and those outlets might then include unnatural perversions. This is why many priests, explicitly forbidden by rules to have sex with women, still remain prisoners to strong sexual desires and then look for their fulfillment through alternative means, such as sex with young boys. The best course of action is to try to sublimate or re-channel the expression of such impulses.

If the *kleshas* are not dissolved at their root they will continue into future lives even if you block them in this life by disciplined restraint. Sometimes those future manifestations, as a type of rebellious reaction to the forced repression of natural energies, will manifest in the form of a mutinous wildness that exhibits stronger "infractions" of the desired virtue than would be the case had there been no restraint at all. The analogy of the preacher's daughter comes to mind – someone forced into a life of artificial restrictions who, once released of parental control, acts out in all sorts of rebellious ways. When Arabs or Japanese travel to other countries where they are released from the repressive (overly strict) behavioral rules of their societies, we also often hear similar tales of flagrant behavior.

This by no means excuses the expression of *kleshas*, but simply explains what happens across lives when *kleshas* are not dissolved at their root. It also explains why you must use meditation practice to dissolve them. Additionally, this makes it clear why parents should strive to help their children transform the seeds of unwholesome behaviors. If they do not work to help their children transform their negative inclinations and behavioral issues when young, improper tendencies can develop into larger personality flaws that will mar the present lifetime and carry over into subsequent incarnations. Parents have a sacred duty to help their children purify themselves of the non-virtuous seeds of errant behavior in the present.

The mechanical repression of thoughts and desires is one way people try to handle them, but is not the best way. The highest way is to achieve *natural restraint* due to wisdom and understanding. You want to use wise discrimination to help ignore ingrained habits and replace non-virtuous ways with virtue. You need to learn how to mindfully watch your thoughts, identify any bad behaviors in the live moment, and transform them through a higher understanding. As Aristotle once said, you try to determine what virtue is and then train yourself to follow that path even if uncomfortable.

Watching your thoughts mindfully becomes the practice of introspection, namely mindfulness. Rather than act on a negative *klesha* we can learn to passively watch it through keen awareness called witnessing, observation or watchfulness. If you don't get entangled in it then you won't follow it and it will leave. If you additionally contemplate the causes behind a *klesha* in order to destroy it, this becomes the path of cultivating prajna wisdom. This is one of the highest paths of spiritual cultivation but hard to do. As Confucius aptly said, "In vain I have looked for a single man capable of seeing his own faults and bringing the charge home against himself." He described the path of wisdom analysis to a tee.

It is a natural principle that if we mindfully watch the thoughts in our minds all the time and by doing so perceive an impulse we recognize as bad, the grip it has on our consciousness will weaken with that insight. This is why we should practice insight meditation to watch our minds, and unfathom the real intentions we have behind our actions.

If a *klesha* keeps afflicting us and pressing upon our mind despite attempts to deal with it through wisdom and restraint, the only alternative left is to use complementary supplements to help free ourselves from its grip.

COMPLEMENTARY STRATEGIES FOR REDUCING KLESHAS

Nan Huai-chin has said, "Within affliction are hidden many,

many seeds of wrongdoings. Many elements of wrongdoing all come from affliction. If we transform and eliminate affliction, and have totally purified ourselves of it, at this point our mental state is comparatively pure and illuminated. Only after this are we capable of examining our own thoughts as they arise and disappear.

"For example, as we sit there meditating, we feel that our mental state is very pure. This is a realm of consciousness. But you should know that when we are in this instant of purity, so many wrong-doings and afflictions are hidden away there. Can you find them? Suppose someone boasts that while he is in this mental moment of purity he has absolutely no afflictions and absolutely no trace of wrongdoing. In that case, this person should not be talking about cultivating practice: fundamentally he does not see the truth! When we are in this mental moment of purity, the roots of afflictions and wrongdoings are still there, more than eighty-four thousand of them. This is a hypothetical number, a metaphor for very, very many. Buddha said: 'In a moment of thought there are eighty-four thousand afflictions.' Thus there are eighty-four thousand methods to deal with these afflictions."[1]

Buddhism actually has specific exercises for transforming afflictive emotions. There are meditation methods for turning greed into generosity, anger into patience, stupidity into wisdom, conceit into humility, and distraction into concentration. Buddhism teaches that if you don't transform the six root afflictions, ten thousand other afflictions will always be ready to sprout. This is true.

Many are the other possible antidotes, other than meditation, that might help you transform your negative *kleshas*. One major strategy for eliminating the hold of bothersome *kleshas* is to ignore them by occupying yourself with other activities until the burdensome impulse goes away. You might divert your energies into another activity that occupies your time, effort and concentration. For instance, men typically refrain from the urge to masturbate by occupying themselves with other activities until bedtime so that the urge disappears when they go to sleep. Some people throw themselves into a hobby that requires concentration so that they can ignore mental annoyances. Some people turn to exercise to use up their excess energy, and thus limit their straying in this way. The idea

---

[1] *To Realize Enlightenment: Practice of the Cultivation Path*, Nan Huai-Chin, trans. by J.C. Cleary (Samuel Weiser, York Beach: Maine, 1994), pp. 291-292.

is to occupy yourself with something else until an annoyance goes away.

We can also try to transform an impulse into a higher alternative, like satisfying the desire to drink carbonated soda by drinking sparkling water instead, and thus become satisfied by the bubbles rather than the sugar. As another example, we might take the impulse of sexual desire and re-channel it into exercise, or work to dissipate it through strenuous *kumbhaka* pranayama practice (holding of the breath). In the effort to stop smoking some people substitute a less harmful habit for this addiction like wearing a nicotine patch, and so one might re-channel a *klesha* in a different fashion until it can be eliminated entirely.

As stated, a spiritual aspirant should always try to transform his or her mental and physical habit energies into something better. However, as can be surmised from these few examples the task is akin to purifying a rushing stream of pure water that is continually being contaminated by a never-ending, onrushing torrent of ever-sprouting *kleshas*. It is hard to go against negative habit energies that continually arise, off and on, to impel us, and it is even harder to root those energies out at their source.

You can use many strategies to help you transform your mind and behavior, but since the stream of *kleshas* is endless most of the transformative strategies will end up tiring your mental energies even though you can somewhat elevate your mind through their usage. The highest attainment is to actually emancipate the mind from all mental tendencies and free it from all mental habits, good and bad. This approach means ultimately cultivating a mental state perfectly free of attachments so that with a detachment mindset the *kleshas* that occasionally arise will not transform into negative deeds. You can cultivate this mental freedom through meditative practice, and the starter practice is insight meditation.

A mind that is trained through meditation to remain balanced and unmoved in the presence of unwholesome thoughts and desires can eventually arrive at a state of detachment, and this enables people to avoid indulging in *kleshas*. However, it requires a constant effort to remain detached from the alluring fulfillment of *kleshas* through thought and deed. Nonetheless if you practice this then with enough work you can eventually abandon old life habits and ways of thought to build a new future.

When you meet a spiritual master they will at times be ruthless in trying to help you cleanse your mind of blemishes, even to the extent of being cruel at the task. A spiritual master can definitely quicken the cleansing of *kleshas*, afflictions, habit energies and *samskaras* (thought potencies) but their methods may be painful. The meditative path for eliminating *kleshas* is longer but the process is often less painful. It is up to you as to which road you want, but having an enlightened spiritual master is actually best.

The best way to succeed with the meditative path of transformation is to employ all the additional help you can get, and not just by having an enlightened teacher who knows your thoughts and mental problems. To help you transform your *kleshas* and *samskaras* other than by meditation there are various complementary practices and activities you might employ.

Detoxing The Body – Supporting the Internal Organs

Some afflictions, for instance, beset us because of the poor health of our physical body as regards our internal organs. Many of our emotional issues have a physiological basis, such as anger frequently arising because we have an unhealthy liver. Accordingly, in addition to vipassana mindfulness efforts to cut off anger whenever it arises, you might be able to reduce the problem by detoxifying your body's liver and supporting it both biochemically with helpful medicine.

By first (1) detoxifying and then (2) supporting the body's organs with alternative medicines you can assist any other efforts to eliminate certain *kleshas* that afflict you and are connected to your physiology.

Your Qi and your consciousness (thoughts) are linked. Your vital energy and your thoughts are intertwined. Pure Qi and smooth Qi circulations produces a pure mind, but dirty Qi and errant Qi flow circulations cause scattered thoughts and errant behavioral impulses. Since poor Qi flow is caused by unhealthy internal organs and faulty biochemistry, you should work hard to help transform your body to a higher state of health in order to deal with bothersome *kleshas*.

Any physical imbalances – even a misaligned spinal column - can lead to a continual onslaught of mental *kleshas* unless addressed, yet you might not know that your physical body is the cause.

Detoxifying and healing the body, so that it reaches a state of structural, biochemical and energetic balance, is one of the first means you might try to help reduce the onslaught of *kleshas*. If you Qi flow is smooth then the thoughts that arise in your mind will reflect less infarctions.

To reduce the physiological influence of your body or mind you must transform them both by opening up the body's Qi channels and purify your Qi. Remember that the health of your Qi and Qi channels is related to your mental activity. You need to open up your Qi channels within your body to experience better mental purity free of *kleshas*. Detoxing the body helps in this task because it helps cleanse the energy flow lines that are intertwined with the development of thoughts and inclinations. Chiropractic adjustments, to help correct spinal misalignments, would be helpful too.

Just as with yoga or the martial arts, bodywork sessions involving deep tissue massage therapy (Rolfing, Hellerwork, etc.) can help you open up your Qi channels. If your Qi channels open then your Qi can circulate more freely within your body. Smoother Qi leads to more peaceful mental states that will reduce the problem of *kleshas* and pave the way for health and spiritual attainments too.

Using Mantras

Reciting mantras is yet another way to help reduce your *kleshas* as well as transform both your mind and behavior. Functioning like prayers, mantras actually request higher spiritual beings to lend their beneficial influences to you so that you can better change situations such as reduce your mental afflictions. In various ways they can help you change your behavior as well as help improve situations for the better.

Reciting mantras or prayers can also be used to occupy your thoughts when negative inclinations attempt to take over your mind. They keep you busy so that you do not engage in indulgences. Affirmations, which are similar to mantras and prayers, are a minor mechanism that can also help you change your behavior if you employ them in the right way.

Mantras, affirmations and prayers can definitely help you change your personality, thoughts and behavior for the better. Whenever you want to purify your mind-stream of *kleshas* and transform your behavior you should always undertake the practice of reciting mantras (or prayers) so that higher spiritual beings might aid you with your efforts. For instance, in the Vajrayana schools the practitioners always pray for spiritual help so that they can abandon violent *kleshas*.

Most who practice meditation do not know that mantra practice is really a necessary companion for the quickest road of spiritual progress, and a powerful assist to meditation for transforming your body and behavior. The question comes down to which mantra is best to use, and there are many to choose from.

Homeopathy, Nutripuncture, EFT and Acupuncture

Sometimes recurring negative thoughts and emotions are due to errant circulatory Qi flows within your body, and sometimes these errant Qi flows can be adjusted back to normal through various forms of energy medicine. If you can straighten out your body's Qi flows through energy medicine, such as by unblocking energy pathways that seem to be blocked or restricted, this is another way to help reduce some emotional issues and bothersome *kleshas*.

Another way of putting it is that by becoming more internally balanced, both biochemically and energetically, you can reduce your *kleshas* and associated wrongdoings. You can reduce the frequency and intensity of your problems. Purifying your body (detoxification) and harmonizing your body's energies are useful strategies for reducing mental afflictions because they make the body healthier and healthier bodies have less negative tendencies.

What are the energy modalities you might try that could possibly help you when you are trying to cultivate a clear mind free of *kleshas*? People usually think of acupuncture right off, but most people don't have access to a good practitioner and cannot see any mental benefits from this modality. A related technique - the tapping method of EFT - can be tried on a daily basis to help you calm emotional issues since it is self-administered and costs absolutely nothing. It is easy to find out about it by watching free videos on the internet. You can look up "Emotional Freedom Technique" or *The Tapping Solution* by Nick Ortner.

Both homeopathy and nutripuncture are modalities that can help supplement or balance any deficient energy flows related to errant body conditions. If you want to transform your mind and behavior, they are augmentative helpmates that might help you transform matters quicker than if you just used meditation alone.

Associating Oneself with Perfuming Influences to Permeate One's Tendencies

Another method for transforming your *kleshas* is called taking the road of "perfuming influences." Just as a rump of meat in a smokehouse will slowly absorb the flavor of the smoke, a set of clothes left in a perfumed room will slowly absorb the scent of the perfume. Therefore, the perfuming strategy for transforming your *kleshas*/behavior is to expose yourself to positive environmental influences that will continually permeate your consciousness. In this way the influences will slowly change the underlying seeds of your thoughts and behavior.

Associating with positive influences will transform you in a positive way while always associating with negative influences is a road to decline. If you always associate with a negative environment you are likely to absorb those tendencies and turn them into negative habit energies. Legends say that the mother of Mencius changed her residence three times on account of concern for her son since the local environments were unfavorable for growing children. This example shows knowledge of the power of perfuming influences for sowing the seeds of future behavior.

Putting yourself in a positive environment where your *kleshas* would not normally arise, or where their opposing virtue is emphasized, is a way to slowly transform them. Associating with positive environmental influences over time will, through permeation, make them better gradually. If you use meditation along with this method then it will certainly help you transform your mind and behavior, which is another reason why individuals choose to associate with the positive influences of a spiritual master.

Reading the right type of books can also help to slowly transform your consciousness and thus gradually help you rid yourself of afflictions if you follow their guidance. This is why I encourage people to read Plutarch's *Lives of the Noble Greeks and Romans*, Nan Huai Chin's *Analects* (of Confucius), *How to Win Friends and Influence People* (Dale Carnegie), and Napoleon Hill's *The Wisdom of*

Andrew Carnegie as Told to Napoleon Hill.

People also like to read motivational or life coaching works by authors such as Tony Robbins, Stephen Covey, Jim Rohn, Brian Tracy, Earl Nightingale, Robert Allen, Wayne Dyer and others.

For transforming your character many people cite spiritual texts for motivation, but the effort must be undertaken step by step and most people fail at this. Therefore I always recommend several books for revealing the actual method that works: *Liao Fan's Four Lessons* (Yuan Liao Fan), *The Autobiography of Benjamin Franklin* (Franklin), *How I Raised Myself from Failure to Success in Selling* (Bettger) and *Move Forward* (Bodri). These few books will help you cultivate virtuous ways and change your personality for the better. If I had knew of any books that motivated people to great merit-making activities then I would recommend them as well.

Relying On A Spiritual Master

As stated, the idea of perfuming influences introduced the strategy of associating with an enlightened spiritual master to help you cleanse your mind-stream of *kleshas* and afflictions, thus calming your mind and improving your behavior. Along with the idea of perfuming influences to transform *kleshas*, people often visit temples and holy men for their wisdom and guidance in this regard.

When you have problems conquering your mind and behavior when meditation is not enough, associating with an enlightened master is another sure strategy to try. Anyone on the meditation path should try to find one or more enlightened gurus to help them transform their behavioral patterns and achieve a subtle body on the way to enlightenment. A true spiritual master is one who can also help you get rid of your *kleshas* just as they might help you get rid of your karma. You must mantra to find one.

How do you know if someone is enlightened? If, for instance, they are a monk/nun/religious head in charge of thousands of students *from a lineage well-recognized to possess a continuous line of enlightened masters* then you can bet that they are spiritually advanced enough to be able to help you. Whether or not you have positive karma with the individual, so that they can help you achieve spiritual attainments quickly, is a different issue entirely. As for helping you transform your *kleshas* and offending behaviors, once again this depends on the karma.

Meher Baba once explained that some people need to become better and others need to become worse off in order to drop free of their *kleshas*. Nan Huai-chin said that some people need to drop to the absolute bottom (such as drunkards, drug addicts or gamblers in some cases) so that they can completely tire of a *klesha* and then become completely free of it. All paths are different; we are always seeking the quickest and most painless way.

Adopting a Strict Ethical Code of Conduct or Discipline

The method of according with well-established ethical codes of conduct and rules of proper behavior generally accepted by society, such as by following the eight-fold path of Buddhism (right view, right thinking; right speech; right action, right living; right effort; right memory; right meditation), is another way to stifle the expression of *kleshas*. According with an ethic code disciplines one's urges and elevate one's life rather so that you don't give into some types of afflictive *kleshas*, negative seeds and baser instincts. This is channeling your thought, speech and behavior through the path of culture, societal norms and discipline.

If you strictly subject yourself to such guidelines then even though they be artificial constraints this is one way of dealing with *kleshas* and denying your mind-stream and behavior an outlet for wrongdoing. For instance, Moslems do not drink alcohol and thereby avoid the problem of drunkenness and its consequences. As a religious rule this then becomes a societal norm reducing certain societal problems. Conforming to the rules of society while following the path of meditation can therefore help you avoid bad outcomes and elevate your mind/behavior over time. However, discipline is an artificial restraint that simply dams up energy without transforming it.

Moral principles promote harmony in social interactions because they channel how society acts. To conquer *kleshas* one should not just practice meditation, but also observe the ethical codes generally accepted by the moral consciousness of the times. Following the proper rules of conduct will reduce behavioral problems so that a society runs well, and is like establishing rules for the orderly flow of traffic on streets. Therefore this is commendable. However, one should not let such guidelines ossify into strict rules never to be broken. Unfortunately, at times only someone enlightened can safely go against the moral codes of the time through a higher or lower octave of ethics.

The problem with the road of following the moral codes of the time, of course, is that strictly adhering to rules of disciplined conduct does not dissolve impulses but simply bottles them up or deflects them without dissolving them. The rules themselves, if they become solidified through ossification, can also cripple society as it advances in awareness. Some say this is what has happened to the Amish, Orthodox Jewish and Sharia law cultures where natural impulses have been thwarted by artificial regulations that were meant only for a different time and different circumstances. In Buddhism one never takes artificial rules and regulations as the spiritual path.

While the seeds of negative *kleshas* will remain within consciousness but not sprout into action due to the restraint of following rules, they will still exist. That negative energy, since the root afflictions are not dissolved, will simply be expressed through another direction or wait for a subsequent life when it can run with unrestricted play. Therefore while this can prevent harmful actions from being born, it is not a way to actually eliminate the *kleshas*. Nevertheless, this road can be of benefit to society.

Visualization Practice To Forge New Neural Paths

In Buddhism some practitioners cultivate meditation on the four immeasurables (infinite joy, infinite compassion, infinite kindness, infinite equanimity) or valiant Qi states (infinite courage, generosity, etc.) as a means of perfuming their deepest consciousness so that better seeds of behavior will become habitual energies over time. This is another road for dealing with *kleshas*.

Visualization practice is another mental programming tool you can use to help deal with *kleshas*, such as bothersome anxiety or fear. As detailed in my book *Visualization Power*, by visualizing yourself performing a new type of perfected behavior in your mind this effort will form new neural pathways in the brain for that desired behavior.

Due to neural plasticity, you can use visualization practices to create new neural pathways in the brain that correspond to generosity, courage, truthfulness and so on, and through this means help replace negative *kleshas*, vices or "sins" with more positive counterparts you have selected. Every time you follow the same mental pathway, including those forged through visualization practice, that specific pattern gets closer to becoming the pattern of unconscious default. Thus, through the daily practice of visualization you can actually build new positive patterns of behavior.

Many NLP practices, such as the "Circle of Excellence," also train you to create positive internal states that you can call upon at will in order to deal with mental afflictions. NLP methods don't dissolve the seeds of *kleshas* but they make it easier for you to re-channel/transform your negative seeds into other impulses whenever you need. If you are trying to transform your behavior, many personal development methods like this are useful companions to the practice of meditation.

Contemplation of Thoughts – Prajna Wisdom Analysis

As previously discussed, one of the most powerful strategies for dissolving afflictions so that they no longer arise is to ponder past incidents of afflicting *kleshas*, along with the harm and wrongdoings they may have caused, with disapproval and a remorseful heart. The spur of regret can definitely help you change your behavior. The more often you examine a negative *klesha* that commonly arises and then mentally give rise to feelings of remorse and repentance for those inclinations, the more that this type of analysis will serve as a type of antidote to the *klesha*.

This practice is called wisdom analysis, and through the fire of contemplation it will help to unravel the hold that a non-virtuous tendency has upon your mind. You gradually work at eliminating a *klesha* by analyzing why it is improper, what harm it might cause, why it keeps arising and what to do about it. This type of introspective awareness will help to consume those tendencies and thus, slowly cuts off afflictive mental knots and compulsions.

The most common form of meditation practice – mindfulness practice or inner watching - instructs you to simply shine awareness on thoughts without becoming entangled with them until they die down. You observe thoughts without acting on them (without giving them extra energy) until the mind reaches a state of quiet because of the passive disengagement. This is passive mental watching that over time leads to detachment. It doesn't mean that you no longer have desires or that your emotions do not arise. It doesn't mean that you have a laissez faire or even negative view of the world that nothing maters. It just means that you can create enough distance from them (detachment) when you need to. You don't act on negative impulses that impel you because you can keep a distance from those impulses. You develop self-control that prevents them from gaining control over you. Detachment, in short, allows you to become the master of your behavior.

On the other hand, contemplation (wisdom analysis) uses discriminative reasoning to help unravel these knots at their root. This technique involves more mental engagement, but produces a deeper and more long-lasting result when successful. Both meditation methods must be practiced on the spiritual path.

Inner Watching

Many Asians are familiar with the Chinese story of Yuan Liao Fan, which can be found in his famous book *Liao Fan's Four Lessons*. I always recommend this book to others, especially as free versions can readily be found on the internet. It is one of the few books that I recommend parents get for their children. Despite having many personality *kleshas*/flaws, Liao Fan was able to transform his character and even change his karmic fate due to simultaneously performing a set of specific cultivation practices: *mantra, witnessing meditation and merit-making.*

Specifically, every day he would mantra for spiritual help to change his fortune, watch his inner thoughts and outward deeds to determine whether they were positive or negative, and strive to do good deeds and virtuous acts instead of wrongdoings. He always recorded his mindfulness efforts in a daily log/journal to track his efforts. In this way, by constantly watching his mind and behavior and recording the plusses and minuses he experienced in trying to transform himself, he was able to change his astrological fate over time.

Benjamin Franklin, in his autobiography, revealed that he used a similar method of ledgering introspection (similar to Liao Fan's ledger of merits and demerits) in order to perfect a set of virtues that he wanted to instill in his personality. His target was character and behavioral transformation, which is actually the true measure of spiritual growth. This is why I always encourage people to also read *The Autobiography of Benjamin Franklin*.

Frank Bettger, author of *How I Raised Myself from Failure to Success in Selling*, copied Franklin's method for business objectives. He applied the method to help him develop specific personality skills for business success. You can find out how others also used similar methods, and how to make them into a daily habit, in *Move Forward: Powerful Strategies for Creating Better Outcomes in Life*. This method of eliminating *kleshas* and changing your fate for the better uses meditation, mantra, and merit-making to succeed along with the standard methods of goal setting and achievement.

If you really want to cleanse your mind and behavior and change your astrological fate, fortune and destiny, you should emulate the methods in *Move Forward: Powerful Strategies for Creating Better Outcomes in Life* as closely as possible. During the day you should watch your thoughts and keep track of any infractions against what is right and proper. You learn to transcend negative thoughts and impulses by witnessing your mind, in effect centering yourself in a higher level of consciousness, a higher body that can detach from the impulses and thoughts you are observing. The more you can do this the more you can cultivate your Qi channels and purify your behavior.

You should do this all the time so that it becomes your new way of living. Furthermore, you should set up a small shrine in your house (such as a section of a table) with a stick of incense and at the end of the day you should formally/ritually report in front of it the day's progress to heaven.

As an admirable example of how you can put this into daily practice, so that this becomes an actual ritual or habit that works, there is the story of a famous king of South India, King Kulashekhara. This king would also watch his thoughts and activities during the day (like Liao Fan, Franklin, etc.) when running the kingdom. At the end of each working day he would then enter his personal shrine and submit a report of the court activities he had conducted to the Deity. He adopted the principle that the kingdom belonged to the Deity and he was just a caretaker serving the function of proper management. In this way he kept a check on his behavior, and never cheated himself on his intentions such as whether he was becoming greedy, arrogant, power hungry and so on.

How great would be the behavior in the nation if every individual were to emulate this practice and do it every day.

This is a daily practice I very much encourage in society in order to help people transform themselves and uplift culture on a vast scale. Every individual and family should have a small table or shrine in front of which they can report their daily doings and personal attempts to elevate their behavior (in the manner described by Franklin or Liao Fan) to Heaven for approval. This will most definitely change the culture of a nation.

SUMMARY

Afflictions or *kleshas*, which are troublesome and annoying, are a basic condition of our mental activity. They are also a type of wrongdoing that defiles your mental state. If you continually cultivate bad seeds in your mind, allowing them to run around unchecked, they will taint the virtuous seeds you have already cultivated and eventually pollute them. This is for certain.

Kleshas usually turn into temporal wrongdoings if they are not eliminated. We must therefore work to make the mental activity by which we carry out activities pure and empty, free of *kleshas*, and the way to do this is through meditation. Meditation can help you purify your mind so that it is free of wrongdoings and afflictions.

One approach for dealing with afflictions is to try to block the *kleshas*, or cut them off, but this is usually inadequate. Another approach is to just ignore them until they go away, but here the problem is that we usually succumb to them anyway. A better approach is to use wisdom to slowly transform bad seeds into good ones, or to surround ourselves with a perfuming environment of positive influences that can slowly encourage good seeds to become adopted as the default natural response of consciousness. There are all sorts of other helpful remedies you can also complementarily use when trying to transform your mental behavior.

You always have a choice on how to act in the world and the discipline of the spiritual path is about how to control yourself and express better behavior. For this objective there are countless methods a man can use to overcome himself and restore propriety.

The path of meditation, for instance, teaches you to always be inspecting your mind and not act contrary to benevolence and righteousness for one moment. In this way you control yourself through self-policing. If you set out to purify your mind by also cultivating the seeds of virtue rather than just refusing to act wrongly then you can slowly become a truly virtuous human being. If you are going to live a long time in a subtle deva body, that is the type of person you must become.

The importance of cultivating good mind-body seeds cannot be overemphasized, and it is especially important not just to learn this yourself but to teach children how to do so. Parents must teach their children how to cut off *kleshas* so that bad seeds don't turn into errant wrongdoing, and how to replace bad habits with good ones if they have already established bad habits. This is especially true during the formative years when children are learning right from wrong and struggling with how to control their impulses and behaviors.

We commonly lament that public morality has degenerated in our times and virtue has vanished in society. The problem is that we do not emphasize methods of self-cultivation such as the meditative methods explained for policing our minds and eliminating errant *kleshas*. Isn't this the most effective path for uplifting society rather than establishing layers of new laws and outward rules of behavior?

Other than personal benefits, this is another reason why you should take up this practice, but how to do so? The methods of Yuan Liao Fan and Benjamin Franklin, seen in this light, would serve both self and society if adopted by everyone on a daily basis. They essentially entail taking up the practice of watching your thoughts and behavior – a continual mindfulness of inner observation – that in turn involves centering yourself in a transcending mental state called emptiness, pristine awareness or witnessing.

This will eventually enable you to detach from bad habit energies as well as cultivate a clear clarity called "being bright." Your mind becomes "bright" when wandering thoughts die down (because you detach from them and don't follow them with energy). Your mind will then always be perfectly clear about whatever arises within it. You simply transcend the habit of getting entangled with thoughts and thereby transform your habit energies through a type of independence.

Most educational systems concentrate on teaching academic topics to children rather than teaching virtuous behavior. They don't teach children how to detach from errant impulses or transform unwholesome tendencies into good ones. Therefore the methods found in *Move Forward: Powerful Strategies for Creating Better Outcomes in Life* are very important for teaching us how to become good people.

The foundation of one's character in life is always established in one's youth. Even the fortune of your life can usually be traced back to your youth and your character traits formed during that period. Think about the methods you can use, in conjunction with meditation, for mindfully policing your thoughts and behavior as well as how you might teach them to children. We must all work at instilling these methods in ourselves and in society.

.

CHAPTER 3
"EMPTY MIND" MEDITATION PRACTICE

Meditation involves cultivating a peaceful mental state absent of *kleshas* (afflictions) and mental bonds that is also pristinely clear, empty and always aware. It always allows thoughts to arise, but does not cling to them. Through meditation practice your consciousness is thus slowly taught to be like empty space which itself lets all things arise within it without interference, but does not cling to anything.

Thoughts will always arise in a mind so there is no such true thing as a mundane state of mental emptiness lacking thoughts. However, there are naturally peaceful mental states largely free of wild thoughts, wandering thoughts and *klesha* afflictions and you can certainly cultivate those clear states through the path of meditation. You can also learn how to become detached from thoughts so that you can deal with them like things, and not get caught up with them to the extent that they then own you.

This is one of the target objectives at the earliest stages of the spiritual path. You want to cultivate a clear mind free of wandering thoughts that can, because it is not prone to distraction and scatteredness, concentrate with clarity for long periods of time. It can ignore wandering through distractions. You also want a mind free of negative *kleshas*, which might otherwise turn into wrongdoing, and replete with virtuous thoughts so that your behavior becomes pure and helpful to others.

On the spiritual trail you must cultivate your mind and body, your consciousness and vital energy. This book is solely concerned with cultivating your mind while *Nyasa Yoga* is concerned with cultivating your internal energy, or Qi. It works on life force cultivation. Together, the two types of cultivation can lead to the first stage of attainment on the cultivation trail, which is the attainment of an independent spirit body, deva body, astral body, etheric body or subtle body that can leave your physical body at will. It takes years of practice to get the *real* kundalini energy to arise in order to generate the deva body because kundalini is far more significant than the superficial Qi feelings of "wind" that typically arise within the body. After it is initiated, it takes twelve years of kundalini constantly flowing everywhere within you to form the subtle spirit body attainment.

Putting the talk of Qi internal energy aside, which is body or life force cultivation, in terms of mental cultivation there are two basic ways to cultivate the mind so that it is free of the *klesha* afflictions so that your mind-stream becomes virtuous and pure.

The first method is witnessing your thoughts without getting entangled in them, and in time they will die down. This method doesn't use discrimination or analysis to unravel mental afflictions and arrive at a clear mental state. With this method you simply witness the thoughts that arise in your mind without adding energy or analysis to them. Because you detach from thoughts while letting them arise freely, they will eventually die down and your mind will slowly become clear and free of afflictions. With this type of practice you don't cling to any mental phenomena that you witness but just observe the comings and going of thoughts without interference. The Zen method of "dropping everything" is a derivative of this method.

The second method is to always mindfully watch your thoughts so that you can immediately identify afflictions when they arise. When an affliction arises in the mind you should try to analyze it to unravel its root sources because this will help loosen its habit energy. This, in turn, will help prevent that affliction from arising again. You should always critically evaluate your thoughts and correct them whenever you find they are going astray.

This route of wisdom analysis, as taught in the previous chapter, uses discrimination and so is called the practice of "prajna wisdom (discriminative wisdom)." This method of analyzing thoughts is an active form of *contemplation* rather than just the passive witnessing or observing of thoughts so that they die down. Using this method, in conjunction with mental witnessing, in time you can produce a relatively clear and pure mental state that we call "empty," "emptiness," "peaceful," "calm," "quiet," "pristine", "clear," or "tranquil" because wandering thoughts have been abandoned. Lacking the normal cacophony of unchanneled wandering thoughts, it is also called "a state of concentration." Because thoughts still arise but without the accompaniment of wandering chatter, it is also called a state of pristine clarity, or pristine wisdom.

Are there other ways to cultivate a peaceful empty mental state that is calm and clear but not a blank state of ignorance? Are there other ways to cultivate a mental emptiness like space that accepts whatever arises within it, and knows whatever rises within it with clarity, but which does not attach to any things that arise?

Yes, but most people practice these other methods incorrectly. The problem with most meditation practitioners is that they start using a certain method but fall into a certain groove of incorrect practice that they then repeat for years, never making any progress. Over and over again they repeat the same mistakes, always clinging to the wrong method of practice. Typically they cling to thoughts without knowing it.

The best way to prevent this is to always shake up their mental routine so that it never falls into the rut of clinging. Furthermore, one of the best ways to insure this is to make sure that they *simultaneously practice several different cultivation methods* - such as mantra, visualization practice, pranayama, stretching exercises, sexual discipline, charity and meditation - that chip away at transforming their Qi and mind *via different principles.*

If you are seeking a variety of different types of meditation practice you might try, you might follow the instructions with *Meditation and Its Practices* (Swami Adiswarananda), *Twenty-Five Doors to Meditation* (Bodri and Lee) or *The Little Book of Meditation* (Bodri). In *Nyasa Yoga* I introduce many types of meditation practices that cultivate your Qi, or inner vital energy. In *Visualization Power* I introduce various concentration practices to help you cultivate your mind and body, and especially the *kasina* practices of Buddhaghosa within the *Visuddhimagga*, an ancient meditation text.

For instance, Buddhaghosa instructed meditators to sit in front of a body of clear water with their eyes almost closed. They were to observe the water without much interest and then to gradually forget their body and mind to become unified with the water. "Becoming one with water," which would help purify their Qi channels, was the water *kasina*.

They might alternatively hold in their mind the fiery image of the sun or a fire while visualizing a flame within their abdomen that would slowly get bigger until their whole body was imagined as being in flames, everything got burned away, and they were left with an empty state of mind. This washing of oneself using fire was the fire *kasina*.

They could find a wall and facing it, visualize that it became empty and then extend that emptiness into their body, which was the earth *kasina*. Their body was to become empty like a sack.

Lastly, they could go to a mountain top and observe the empty sky of endless space, extend that emptiness to understand their body and then merge with the vast, endless universe. This was the space *kasina* that helps you cultivate an empty mind. In Mahamudra practice, popularized in Tibet, many people practice in a similar way.

As to emptiness meditation itself, the problem is what type of practice can help you cultivate an empty mind free of afflictions, a mental space that provides an inkling of what "mental emptiness," "no-thought," "purity of mind" or "mind essence" entails.

The best way to pursue "empty mind" as a target is to *practice a different type of emptiness meditation every week so that you do not settle into any set pattern of incorrect technique.* Because people usually select one technique, cling to it and then practice it incorrectly for years without progress, by rotating through a different technique each week (or every two weeks, etc.) you will prevent this problem and eventually achieve a clear mind free of afflictions.

This is a superior way of practicing rather than just using the same technique over and over again with mental clinging, or repeating errors forever. It is one of the quickest ways to help you generate an empty mind free of *kleshas* and attachments.

The Zen school advises practitioners to cultivate a pristine clear (empty) state of mind through meditation instructions such as "Let your mind be empty like space," "Drop everything and see what you turn out to be," "Emptiness is my home. Be like the emptiness I truly am," "Imagine what you were like before the universe was even born," "What were you before your parents were born? Be like that empty non-existence."

Typically you start out in these meditations as a conditioned being with limiting adjuncts and try to become unconditional. You try to use any mental trick that will help you to let go of clinging to consciousness; the target is to let go of clinging to get a taste of empty mind, no matter how briefly, rather than that there is a perfect logic to the method.

Other traditions use meditation approaches or descriptions such as the following sadhana that you might try:

- Set your mind on the highest ether of consciousness that is above all thought-constructs. Let go of thoughts and remain there.

- You should concentrate intensely on the idea that this universe is totally an ephemeral, effervescent illusion populated by transparent images like mirages. Let go and let your mind become like the empty void in which they appear.

- Go to an empty plane and stare into space. Take no notice of the clouds in the sky but become the space itself, infinitely everywhere. Become that endless space. Rest in that state ignoring any thoughts that arise not without suppressing them. Let them appear with clear knowing but don't attach to them since you are bodiless space.

- Imagine that, like a fish, you are swimming in an infinite ocean of pure consciousness without any obstructions whatsoever. Now, maintaining that imagination, imagine that you lose your fish body and you become a bodiless observer within an ocean of consciousness. You become the ocean of emptiness itself.

- Imagine you are a pot of water immersed in water, and what it is then like if the pot breaks and there is water both inside and outside. Now imagine as if you are a pot of air resting in space, and similarly the pot disintegrates. What are you now like?

- Imagine that you are a point of light within an ocean of infinite light. Next, try to feel that you are that ocean of light, which has no form. Make that point of light merge in the infinite ocean.

In some of these approaches you are the center of your consciousness and try to feel that you are infinite, and in others you try to make the infinite the center of your consciousness and think of yourself as a manifestation of that infinite. You must try each of these ways to see what works best for you. When you find that your internal energy stirs because of using some technique then that is a good sign of progress.

The *Vijnanabhairava*, which is a how-to meditation book from the tradition of Kashmir Shaivism, contains instructions for practicing over one hundred different types of meditations. Several of these meditation practices embody different . roads to cultivating mental emptiness. In order to avoid getting into a rut, I suggest you devote yourself to a new one each week and cycle through them on a yearly basis. This is one of the quickest ways to develop meditation progress! Some of the relevant emptiness meditation practice instructions are:

- Visualize the Qi of your body arising from the root chakra as getting subtler and subtler until at last it dissolves into emptiness and remains there. Let your mind become empty like the final dissolution state of that Qi.

- Fill the center of your brain with Qi (visualize it coming in the brain from the spine, or draw it into the head from the cosmos, or imagine it being a projection into your head from a spiritual great or your master, etc.) and keep letting go of any thought-constructs. Let your mind become un-minded. Your consciousness will eventually become empty if you continue letting go of whatever arises within your mind after bringing Qi into your head. Instead of the center of your head, you can alternatively bring your Qi to a position behind the center of your eyebrows, let go, and practice watching thoughts without grasping them until you settle into a state of quiescence.

- Meditate by locating your consciousness in your heart, holding your thoughts and energy there so that discursive thought disappears. Upon its disappearance stay absorbed in that emptiness. Alternatively, restrain your mental activities in the heart chakra (or on a flame that appears inside it) and try to cultivate an empty mental state therein by holding your energy there while rejecting thoughts.

- Recite the sound "Aum" and observe the void of emptiness at the end of the protracted syllable. Doing this each time, you will eventually attain an experience of mental emptiness.

- Imagine that you are empty space in all directions simultaneously without any thought-constructs, experiencing emptiness all around you. Imagine being the spatial vacuity in all directions around you and rest your mind in that state. If anything arises, let it arise within you without interference (just ignore it) because you are just infinite emptiness, bodiless like space.

- Imagine there is endless space above your head, below your feet and within your heart. Rest your mind in that visage of empty space without holding onto any thoughts that arise. Then simultaneously imagine that the upper part of your body (where consciousness resides) becomes void and the lower side of your body becomes void. In the upper half of your body there is nothing, in the lower half of your body is nothing, in your consciousness there is nothing and in everything everywhere there is nothing. Rest there.

- Contemplate that the constituents of your body (like the bones, flesh, etc.) are pervaded with mere vacuity (emptiness). Imagine that they are all empty inside. In other words, imagine that there is nothing inside your

45

body's components. In time, the contemplation of having empty body parts will become steady and you can then extend the idea of emptiness to resting your mind in empty space.

- Contemplate that the skin of your body is like an outer wall and that there is nothing inside it but empty space. After you imagine that the body becomes like an empty sack, imagine that your mind becomes limitless, infinite in all spatial directions. All things you experience appear within this infinite spaciousness, but you know them without attaching to them because nothing is you, you are just the empty space that cannot attach to anything. Rest your mind in empty space like that.

- Bring your mind and your senses into the interior space of your heart – the ether or voidness of the heart - and exclude everything else from consciousness.

- Penetrate all the various parts of your body by consciousness, feeling all the parts of your body as a unified wholeness of soft energy. Next bring your mind into the brain and dissolve its thoughts into emptiness by letting go and letting them dissolve away.

- Imagine that the whole universe is successively dissolved from a gross state into a subtle state, from a subtle state into emptiness, and then from emptiness into an even more transcendental formless supreme state that lacks any attributes or distinctions. Allow your mind to be dissolved away the same way into pure empty consciousness and then the emptiness of non-existence. This is called the technique of *sadadhva* where you trace the entire universe back to its source.

- You should concentrate intensely on the idea that this universe is totally void, without substance, completely empty. Imagine that it is a nothing. In that emptiness (void) let your mind be absorbed.

- You should cast your eyes in the empty space inside a jar or any other empty object leaving aside the enclosing partitions. Let your mind get absorbed in that empty space, and then imagine that your mind then becomes absorbed in a total void of infinite emptiness. Let yourself become identified with that infinite voidness.

- Cast your gaze on a region in which there are no trees, such as going to a mountain plateau or high wall and looking into the empty sky. Let your mental state become like the empty sky you observe. Let thought-fullness become thought-lessness. Let your thoughts dissolve as you become the empty space. Cast aside the body and ignore the fluctuations of your mind as you become the empty space you see.

- Contemplate with an unwavering mind that your whole body together with the entire universe simultaneously are the nature of consciousness. Since your consciousness is what sees everything as pictures, then what you are seeing is only consciousness (only images within your mind). Therefore the body you normally take yourself to be and the universe you see are just mental images of consciousness-only. Your existence is just an image in the mind so let it go. Stay in that realization. The "you" ("I") that you take yourself to be is fundamentally just pure consciousness that has absolutely no perturbations like space. Stay like that.

- Contemplate that your whole body and the universe simultaneously are in their totality filled with bliss. Afterwards try to feel fully permeated/saturated with this bliss, let go of all consciousness and let your mind rest in this blissfulness feeling without thinking.

- Concentrate on yourself in the form of a vast firmament, boundless and unlimited in any direction whatsoever.

47

- One should contemplate thus: "Within me the inner apparatus consisting of the mind does not ultimately exist for it is just brought about by the combination of energy forces in a particular structure that make consciousness happen. In the absence of thought-constructs, I will be rid of all thoughts and will therefore abide as pure empty thought." Try to become that ultimate state free of thoughts but without suppression.

- Observe your mind and any desires or afflictions that spring up. When you observe a desire or affliction that springs up, put an end to it immediately. Don't let it function at all. Let the mind become absorbed in that very place from which it arose. In time the mind will become pure and clear like space.

- Consider, "When knowledge has not arisen in me, then what am I when in that condition?" Become absorbed in the reality of that emptiness.

- After rejecting attachment to your body, you should with a firm mind that has no consideration for anything else contemplate thus, "I am everywhere."

- Cast your gaze on an object, withdraw it and slowly eliminate all knowledge of that object along with all other thoughts so as to abide in non-knowing.

- When a person perceives a particular object, absence is established regarding all other objects (including what you perceived just prior to this object). If one contemplates on this vacuity with a mind freed of all thought, then even though the present particular object is still known or perceived your mind will settle into a tranquil state.

- Fix your mind on the vast, limitless external space that is empty and without support. By prolonged concentration practice on becoming boundless external space, you will gradually acquire the capacity of mentally becoming like supportless, objectless, vacant space. Let your mind become absorbed in this experience.

- Towards whatever object the mind goes, one should remove it from there immediately by that very mind, and thus by not allowing it to settle down anywhere – by making it supportless – one will become free of agitation. Just push the mind away from any point upon which it settles. Wherever the mind moves, push it onto another object. Do not attach to any thoughts that arise within the mind.

There are countless forms of spiritual cultivation, and meditation is just one of them. There are also countless forms of meditation practice that operate using different principles of mental calming. Rather than focusing on mental objects (such as physical sensations, images of masters, etc.) in order to engender states of concentration, each of the ones just featured approach the target of cultivating an empty mind in a different way.

There are many other approaches possible, and these represent just a few meditation examples you might try from the tradition of Kashmir Shaivism. One of the main ideas you can derive from these meditations is that you can center consciousness on formless, bodiless, infinite space in order to cultivate an empty mind. This is an alternative approach to watching or analyzing thoughts.

The *Jnana Sankalini Tantra* says, "One whose mind is fixed on the formless becomes formless. Therefore through every effort, go beyond form." In this pursuit, it is actually much easier to start with images that suggest the infinite than to try to immediately cultivate the abstract idea of infinity. Through gradual approaches of approximation you can use images to cultivate to the imageless.

For instance, you can initially set the mind on the image of the sky, space, an ocean or vast emptiness and in time the mind can become empty or formless with such practice. Even the mathematical concepts of infinity that mathematicians play with (Cantor sets, etc.) can be used as a mental means to help you stop thoughts and reach a stage of emptiness if, once pondered, you then cast thoughts aside to rest in an empty mind.

If you can somehow identify yourself with images of infinity this mental approach might help banish thoughts or lead to a state of detachment. Sometimes the key to meditation is to also mentally think "I am as infinite as the sky," "My consciousness is as infinite as the sky," or "I am one with the infinite space in all directions, bodiless, formless." Some of the *Mahavakyas* of Hinduism ("I am Brahman," "This Self is Brahman," "Consciousness is Brahman") are meditations that embody this approach to some extent.

For any of these techniques the objective is not actually to make the mind blank or suppress it but to so free it from following thoughts (becoming entangled with them) so that they die down to leave the mental realm clear. In freeing oneself of thought attachments one's natural Qi circulation is sure to arise and start opening up one's obstructed Qi channels. With better Qi flow your mind becomes more stable and clear, and this is how meditation produces a peaceful mind.

Of all these possibilities, the best meditative means for achieving an empty mental state that is largely clear of wandering thoughts (and *detached* from thoughts) is the one that seems to work best for you. The best one is the one that helps you the most, but the only way you can find that practice technique is if you try each of these sequentially, one week at a time.

A common problem with meditators is that people commonly attach to one particular method of meditation that they cling to for decades. However noble this is, if they practice incorrectly, such as with clinging, they will get nowhere. To prevent people from falling into a mistaken groove that will not result in progress you should try practicing a different type of emptiness meditation on a regular basis. Just as Shakyamuni Buddha advised monks not to settle down in any location so that they did not form attachments, one should hold fast to certain cultivation practices and rotate through others in order to maximize one's progress.

It is standard practice that after a session of mental witnessing practice (mindfully watching your thoughts) and after practicing prajna wisdom type contemplations (that analyze your *kleshas* during meditation in order to dissolve them), you should always end the practice session with some type of emptiness meditation where you rest your mind as empty space. This will bring you the highest progress in the quickest amount of time.

CHAPTER 4
UNUSUAL PHENOMENA THAT MIGHT APPEAR DUE TO YOUR MEDITATION PRACTICE

It is now perfectly clear that the most fundamental spiritual practice is meditation and the two basic types of meditative practice either use discrimination (analysis of the contents of the mind) or do not use discrimination (witnessing meditation).

In previous chapters we have gone over these two meditative techniques. They cannot be emphasized enough in order that you clearly know how to cultivate your mind. For instance, there is the meditation practice of eliminating *kleshas* using contemplation (wisdom or discriminative reasoning) in order to bring about a clean mental state, and the alternative practice of cultivating mental emptiness directly that corresponds to various types of "emptiness practice," including mental witnessing so that thoughts slowly die down.

The two basic meditation techniques are explained in the Analyzing Yoga chapter of the *Sandhinirmocana Sutra*, which explains that meditation can have (1) content available for contemplation or (2) content not accompanied by reflection/analysis. This is basically (1) using the discriminative ability of consciousness (contemplation practice) and (2) not using the discriminative abilities of consciousness during meditation practice (emptiness meditation). You are either using discrimination or not using discrimination (analysis). If one succeeds at these meditation practices they can reach the stage of an enlightened Bodhisattva or Buddha. A Bodhisattva is enlightened with a bit of remainder, but a Buddha is fully enlightened and has reached the full stage of non-duality.

The teachings within the *Sandhinirmocana Sutra* became the basis of Asanga's *Yogacarabhumi Sastra*, which in turn became the basis of Atisha's *Lamp for the Path to Enlightenment*, which in turn became the basis for Tsong Khapa's *Lam Rim* (*Great Stages of the Exposition of the Path*). All of these books greatly influenced Asian culture. We absolutely must say that meditation was a core element in fashioning Asian civilization.

Similarly, the idea of mental witnessing used in Confucian introspection practice (Confucians cultivate their mind by watching it carefully) was taken up by Wang Yangming, who greatly influenced pan-Asian culture with his teachings. Christian contemplation teachings strongly affected European culture as well, so do not underestimate the importance of mental watching and mental analysis. Cessation-observation (witnessing) practice is the foundational bedrock of moral and spiritual development in countless religions and cultures, but today people hardly teach it.

This is why I recommend that everyone emulate the practice of Yuan Lao Fan and Benjamin Franklin in keeping a daily record of their thoughts through mindfulness observation, and at night ceremonially making a formal report of their daily efforts to heaven. This will do more towards improving your personality and fortune than 10,000 meditation sessions, reading 10,000 meditation books or attending 10,000 meditation retreats. It employs a feedback mechanism of self-correction. *If a cultural group adopted this daily practice of mental witnessing and contemplation it would soon have outstanding citizens and accumulate enough merit to become predominant in a nation.*

By practicing meditation you begin to lay a strong foundation for a better life. At the lowest level of achievement your mind will start to become clear of wandering thought clutter so that you can concentrate with clarity. With a clear mind you will begin to see your own thoughts and behavior rather than simply get caught up in them, and through that heightened awareness you can then start making better decisions in life. Through concentration you can develop the grit and perseverance to work through problems.

All this will improve your personality and behavior and

change your fortune for the better. Through this avenue of progress you will actually change your astrological fate and fortune. In this way the road of meditation practice becomes a method of self-improvement that transforms your life for the better.

At a higher level of achievement, meditation will start to significantly purify your Qi, which is the vital energy of your physical body. This is the life force energy of a body also known as prana. As this happens all the Qi channels (*nadis*) will start to open within your body, which can actually cure many disease states and illnesses. Therefore many devas train on how to do this to help people. Opening your Qi channels will subsequently produce greater health and longevity. Meditation is thus a way to improve your health and longevity as detailed in *Look Younger, Live Longer*. Health and longevity are the next two of its many benefits.

In addition to the physical and mental benefits or the ability for meditation to change your life, there are also the possibilities of higher spiritual attainments due to meditation. As explained, the first milestone of the spiritual path is the attainment of an independent deva body, which is a subtle body made of Qi that can leave your physical body at will.

As Meher Baba explained, this subtle body composed of purified Qi, achieved through the path of meditation, can leave the physical body during sleep or wakefulness. Conscious separation of the subtle body from the outer vehicle, the physical body, is achieved when you can take off the external body as if it were a cloak and use this astral body for undertaking journeys. This achievement brings the opportunity to cultivate one's spiritual advancement even further.

Those who have a near death experience from surgery or suffer accidents where they find themselves thrown out of their physical shell essentially experience a weaker form of this subtle body, namely the body one uses after death. The first major milestone on the spiritual trail is to cultivate this independent body so that it can leave and re-enter your physical shell at will, so Buddhism also calls it the will-born body. This is the "initial fruit" of true spiritual cultivation practice although no one tells you. This achievement is why saints develop superpowers and can perform miracles.

To achieve this subtle body you need merit because its attainment requires help from higher spiritual powers. No one will help you if you are an evil human being. You need to be a virtuous person who is following the spiritual path. If you lack sufficient merit then the attainment of the subtle body, or deva body, will be impossible despite your spiritual efforts. You have to practice merit *and* cultivate spiritual practice, including the practice of Qi energy work of some type (*nei-gong* practices), in order to reach this attainment easily.

Remember that when we say that meditation opens up your Qi channels we are not just talking about acupuncture meridians. Qi channels include all the atomic bonds within the atoms and molecules that make up your physical structure. When they all are transformed through meditation practice (due to the stirring of inner vitality and inner energy work) you have strengthened a pre-existing inner etheric body double that duplicates your physical body, only this vehicle can leave your physical shell at will; you don't have to wait until you die This is not anything supernatural or un-scientific. Consider that a lower grade version of the subtle body attainment is ejected from the physical shell upon death and in near-death out-of-the-body experiences, which is why people report about it. However, a subtle body strengthened through meditation work and other spiritual practices that move the Qi, being will-born, has higher powers and abilities.

The key to the highest spiritual attainments is not just to cultivate your mind through meditation, but to also cultivate your body's Qi or vital energy through special practices such as detailed in *Nyasa Yoga*. You should not just practice meditation, but also various forms of inner energy work called *nei-gong*. To do so and achieve the subtle body quickly the cardinal principle is to *simultaneously* practice, on a fixed schedule, *several entirely different* types of spiritual cultivation because they work at producing the final result via different principles, and since you cannot predict which principle will work best for you then you should wed yourself to several. Such practices that cultivate your Qi based upon different principles include:

- Mantra recitation
- Visualization and concentration practice
- Pranayama
- Asanas (yoga, martial arts, stretching)
- *Nei-gong* inner Qi movement work

- Cosmic energy absorption (from the sun, moon, etc.)
- Qi supplementation methods (from the diet, herbs, minerals, remedial measures, environment)
- Matching yourself with earthly and cosmic transformations
- Mental unification with a guru's higher bodies
- *Bhakti* yoga (and other forms of reverence)
- Disciplined sexual practice

Using different cultivation practice techniques, which work on entirely different principles to transform your Qi and mind, you can finally start to move the superficial Qi currents within your body. From an initial trickle of Qi energy can eventually appear a flood of Qi channel transformations just as it is said that the flapping of butterfly's wings can eventually produce a hurricane. When your Qi starts to move this will eventually open up all your body's Qi channels if you keep going so that the etheric subtle body double, which is normally referred to as an astral body or spirit body, can readily strengthen.

Typically you will see the astral body double referred to as a subtle body, deva body, deity body, impure illusory body, *suddha deha*, *yin shen* and so on. As stated, the people who attain this achievement will never tell you they have it for obvious reasons. These are the "masters" of the spiritual path available in each and every spiritual tradition. They receive titles like saint, sage, master, guru or sadguru, but the common denominator is that they have all achieved one or more extra bodies composed of higher substances than matter. With those bodies they can do special things to help others.

After this subtle body attainment, further spiritual cultivation *of that astral Qi body* will produce an even higher spirit body produced from within it, composed of a yet higher etheric substrate, through a more advanced cultivation process. That next body is the Causal body said to be composed of Shen (spirit energy), and repeating the process there are higher bodies still as explained in *Move Forward* and *Nyasa Yoga*. This process is commonly discussed by Taoism, Vajrayana Buddhism, Hinduism, Yoga and works by spiritual masters such as Meher Baba, Nan Huai-Chin and traditions like Kriya Yoga, Bihar Yoga, Bahai and Sufism.

Vajrayana Buddhism describes the road to this initial subtle body achievement by dividing the entire spiritual path into a "generation stage" and then a "completion stage." There are many alternative interpretations of these stages. For instance, the generation stage entails all the spiritual cultivation practices you undertake (such as using deity yoga) prior to generating an independent subtle body, and the completion stage pertains to the cultivation path necessary after it is achieved to manipulate your winds (Qi or energy) to attain yet higher bodies and enlightenment. Alternatively, the generation stage refers to the practices necessary to get to a kundalini awakening, and the completion stage refers to all the *nei-gong* practices of inner Qi manipulation is order to complete one's deity body or deva body.

Many stages of yoga can be partitioned into generation and completion stages just as every yogic achievement can also be partitioned into the four stages of *prayoga* (warming, summit, forbearance and highest attainment). The meaning will depend upon your teacher, but the point is that there are practices you must perform prior to attaining the deva body as well as afterwards because the deva body attainment is the first milestone on the cultivation path of the *sambhogakaya* Reward body (also called an Immanence body) that masters of all paths must attain.

Prior to the attainment of the spiritual body you need to devote yourself to many cultivation practices and you will consequentially experience many physical symptoms arising due to your practices. Therefore on the one side you have mental cultivation involving emptiness or witnessing meditation, the elimination of negative thoughts tendencies (*kleshas*) and errant, non-virtuous behaviors. On the other side you have the cultivation of the inherent subtle energy of the physical body, known as your original Qi, prana or *real* kundalini energy. Pursing both mind and energy is mind-body cultivation, or the Yogacara-Madhyamika (energy-emptiness) split of the esoteric schools.

If you cultivate your Qi energy well enough you will not only experience many physical symptoms related to inner Qi movements but will eventually achieve what the Yoga schools call a "kundalini awakening." This is when your original Qi, Yang Qi or real Qi finally arises in your body. This is the real prana of the physical body.

Vajrayana refers to some related milestones along this way with references to opening up the body's central *sushumna* channel whereas Yoga schools refer to opening up the *ida, pingala* and *sushumna* (left, right and central channels) within the spine. The Chinese cultivation schools, such as Taoism, talk about kundalini in terms of Yang Qi and Qi rotations within the body that open up the front and back Qi channels, called *jen mai* and *tu mai* respectively. It also uses terms such as the microcosmic circulation, macrocosmic circulation, rotation of the river chariot, and greater (or smaller) circulation of the front and back channels. These names refer to the movements of Qi (prana or kundalini) within the body once it becomes initiated.

In regards to this Nan Huai-Chin wrote:

By following the usual principles of meditation, the *Great Circulation of Heaven* and *Small Circulation of Heaven* described in Taoism will regularly occur if one can open up the back and front Qi channels of the body. What about the three Qi channels [*ida, pingala* and *sushumna*] and seven chakras of esoteric Buddhism? What happens when they are all open and one is within the scope of the cultivation of the Tao? This is a very important question. The opening of the front and back Qi channels and the rotation of the river chariot [Qi flows in circular orbits] are believed, by the Taoists who practice to become sages, to be the highest secret.

People often believe that the rotation of the river chariot is all-important and fail to ask the main question, which is how long should the Qi be rotated. One should be aware be aware that the rotation of the river chariot and the opening of the eight extra meridians are not the ultimate achievements in the cultivation of Tao. Strictly speaking, the rotation of the river chariot and circulation of Qi in the eight extra meridians are good for health and rejuvenation, but they are merely the groundwork for the cultivation and achievement of Tao.

After the Qi within the body begins to rotate and the Qi circulates in the eight extra meridians for a certain time, at an optimum stage Qi will automatically cease to rotate. The Qi does not rotate because of its fullness.

The body will gradually feel light, clear, warm and soft and one will reach the state of "forgetting the body and emptiness of self." Only at this time will one suddenly introspect and recognize the roundness and illumination of the origin of nature and life. One can actually separate from and unite with the later heaven body, which has shape and form, and then combine this original nature once again with this later heaven body (or furnace), and mind (cauldron) to continue cultivation. In his way one can either separate or unite with this body and mind and build a solid foundation for the cultivation of Tao. At this stage one can genuinely claim to have the *initial fruit*.

... Very few can achieve genuine rotation of the river chariot and circulate Qi among the eight extra meridians. Even fewer really understand the stage of separation and unification of body, mind and the origin of Nature. Therefore, even if one sincerely wants to teach this, a student with the ability to receive this supreme instruction is rare. After this stage, a person goes beyond earthly things and enters into the metaphysical realm. Even if a teacher wished to describe this in detail, a student with the wisdom and experience to receive these instructions beyond the realm of the human world would be exceptional.[2]

Prior to the achievement of the deva body, along the trail of meditation many people will experience a wide variety of physical sensations or mental phenomena but won't be able to comprehend them correctly. People typically interpret these experiences in a way that attaches to them greater significance than they deserve, and assume that they are high stages of attainment when they are really just minor phenomena corresponding to superficial Qi flows within the body.

If you do not achieve a continuous macrocosmic circulation of Qi within your body then any Qi flows you feel are not yet the *real* kundalini, but just Qi winds moving within the body that produce unusual temporary sensations. Once the real kundalini is initiated the process goes on *continuously, without stop, for years* and is eventually felt in every cell of the body. The full body Qi rotations for prolonged periods of time culminate, after many years, in the attainment of the

---

[2] *Tao and Longevity: Mind-Body Transformation*, Huai-Chin Nan, trans. by Wen Kuan Chu, (Samuel Weiser, Maine, 1991), pp. 78-79.

deva body attainment. If you are not experiencing this, the experience of Qi sensations within your body must be considered as manifestations of temporary Qi winds. This is called Fan Qi or wind Qi so that it is not mistaken for real kundalini energy, or original Qi.

Indian culture calls the arising of your Qi the kundalini or Shakti phenomena. As does Chinese culture, Yoga states that only spiritual exercises will activate your kundalini and once arisen it will begin to go through and purify your Qi channels (*nadis*), which is what will make a spiritual body attainment possible. What is rarely discussed in spiritual texts is that Qi channel blockages within the subtle body contribute to the predominance of *kleshas* in the mind-stream. Since meditation opens up any Qi meridian blockages, you don't just use it to destroy the *kleshas* and become a better human being but to finally attain the macrocosmic Qi circulation within.

Predominant among the spiritual exercises that you can perform to wash your Qi channels – as detailed in *Look Younger, Live Longer* and *Nyasa Yoga* – are pranayama techniques. As Swami Muktananda once wrote:

> Often, when Kundalini first becomes active, you feel heavy-headed and sleepy. This is a result of the movement of prana, and it is a sure sign that the Kundalini has been awakened. As Kundalini moves up through the sushumna, She transforms the body and makes it fit for spiritual sadhana; it is only after the body has been purified that the Shakti can work with full force. The basis of all disease and pain is the impurities which block the flow of prana in the nadis. These blockages are caused by imbalances and disorders in the three bodily humors – wind, bile, and phlegm – due to undisciplined habits of eating and immoderate living. In order to purify the nadis, Kundalini inspires the various hatha yogic movements or kriyas, which take place in the physical body. In the form of prana, She penetrates all 720 milllion nadis, consumes all the old decaying fluids, then releases vital energy into them all. As the nadis become filled with prana, the body becomes rejuvenated from within. It becomes strong and firm, with all the suppleness of a child.
>
> Sometimes during this process, latent germs of diseases

may be brought to the surface, and as a result, the person may start to suffer from that disease. However, this is happening to expel this disease from the system permanently, and there is nothing to be afraid of. ...

The purification of the nadis is purification of the entire system. The same blockages which cause diseases also give rise to such feelings as aversion, hatred, lethargy, dullness, and greed, and these qualities also disappear when the nadis are washed by Kundalini. When the nadis are cleansed, the mind is purified. The mind is intimately connected to prana. When the prana becomes uneven, the sense of duality arises, and the mind keeps weaving new webs of thoughts and fantasies. To control the mind, to make it still and even, yogis try to control the breath. This is why they practice so many different kinds of pranayama, or breath control. During the process of Siddha Yoga purification, natural pranayama begins to take place. The prana and apana (the outgoing and incoming breaths) become even, and eventually the breath begins to be retained within. This is called kumbhaka. Shaivism says that to keep controlling your breath is not true kumbhaka. In true kumbhaka, the prana and apana become one. At that point, prana does not go out, nor does apana come in. When prana stops, the mind becomes still, and you experience supreme tranquility. Great beings are in this state of inner stillness. If you look at the picture of my Guru, Nityananda, you will see that he has a big belly. This is not because he ate too much but because of the inner kumbhaka.[3]

Many physical phenomena commonly happen to meditators who begin to practice, pranayama, visualization, mantra, yoga, asanas and of course meditation. Unfortunately, they always become confused about these phenomena and often confuse the lesser for the greater because of a resemblance. In order to help meditators become more knowledgeable and avoid interpreting these phenomena as higher than they are, here is a list of some of the things you will commonly encounter due to spiritual practices:

[3] *Kundalini: The Secret of Life*, Swami Muktananda (SYDA Foundation, New York, 1994), pp. 28-29.

Physical Sensations

The *Hatha Yoga Pradipika* states that those who practice pranayama and meditation will experience three successive symptoms or signs. This includes the physical signs of perspiration, quivering or shaking. The *bhakti* tradition of devotion states that practitioners may go through spiritual emotions and physical signs of stupor, perspiration, horripilation, choking of voice, trembling, paleness of complexion, tears, and loss of consciousness. There are far more possibilities than this.

Buddhism provides an extensive list of the different types of physical sensations you might start to experience due to meditation practice. They are all the result of Qi starting to move within your body. The short list of possible sensations this might cause includes pain, itching, coldness, warmth, weightlessness, heaviness, roughness and smoothness.

The longer list of possible sensations includes feelings of cold or coolness, heat or warmth, lightness, heaviness, roughness or coarseness, dryness, slipperiness, granular feelings, hardness, softness, tenderness, weakness, hurriedness or urgency, a feeling of being internally stuck, internal movements, itchiness, energeticness, slowness, soreness, aching or pain, swollenness, numbness, fullness, feelings of floating or sinking or being solid, feelings of being tired or rested, feelings of being sick or lost or drained, and the feeling of being courageous, scattered, dreamy, peaceful or quiet, old or dead, and hungry or thirsty.

If you experience any sensations like this due to meditation, this is normal. Don't be alarmed. The feelings arise due to transformations of your Qi and Qi channels. There are many physiological reactions like this that correspond to the opening of Qi channels, most of which can be found in Nan Huai-chin's *Tao and Longevity: Mind-Body Transformation* and *The Little Book of Hercules*. The most important sensations usually involve the feelings of warmth and coolness that correspond to transformations of the Yang Qi and Yin Qi within your body whose discussion follows.

Feelings of Heat & Warmth or Coolness & Cold

Most of the Qi transformations that happen to you due to meditation and other spiritual exercises are eventually accompanied by feelings of warmth and heat, although sometimes you will feel coolness and cold. The difference is as follows.

When your Qi starts working through your subtle body to open its Qi channels due to spiritual practice, it will encounter obstructions that cause friction. This friction will give rise to the feelings of blockage, being stuck inside, irritation, warmth and heat. Thus, people who mantra for hours will commonly feel warmth in their body as the Qi encounters friction as it starts opening up their energy channels due to this practice.

Those who perform visualization practice on any section of the body, which brings Qi to that region, will also feel a corresponding warmth and heat as the Qi channels in the vicinity start to open. For instance, if you imagine that a particular bone inside you shines with a bright light, this visualization practice will produce warmth and heat around the bone. The concentration on the bone will bring Qi to the area, the Qi will open up the channels in the vicinity, and heat will be the net result of this process.

Any type of method that brings Qi into a body, such as Qi help projected from a deva or spiritual master, is also usually accompanied by warmth. This is because Yang Qi is generally warm by nature. If it is being projected in order to help open Qi channels, that opening will usually be accompanied by warmth.

If one has a lot of heat rising in the body from meditation, such as due to a minor kundalini arousal, it is possible to experience dry skin and chapped lips. If one does a lot of pranayama practice, this is often followed by feelings of warmth in the belly and extremities as well as by shaking, perspiration or skin rashes due to poisons being eliminated from the body.

Your body has both Yang Qi and Yin Qi, which are basically warm Qi and cool Qi represented by the sun and moon, or fire and water. Most spiritual texts talk about Yang Qi but rarely about Yin Qi, which corresponds to the sensation of cold or coolness in the body during some stages of cultivation.

For instance, one stage of cultivation called "coolness and lightness" (*ching an* – see *Tao and Longevity: Mind-Body Transformation*) is often accompanied by feelings of coolness all over the body that you might compare to a light breeze, air conditioning, the melting of dry ice or the feeling of cool vapor rising from the body. This coolness experience often appears as the energy channels of your body are being transformed.

A more serious stage of Yin Qi transformation will produce sudden chills and shaking, similar to malaria or fever, where you might even find your teeth chattering from the cold you feel all over your body. When this occurs you might need to climb into bed for a half hour or so until the Yin Qi from the body is released from your obstructed channels. Since this type of shaking rarely lasts more than a half hour, something more serious than this reaction is probably the sign of a medical condition.

Whenever anyone does feminine, lunar or water-related sadhana practices, one should expect to feel coolness in the body as the Yin Qi is being purified and Yin Qi channels start opening. You can also feel cool Yin Qi when you deal with sickness, ghost sadhanas, funerals and other ceremonies or practices related to Yin Qi. Some people feel chills or sharp pains in the legs whenever people talk about sickness or unfortunate things, and this is also an indication of the Yin Qi channels opening.

During certain stages of cultivation, devas often expose practitioners to illusory situations (such as being attacked by ghosts or demons) that arouse extreme fear and anxiety. Normally people feel a bit cold under such circumstances. The purpose of making them afraid is so that these emotions stir/activate their Yin Qi so that the appropriate Yin Qi channels can be opened.

While people can have Yang Qi blessings from spiritual beings that feel like bliss, there are Yin Qi blessings as well that involve cultivating your Qi channels. Chinese herbal medicine has various formulas, as does Ayurveda, for dealing with Yin Qi excesses and deficiencies in the body but only a wise master can tell whether you need these for cultivation purposes.

Vibrations – Internal Qi Movements

As the Qi begins to stir within your body due to meditation practice, you will often feel all sorts of strange movements and vibrations within your body. Ramakrishna presented a poetic description of these vibrations saying that the kundalini motion inside you might feel like the movement of an ant, a fish, monkey, a bird or serpent. Of course, there are thousands of different sensations possible when kundalini arises, so this sentence is misleading if you confine yourself to just these five types of sensations. Basically, you will start to feel all sorts of energetic movements inside you when your Qi starts to move, which can and must happen on the spiritual path. When it first starts to stir, however, this is just wind Qi rather than the real Qi or real kundalini of the physical body.

For instance, it is common to feel the Qi moving or even rotating inside you after Qi channels open. You might feel the front-back microcosmic Qi circulation up the spine and down the front of the body as described in Taoism, Yoga and the Vajrayana traditions. You might feel the individual major Qi channels (acupuncture meridians) described by Taoism, Yoga and Chinese medicine. There are so many ways to describe the fact that you might feel energy not just moving but rotating in specific patterns inside you. Sometimes this will produce headaches or heart palpitations. *Tao and Longevity: Mind-Body Transformation* has many descriptions of such phenomena as does *The Little Book of Hercules*.

You might also feel pumping at the back of your heels (as represented by the feathered wings on the heels of the Greek god Mercury), Qi wiggling at the base of your spine, or energy pumping through it. You might feel various pumping sensations in your sacrum (the "sacral chakra") or lower abdomen and at other body locations. Even if a location is not specifically mentioned in any books, you must remember that the sensation of energy pushing inside you is due to Qi movements trying to force open obstructed Qi channels. Your situation, however unusual, is not any different from this.

In general, you will feel movements inside your head, chest, abdomen, appendages, bones ... simply anywhere and everywhere inside your body when your Qi begins to move. Until you have the real kundalini awakening, which is followed by many months (and then years) of full body Qi movements without interruption, the sensations are all to be considered *wind* Qi rather than the *real* Yang Qi of the body.

The sensations you feel of wind Qi correspond to the opening of the tissues in your subtle body, which we call Qi channels in the physical body, and prepare you for the real kundalini awakening. Often you will feel your entire body being shaken when your Qi first starts to stir, and you might even feel as if there is an entire inner scaffolding within the flesh that can be grabbed and shaken. All sorts of strange sensations are possible.

One of the worst feelings is a type of vibration or motion of Qi within your head that is so severe that moving your head in any direction brings pain, and you must lie down for a day or so until it passes. When this happens I have no good advice other than to find a position that is comfortable until this goes away. This stage, which is meant to open the channels in your brain, is very painful.

When the real Qi passes through your brain stem – at the stage of a kundalini awakening – this also produces severe pain for a few seconds until the channels in the brain stem are finally opened. The biographical story of Zen Patriarch Huike says he heard celestial voices to "bear the pain in your head as your skull bones are being opened" when this happened. The actual truth was that he head voices telling him to bear the pain as the brain stem was being opened. The voices were due to devas who were working on opening his Qi channels.

Changes in Respiration

There have been many scientific studies proving that meditation can slow your heart rate, reduce your blood pressure, and stimulate hormonal changes in the body. Many physiological changes caused by meditation have already been recorded by modern science. Of course during meditation it is common for your respiration to slow down, but during the course of meditation practice it is also possible for a practitioner's breathing to slow to a seeming halt. This is not anything to worry about when it happens because the body is doing this naturally. If this wasn't something that was supposed to happen due to meditative relaxation then the body wouldn't let it happen! Therefore there is no reason to police it or worry about it. In fact, you want this to occur for longer and longer periods of time if possible.

Just as it is possible due to meditation to feel internal pumping in the abdomen, as a type of embryo breathing, your breathing can at times speed up or slow down due to cultivation progress. Overall, however, it should become slower, smoother and deeper over time. In other words, it should become more smoother and more regular. To help attain this type of progress, all meditation practitioners are advised to practice pranayama exercises, namely *kumbhaka* breath retention exercises. This is one of the fastest ways to make progress at spiritual cultivation, yet few masters stress it.

The best way to open Qi channels quickly is actually through pranayama practice. I particular recommend the nine-bottled wind practice, detailed in *Nyasa Yoga* and *Visualization Practice*, as well as the eight *kumbhaka* pranayama techniques, called pots, from the *Geranda-Samhita*. The longer you can hold your breath, by combining the methods of freediving with standard *kumbhaka*, the better will eventually be your progress in meditation.

When people have done so much energy work that their Qi has become imbalanced, a sure remedy is to practice the nine-bottled wind pranayama technique as well as the bellows breathing and shining skull pranayama methods of Hatha Yoga. However, many masters have favorite pranayama techniques other than the ones I have listed.

In his *Raja-Yoga*, Swami Vivekananda stated:

> After one has learnt to have a firm, erect seat, one has to perform, according to certain schools, a practice called the purification of the nerves [Qi channels]. This part has been rejected by some as not belonging to Raja-Yoga; but since so great an authority as the commentator Shankaracharya advises it, I think it fitting that it should be mentioned, and I will quote his own directions from his commentary on the Svetasvatara Upanishad: "The mind whose dross has been cleared away by pranayama becomes fixed in Brahman; therefore pranayama is taught. First the nerves [Qi channels] are to be purified; then comes the power to practice pranayama. Stopping the right nostril with the thumb, draw in air through the left nostril according to capacity; then without any interval, eject the air through the right nostril, closing the left one. Again inhaling through the right nostril according to capacity, eject through the left. Practicing this three or five times at four periods of the day – before dawn, during midday, in the evening, and at midnight – one attains purity of the nerves [helps open the Qi channels] in fifteen days or a month.

Then begins pranayama." Practice is absolutely necessary. You may sit down and listen to me by the hour every day, but if you do not practice, you will not get one step farther. It all depends on practice. We never understand these things until we experience them. We have to see and feel them for ourselves. Simply listening to explanations and theories will not do.[4]

The venerable Shankaracharya quoted the sage Yajnavalkya on some alternative pranayama techniques one might try:

Thinking of [the seed-word] Hum, at the junction of the pingala and the ida (the right and the left nostrils), the ida should be filled with external air in twelve seconds; then the yogi meditates on fire in the same place, with the word Rung, and while meditating thus, slowly ejects the air through the pingala. Again filling in, through the pingala, the air should be slowly ejected through the ida in the same way. This should be practiced for three or four years, or three or four months, according to the directions of a guru, in secret (alone in a room), in the early morning, at midday, in the evening, and at midnight [until] the nerves become purified. Lightness of body, clear complexion, good appetite, and hearing of the Nada are the signs of the purification of the nerves [Qi channels]. Then should be practiced pranayama, composed of rechaka (exhalation), kumbhaka (retention), and puraka (inhalation). Joining the prana with the apana is pranayama.

After filing the body from the head to the feet in sixteen seconds, the prana is to be expelled in thirty-two seconds, and for sixty-four, kumbhaka should be practiced [16:64:32].

There is another pranayama, in which kumbhaka should first be made for sixty-four seconds, then the prana should be expelled in sixteen, and the body next filled in sixteen seconds [16:64:16].

---

[4] *Vivekananda: The Yogas and Other Works*, Swami Vivekananda, (Ramakrishna-Vivekananda Center, New York, 1971), p. 587.

By pranayama the impurities of the body are expelled.[5]

The sage Yajnavalkya also provided an entirely different set of directions, similar to Nyasa Yoga, which you can also use to purify your Qi channels:

> The following pratyahara is the greatest yogic practice and is praised and followed by yogis always. Having drawn the prana from one point to another, holding it in the eighteen vital points (marmasthanas) is spoken of as pratyahara. The Asvini Kumaras who are the best among the physicians of the celestials (devas) have spoken thus of the vital points in the body, for the attainment of liberation from yoga.
>
> I shall explain all of them in an orderly manner. Listen, disciplined [Gargi]! The big toes, the ankles, in the mid-shanks, the root of the calves, the knees, middle of the thighs, the root of the anus, the center of the body (dehamadhya), generative organ, the navel, the heart, and neck pit, Gargi. Then, the root of the palate, the root of the nose, circular orb of the eyes, the center of the eyebrows, the forehead, and crown of the head. …. These are the vital points. …
>
> Some skilled yogis speak of [another] pratyahara. Listen beautiful [Gargi], I will tell you [about] it. During the practice of pranayama, the prana must be held by the mind from the big toe to the crown of the head, like a totally filled pot. Drawing [the prana] from the crown of the head, one must focus it in the forehead. Drawing [the prana] from the crown of the head, one must focus it in the forehead. Again, drawing the prana from the forehead, one must focus it between the eyebrows. Drawing [the prana] from the center of the eyebrows one must focus it in the center of the eyes. Drawing the prana from the eyes, one must focus it in the root of the nose. From the root of the nose, one must focus the prana in the root of the tongue. Drawing [the prana] from the root of the tongue, one must focus it in the base of the throat (neck-pit). Drawing the

[5] *Vivekananda: The Yogas and Other Works*, p. 690.

prana from the neck-pit, one must focus it in the center of the heart, from the center of the heart one must focus it in the center of the navel, again from the center of the navel one must focus it in the generative organ and then from the generative organ one must focus it in the abode of fire (dehamadhya), from the dehamadhya (center of the body), Gargi, one must focus it in the root of the anus and from the root of the anus in the [mid-] thighs, then from the mid-thigh in the center of the knees. Then, [from the knee] one must focus the prana in the root of the calf, from there in the middle of the shank, and drawing [the prana] from the middle of the shank in the ankle. From the ankle, Gargi, one must focus it (the prana) in the big toes of the feet.

The wise one who, drawing the prana from point to point, focuses it in the above said manner, will be freed from all bondage and will live as long as the moon and the stars exist (will attain liberation). This [pratyahara] is praised as the means for the fruition of yoga even by Agastya (one of the great sages). Among the pratyaharas, this one is considered as the best by yogis.[6]

Sensations Inside Your Appendages

As stated, due to meditation it is possible at times to feel Qi energy moving inside your various appendages, specifically the arms and legs or even the nose, ears and sexual organs. If you are a male who is young and healthy, while meditating you might also feel your scrotum tightening. You can sometimes feel your Qi move in various repeating patterns within you such as orbits too.

Practicing the exercises laid out in *Nyasa Yoga* and other tantric yoga texts will help smooth out any aberrations within these energy patterns. Some of the best books to guide you include *Yoga Yajnavalkya*, *A Systematic Course in the Ancient Tantric Techniques of Yoga and Kriya* (Satyananda Saraswati), *Dharana Darshan: Yogic, Tantric and Upanishadic Practices of Concentration and Visualization* (Niranjanananda Saraswati), *Kriya Secrets Revealed* (J.C. Stevens), *Hatha Yoga Pradipika*, *Tibetan Yoga and Secret Doctrines* (Walter Evans-Wentz), *The Six Yogas of*

---

[6] *Yoga Yajnavalkya*, trans. by A.G. Mohan with Ganesh Mohan, (Svastha Yoga Pte Ltd, 2013), pp. 75-79.

Naropa (Glenn Mullin), *Readings on The Six Yogas of Naropa* (Glenn Mullin) and finally *Roots of Yoga* (Mallinson and Singleton).

To develop the deva body you need to eventually reach a point where you feel the entire body of Qi within your limbs and your body as a single whole. Within this whole body feeling your Qi must begin circulating for years, twelve to be exact. To reach this attainment you must go through various stages of preparatory progression, which you can actually practice to attain.

The initial stage is to feel random internal Qi movements, which tends to happen to most meditation practitioners after awhile. This is the phenomenon of wind Qi starting to move within you. Next you will feel your Qi moving in particular patterns, and will eventually reach the stage where you feel the entire Qi of your body's trunk and limbs. You have to work hard using many exercises to reach this attainment for the objective is to open all the channels in every cell and atomic bond. This is why it is figuratively said that the body is a meshwork composed of 72,000 Qi channels. The *Prapanchasara Tantra* also says there are 300,000 channels networking the body while the *Shiva Samhita* ramps this up to 350,000 channels. All these numbers are just figurative ways of saying that you must transform the Qi within every cell and tissue of your body.

All you have to know is that you are trying to purify an exact etheric duplicate of your body by activating your Yang Qi to pass through every one of its components, and this is the meaning of "72,000 Qi channels." By doing this you can attain the subtle deva body. Actually, you already have this subtle body within you because it is ejected upon death. However, that body is not purified. What you are trying to do is activate your real kundalini so that it passes through all of its tissues to open up obstructions, thus purifying it. In this way it will attain an even higher stage of purity. Through spiritual exercises you can attain mastery of this body while alive and then use it at will, which is the first genuine success stage of the spiritual path.

There are many sensations common to practitioners who begin to purify the inner subtle body. A common sensation due to meditation is to feel as if the entire body is like an empty sack. It is also common that an appendage, such as an arm, temporarily feels entirely vacuous or empty inside. Some body parts might feel like they are becoming larger. You might even feel body parts disappearing or simply getting lighter or heavier. You might feel sinking or rising feelings of the body's energy, or sideways movements of your Qi too.

The Little Book of Hercules describes several milestone *gong-fu* stages along these lines. One unusual phenomenon occurs when the front Qi channels (*jen mai*) in the body start to open and the chest the temporarily feels as if it is enclosed by an impenetrable barrier like armor. In Chinese culture this is symbolized by the story of Sun Wukong (the Monkey King) getting his armor when retrieving his staff from the bottom of the ocean (symbolizing the Yang Qi or real kundalini rising from a person's perineum). In Greek culture it is symbolized by the story of Hercules strangling the Nemean lion and then wearing its impenetrable hide.

Another particular milestone on the cultivation path is when the Qi channel meridians running down the inside of the legs to the big toes start to open. When this happens you might feel the actual channel lines tracing out their existence. To some practitioners it feels like a line of dry hot Qi along the meridians when those channel lines open.

Afterwards you might immediately start having sinus problems, where your nose drips mucus for no reason whatsoever, because the nasal cavity then beings clearing out. This phenomenon, which is not due to sickness or allergies, will probably happen several times during the cultivation path and is explained in *Tao and Longevity*. During many stages of transformation you will often find the nasal cavity acting up because Qi channels in this vicinity are being cleansed, thus pushing out sinus fluid.

Something similar happens when the prostate and scrotum channels are being opened. As Nan Huai-chin mentioned about the sinus problems, the only thing you can do is swallow the mucus until the cleansing disappears, although neti pot washing of the cavities (with water salt and baking soda) may help. Acupuncture might help as well. Along these lines, be careful not to confuse actual sinus problems with Qi channel cleansings caused by advances in your Qi purification efforts.

A similar phenomenon may happen to men as the channels within their prostate and generative organs start to become cleansed by Qi. Men will often find clear prostate fluid in their urine for a short while when the generative organ channels are being opened, or suffer dreamless wet dreams during their sleep. Unusual things can also happen to a man's penis during the various stages of Qi channel purification, such as it being temporarily pulled into the body (called becoming retractable) for a short period of time. As these things are temporary most male cultivators usually pay them no special heed.

Women will experience unusual phenomena related to their vagina as well. It is common for some women to lose their menses due to substantial cultivation progress, and then to regain it again after they pass through the requisite higher stages of attainment.

Skin Problems

As the Qi pushes through your Qi channels to cleanse them most people will develop some sort of detoxification reaction, namely various types of skin problems. These skin problems may last for years or be temporary, and may or may not be accompanied by itching.

It is common to develop skin rashes due to the purification efforts of Qi pushing the obstructions and poisons out of your Qi channels. Irregularly shaped or even circular rashes might form on body parts that you are working on through yogic practices. The problems may seem similar to eczema or psoriasis and respond to a better diet, but the real cure usually centers around herbal detoxification regimes to help quickly clean the body. Sometimes there is nothing you can do to speed the progress of poisons being ejected from your body due to the strong Qi purification being undergone within you. Even the finest forms of nature-based healthcare will often fail you until all the poisons are ejected from your body.

Sometimes a meditator will even find a residue line building up underneath the fingernails, which indicates that poisons are being pushed out of the heart channels. Taoism practitioners usually cut the skin right under the fingernails when this happens so that the released blood can then push out the accumulated poisons. In Chinese medicine people also sometimes cut the top of the ears and squeeze out congealed blood in order to improve stagnant blood circulation.

There are other various remedies to dissolve internal blood clots and improve blood circulation you might try to help speed the processes of detoxification and body purification. These would involve ingredients such as fish oil, nattokinase, red ginseng, raw tienchi powder and other substances.

At very advanced stages of cultivation there are stories of poisons and pus being pushed out of the body due to the force of strong Qi currents, as was the case with Yeshe Tsogyel, or even one's blood being pushed through the skin as was the case of Ramakrishna due to so much excellent cultivation work. The Yoga schools commonly tell you that the physical body will be *purified* through the "fire of yoga," and the meaning is that there will be all sorts of exudations due to the frictional pushing of kundalini trying to force its way through obstructed Qi channels.

Sweet Saliva

Another unusual and unique phenomenon caused by meditation is a sweet taste that appears in the mouth, namely sweet saliva, which appears at a certain stage of meditation progress. The practitioner's saliva becomes very sweet, and this sweet taste seems to vary over time in terms of its thickness and sweetness. This phenomenon of sweet saliva can turn on and off for years, and is temporary rather than permanent in nature.

This sweet saliva goes by many different names such as ambrosia (Greeks), soma or amrita (Hindus), Grail wine (Christian mystics), and sweet wine (Sufis). Some cultivation books say it is due to the pituitary gland of the brain secreting hormones while others say it is due to reactions at the front of the head. Others suggest transformations in the salivary glands. In any case, this signifies a good stage of cultivation progress.

For more information, the sweet saliva phenomenon is clearly mentioned in the medieval *Atalanta Fugiens* from Europe, *Tao and Longevity* (Nan), *The Little Book of Hercules* (Bodri), various yoga books, and *A Systematic Course in the Ancient Tantric Techniques of Yoga and Kriya* (Satyananda Saraswati), which contains the largest collection of information on this phenomenon.

Whole Body Sensations

One of the common reactions after someone does a lot of meditation or *nei-gong* inner energy work is that they feel "shitty" the next day after waking up from sleep. It is hard to describe this feeling other than that they feel blocked up or stuck inside all over their body. Sometimes a practitioner's muscles will be locked the next day after strenuous cultivation practice and they cannot move, but this always wears off. Often people will just feel terrible, such as incredibly tired the next day, after the initiated Qi has been opening Qi channels due to all the great meditative work they did during the day.

These feelings are all proper signs of progress.

While over the long run meditation will cause people's bodies to become softer and warmer because the Qi channels open, you have to go through lots of other different transformative processes, sometimes including uncomfortable feelings like this, to make progress. You shouldn't get frightened about them but just consider the uncomfortable feelings of blockage as a normal affair just as it is normal to feel sore after a lot of sports activity or exercise. The book, *Tao and Longevity* by Nan Huai-chin, explains some of the major physical reactions you will feel in your body along these lines. Even going through puberty we suffer uncomfortable feelings, but this is normal as the body grows and matures. The case of meditation purification is no different.

Strange Emotional Outbursts

During the preparatory process of preparing for kundalini's arousal, any Qi initiated due to meditation will eventually pass through your internal organs. This is likely to cause emotional eruptions for a short period of time until the organ channels become sufficiently unblocked.

Many people know about the emotional-physical correspondences discovered by the Chinese that the health of the liver is related to anger, violence, hatred, brutality, impulsiveness and bad moods of irritation; joy, kindness and love are related to the heart; grief, shame, and pessimism are related to the lungs; and fear, anxiety and dread are related to the kidneys. Western energy and bodywork researchers have actually gone past the Chinese indications and discovered many more correspondences than this, including emotions attached to different body parts other than organs. Nutripuncture also catalogs different types of emotional imbalances when your organs are too strong or weak.

As your Qi (activated by meditation) passes through your internal organs, which cleanses the etheric double of the organs within your subtle body, emotional outbursts and eruptions along these lines will commonly happen due to the energy encountering blockages. It is said that spiritual cultivation will not only awaken the angel in us but also the devil when nonspiritual tendencies are forced to the conscious level. producing emotional eruptions, When your Qi runs through an organ this often produces emotional eruptions. These unfortunate reactions are to be expected unless the organs are very healthy.

Meditators will sometimes find themselves crying for no reason at all when their kidney Qi is being cleared. Shakyamuni Buddha said, "they might find themselves spontaneously bursting into tears (under all sorts of random circumstances)." They might find themselves becoming overly fearful at certain situations when the kidney or Yin Qi of their body is also being purified. In fact, in some cultivation schools it is common for an enlightened master to throw students into situations that cause them to become extremely afraid in order that the Yin Qi of their body can be purified and appropriate channels opened. They might suddenly be shown some fake supernatural sights that will frighten them (the visions caused by their master) and a master will use this opportunity to work on their now activated Yin Qi circulations.

The point is that many unfavorable reactions occur when the Qi provokes emotional reactions as it starts poking through obstructions that involve our internal organs. We can become emotionally vulnerable in particular ways until those organ channels open. This is why in some cases various emotional reactions are desired by enlightened masters to help you purify your Qi channels. During those instances you might sometimes have a very clear mind that seems entirely separate and detached from the emotions you are experiencing.

This is particularly the case with anger, as anger issues usually arise on the spiritual path when Yang Qi passes through the liver and gall bladder organs or meridians. At that time, irritation that turns into violent anger or rage must be guarded against, as explained in *The Little Book of Hercules*. Martial artists who start to open their liver meridians commonly experience this type of problem too because it is due to better Qi circulations being established when blockages are being cleared from the liver.

Whenever Yang Qi arises within your body it is possible to feel over-confident, tremendously bold and courageous, angry and wrathful, or excessively proud. Representative emotional reactions, and many others that occur as your Yin Qi and Yang Qi are being provoked, are explained in the second set of ten delusional meditation states mentioned in the *Surangama Sutra*, which you can find in chapter six.

Visions

It is common to at times see strange visions, both internal and external, on the cultivation path of meditation. However, always remember that the visions are not due to you having attained superpowers or supernatural vision. If that were so then you would be able to readily see supernatural visions at will. Since you cannot, therefore you do not have such powers. They are visions being given to you. Whatever strange notions people strongly believe are typically revealed within their dreams or visions, and so what you might see is often just the product of wild imagination. Unfortunately, people become infatuated with and misguided by this irrelevant stuff.

Many mystical experiences are also just the results of spiritual hopes and fervent imaginations caused by Qi impinging upon certain centers of the brain. Swami Vivekananda once wrote, "When the meditation is deep, one sees many wonderful things." Nan Huai-chin wrote this is usually due to deep-seated psychological tendencies being stirred by Qi within the brain and then interacting with consciousness.

Please remember the rule that a genuine spiritual realization must:

- Never contradict critical human reasoning and analysis
- Always be conducive to the happiness and welfare of all beings

If one does not hold to these rules there is the danger, as has been repeated throughout history, that some one-time strange dream, vision, hallucination or imagination (uch as of God speaking to you or commanding you) will lead to great harm and wrongdoing such as wars, murderous blood sacrifices, self-immolation, individuals giving away all their riches, and other forms of great harm.

People have often lost their family fortune, their career, their health or even their life due to self-delusion and self-deception connected with dreams, visions and other non-repeatable mental experiences. Believing in them and then acting upon them often leads to ruin or humiliation. One must always look at any "spiritual" dreams or visions with critical examination, typically ignoring them entirely. You must use common sense and wisdom to guide yourself in the world. Wise spiritual practitioners must always warn other spiritual adherents about this rule and not take dreams or visions seriously.

That being said, sometimes the visions people see (despite their wide variety) are actually given to practitioners by devas and enlightened teachers on the cultivation path for a purpose. However, this is rare and not to be expected, and still the rule of wisdom is to be followed because usually those interventions are misleading. Furthermore, they usually contain no useful information because no higher guide wants you to become dependent upon them.

On the road of cultivation you must become dependent only on wisdom and clear consciousness. Spiritual individuals should not develop a mystical mind that eschews rational logic, and so visions are not to be expected or used for guidance. For guidance and proper decision making use your own clear reasoning and analysis instead.

As your mind is to be developed on the spiritual path, always look to wisdom, logic and rational analysis for guidance rather than turn to superstitious mysticism wherein you can easily be cheated or fall prey to self-deception. Spiritual practitioners too often become overly mystical or superstitious and then lose their mental balance. In attributing visions to gods, goddesses or other spiritual beings, there is a great danger that this will open the door to self-delusion, exaggeration, wrong thinking and harmful acts. This is yet another reason why such things are rarely given.

Sometimes someone is truly given a spiritual vision to help them, such as for motivation or inspiration, but when it is truly due to a spiritual being it is typically just the devas practicing their powers without any regards to your well-being and how you will react. It is miserable to go through such experiences when you and the people around you don't understand what is going on.

"Devas" means heavenly beings, which includes people who have passed away (such as your parents and ancestors) and not yet reincarnated. It also means angels or *dakinis,* and spiritual cultivators who have already attained a subtle body and therefore are now considered spiritual masters. Who is a deva? Someone just like you who has passed away and not yet reincarnated or a person like who has become a spiritual master; "Heaven" is the subtle plane around us on this earth, though if you cultivate to a higher stage of spiritual attainment you can then travel to other planes (realms) and planets. When one attributes phenomenon to a "deity," that deity is usually just a human being who has some stage of spiritual attainment and/or powers (enlightenment) and then masquerades as some spiritual great in order to help others.

You can read about some representative types of visions people typically see due to delusion-inspiring devas in the "50 Delusive Mara States of Practitioners" found in the *Surangama Sutra.* They are caused by devas and spiritual masters when helping to open the Qi channels of advancing practitioners. The visions they put into your head when doing this usually have no meaning whatsoever, but people mistakenly think they are enlightened or special when they occur.

For instance, Christian practitioners might see visions of internal flames within their heart after reciting Christian prayers centered in their chest, such as the Prayer of Jesus. No such flames, even in etheric form, actually exist as this is just a typical false illusion commonly given to ardent practitioners of that method. Due to Biblical influences, Christians might also see visions or have dreams of spiritual beings with the head of an ox, horse, lion, eagle or whatever because of what they read of such beings in the Old Testament or Book of Revelations. No such strange looking beings actually exist, including angels being people with feathered wings. Wouldn't it be terribly uncomfortable to have such a body at a higher stage of excellence?

Such visions are common in Christianity because centuries ago, in a largely agrarian and uneducated society, someone saw that type of fictitious vision created by some playful master and his disciples, the tale of the vision got turned into a religious text, and then the same images were repeated over and over again because of cultural expectations that this represented true spirituality. This happens in every culture, and thus common visions differ by religion, nation or community.

Let's again consider the event of seeing fictitious images of angels with wings. Wouldn't those wings be uncomfortable to sleep with given that an angel is considered to be at a higher stage of spiritual excellence? The subtle body that you attain as a spiritual practitioner (or upon death) lacks wings, and yet you can quickly get from one place to another because it is a Qi body. Unfortunately, people see visions of many strange things like this, which may or may not have a religious connotation, and mistakenly think they are real and represent true reality. They are just deceptions, illusions or delusions given by devas practicing how to project their powers of visualization into specific parts of your brain, or simply just imaginations. The top two levels of Desire Realm devas, as explained by Buddhism, are particularly adept at playing with giving visionary experiences to ardent spiritual practitioners. Critical thinking is your weapon against being taken in by such deceptions.

In the cases where you hear the story of a master talking with deceased spiritual greats (such as when Jesus' disciples saw him speaking with Moses and Elijah, or Sufis saw their master speaking with various Muslim forefathers), these were also fictitious projections into the minds of the believers that made their way into print. This is clearly explained within the last chapter of the *Surangama Sutra*, which explains the typical types of mara delusional meditation experiences. Once you attain a deva body and you can enter the minds of others, you learn to do all sorts of mental tricks like this.

If a vision occurs to you where you see a spiritual great, such as in a dream, ask how you could possibly know who that person was if you had never seen them before and you are not given their name? Such information is also projected into your mind during visions so that you can interpret them according to the master's wishes. In the *Surangama Sutra* you can read about all sorts of fake visions projected into people like this, some for play and some for sport. Ignore them.

A famous Taoist story along these lines occurred in the life of Lu Yan (later known as Lu Dong Bin), who was once studying to become a Chinese official. At an inn he drank some wine and then fell asleep at the table, dreaming that he took the imperial exam, passed with excellent marks and was awarded a prestigious office. In the dream he also became married, had a son and eventually became prime minister. Attracting the jealousy of others, he was accused of crimes and then through various events lost his office, wife, children and money. He woke up from his dream when he was dying in the street. The entire dream, which covered eighteen years of his life, had taken place during the short space of time that it took to cook a meal of yellow millet, and so it has become known as the Yellow Millet Dream.

Unbeknownst to him, this dream was being given to him by the Taoist master Zhongli Quan at the inn in order to make Lu Dong Bin realize the uselessness of a life that pursues power, position and profit. It was meant to encourage him, because of his past life efforts, to once again start cultivating the Tao. After Lu Yan awoke, he abandoned his pursuit to become a government official and entered the cultivation road of Taoism to become an immortal sage. He eventually became enlightened.

The images (visions) one often sees during cultivation are normally reflective of the country, race, culture and religion of the practitioner. For instance, Chinese practitioners might see visions of dragons, Chinese protect gods and deities, Kuan Yin, Lao Tzu, and other Chinese personages during the course of their meditation progress. They might see flames on their shoulders or proceeding out of the top of their head (since in Chinese culture this denotes a virtuous person), all of which are also fake visions. A practitioner might even see visions of unusual things within their own or another person's body as this is a type of meditation practice used within Buddhism and Taoism.

Shangqing Taoism teaches by using descriptions of deities residing within your body so that cultivation practitioners do not become frightened when they discover that devas are the ones who must enter into them to help open up Qi channels. This school has teaching equivalents with the tantric schools of India and Tibet along these lines. These schools all use colorful pictures of meditators with Buddhas and their consorts living within their bodies in order to open up the Qi channels. No one lives inside you but devas will enter into you or project their energy into you to help open up your Qi channels.

Incidentally, it is through sutras that Buddhism prepares its practitioners for the fact that devas must enter into their bodies to open Qi channels. Various sutras state that Bodhisattvas, such as Kuan Yin (Avalokitesvara), have pores within their body that are entire worlds with many beings inside them. A slow indoctrination along these lines helps prepare practitioners to accept the fact that Buddhas, Bodhisattvas, saints, sages, masters, gurus, devas and deities are the ones who must enter practitioners' bodies to help open up their Qi channels, and are the ones who sometimes give them inspirations or thoughts that solve problems. The Tantric yoga schools and Buddhist Vajrayana also shows pictures of deities within your body to help prepare you for this truth.

Buddhist practitioners who meditate will sometimes see visions of Buddhas and Bodhisattvas (Amitofo, Shakyamuni, Vairocana, Kuan Yin, Manjusri, Samantabhadra, etc.), protect gods, *asuras* and heavens (or hells) given by their master or devas. In certain cases they might see Buddhas above their head or chakras projected into the sky above the skull. Once again, these are all illusions given to them by devas entering their brains and projecting visions into the nerves.

A special category of this type of activity includes visions or dreams of hell, given to people with the appropriate karma, which usually involve fanciful images along with feelings of emotional despair, rage and agony. The tales of such visions – which are found in countless cultures even though the representations are always different – are often made into stories passed down through generations that have provided a tremendous beneficial force in society for the eschewing of non-virtuous ways.

Hindu practitioners who ardently meditate might see visions of Shiva, Vishnu, Brahma, Krishna, Lakshmi, Kali and other spiritual greats. They will also be commonly given visions of strange beings mentioned in Hindu legends. As with every other religion, it is also common for expectant Hindu women (as well as pregnant Christian, Buddhist, Moslem, etc. women) to receive dreams of light-filled rooms and other auspicious events when they become impregnated or are just about to give birth to a future master.

In certain cultivation traditions, special visions become a specialty taught to all the lineage's devas so that they can give them to practitioners to help guide them. For instance, in the Nityananada-Muktananda tradition, the devas are taught to project the image of a blue sparkly point into practitioners to let them know they are on the right cultivation path. In the Aghora and Kali traditions, practitioners often see specialized visions too that they have come to expect due to teachings. Traditional lineage-dependent visions are to be contrasted with cases where no specific vision content is expected, but just a general framework of a visionary expectation, as is normal with American Indians on vision quests.

The Tibetan esoteric Yoga traditions, such as the Six Yogas of Naropa, also have specific vision expectations that are given to ardent practitioners. If a meditator is training in the Tibetan Vajrayana tradition then they are taught to expect to see visions (like stock images used again and again) of one type of Qi dissolving into another type, such as water element Qi dissolving into fire element Qi or "fire element dissolving into the wind element" and so on. They are taught to expect "signs of elemental dissolutions" that will arise because of good meditation work, and which will produce visions like that of a butter-lamp, firefly-like sparks, smoke and mirage. Actually, there are no such things as the elemental dissolutions described in these texts, which is why they are not found in other cultivation traditions.

These are all fictitious visions (illusions) commonly given to Vajrayana practitioners at a certain stage of their yogic practice. They were designed ages ago as milestones to encourage people in specific practice vehicles. Because practitioners all know about these visions they are used over and over again when they don't really correspond to any stages of Qi dissolution at all (or any such biophysical or etheric process). There is no such thing as one type of elemental Qi types dissolving into one another due to cultivation practice. Someone made that false explanation up ages ago as a mechanism for guiding concentration practice, it became part of the tradition, and both devas and masters since that time commonly practice by generating derivatives of these standard visions in order to motivate people during their course of meditation practice. Of course, no such dissolutions really exist.

As the *Lotus Sutra* of skillful means explains, most practitioners do not know that much of cultivation practice and progress is actually based on deceptions like this. Even a master will not tell you what is truthfully going on. Unfortunately, masters and their deva students are just human beings with etheric bodies, and get carried away when they develop these powers and want to practice them. This typically results in all sorts of problems for practitioners.

Another vision common to Tibetan meditation traditions is to see snakes, scorpions, centipedes and forms of smoke or dirty Qi passing out through the toes as one cultivates the feet with Qi energy. This is to encourage people to work harder at cultivating the feet and leg Qi channels, which are very hard to open. It is extremely hard to open the foot Qi channels on the cultivation trail, and you are advised to use yoga, Pilates, stretching and any other methods to stretch all the muscles and tendons in the feet and lower legs to help this effort.

The idea of seeing red and white bodhicitta, or "drops," also gives rise to fake visions. Any visions of seeing networks of Qi channels (*nadis*) within your body are fake as well. There actually is no such thing as drops melting due to the warmth of cultivation practice as found in ancient Vajrayana yoga texts, but since this helps practitioners develop concentration no modern masters ever explain this to students since everyone is in on the gag. The Taoist tales of seeing internal organs are also fictitious illusions created and projected by practicing devas and masters. This doesn't mean you don't have internal organs or that Qi channels don't exist. It just means that what you are seeing is not your internal organs or Qi channels.

When practitioners attempt to master the visualization sadhanas of Buddhist deities such as Green Tara, Vajrayogini, White Mahakala, Guhyasamaja, Chakrasamvara, Yamantaka, and so forth they will commonly have imaginary pictures projected into their mind by various masters (and devas) during those practices. This is then taken by the practitioner as a blessing, empowerment or sign of approval for their progress. The same thing happens for Hindus undertaking Shiva, Krishna, Narayana, Ganesha, Kubera, Surya, Kali, Durga, Lakshmi, Devi, Dhumavati, Matangi and other deity sadhanas. No such beings exist, but a master and his deva students will commonly masquerade as those beings because people call on them for help. Other people looking at the practitioner might also see them overlaid with the visualized deity because those observers are given visions as well that provide this type of illusion. No one, however, ever turns into these fancifully imagined deities.

Such tantric visualization sadhanas are just used as *nei-gong* instruction vehicles to help students cultivate their Qi and channels.

Hundreds of years ago this was the method that inspired practice as well as keep the practice vehicles alive through the generations, and this type of skillful means (deceiving practitioners in order to keep them meditating and making progress so that they can finally attain the deva body) has continued until today. This is skillful means.

During meditation practice it is common for practitioners to also see Buddhas, chakras, stars, galaxies, or other images above their head. When this happens, the idea is that the practitioner should concentrate on pushing their Qi far above their head so that it is pulled upwards out of the two spinal nerve channels within the brain. These two nerve channels, which you can see in DTI diagrams, are symbolized by the horns of Isis holding a sun above her head.

Yoga practitioners are commonly given visions of bright lights within the body or head just as described within many yogic texts. They are also commonly given various visions of gods, deities and past masters all of which are fake. Reminiscent of the Tibetan Vajrayana tradition of elemental dissolution visions, the *Svetasvatara Upanishad* says that when practicing meditation an aspirant might see visions of a snowfall, radiant smoke and the brilliant sun.

Because of expectations like this (of sequentially seeing visions of snowflakes, smoke, the sun, a sky or ball or fireflies, a flash of lightning, the luster of a crystal or the moon) an expectant individual will often see them because devas will project them into their brains. All devas love having the chance to practice doing this so just ignore any visions you ever see. Once again these are all just mental projections that devas practice putting into people's minds when they are working on those individuals to transform their Qi channels. Always ignore such things. If you have a vision of Jesus or Krishna, for instance, it is exactly the same thing. It is never real.

In ancient times many Buddhists would practice the kasina meditations in the *Visuddhimagga* (*The Path of Purification*) of Buddhaghosa. The *Visuddhimagga* says that at a certain stage of trying to visualize the earth, water, fire, wind or space elements they would "apprehend a sign" arising within them, but the text never specifies what the "sign" is supposed to be. Just as in the Vajrayana schools, the signs were always visions, given by whomever was overseeing the process of helping to open the practitioner's Qi channels, and when given there was usually a sub-carrier thought also projected that this vision was the sign or mark referred to. Usually you are not just given a mental picture as a vision but a particular thought on how to interpret it just as when seeing a spiritual great in a dream you also know who they are without words.

Most spiritual practitioners struggle for years cultivating meditation and ardently seek signs of their progress, so the various traditions have all developed visions to reassure practitioners that their efforts are not in vain but bearing progress. In Taoism these are called "signs of proof" (*zhengyan*), "signs of response" (*yingyan*) or "news" (*xiaoxi*). These are regarded as proof of an individual's excellent work at spiritual progress. In many traditions, for instance, the aspirant is taught to expect certain visions after reciting a certain number of prayers or mantras, which then shows that their cultivation is on track. This is not just the case with eastern religions but also the case in Judaism, Islam and Christianity. "Signs" help resolve practitioners' doubts about the path and their personal practice.

Some cultivation individuals will work hard at meditation and then see images of colorful round chakras, which again are entirely fictitious visions because, as explained in *Nyasa Yoga*, the chakras just refer to sections of the body. Many people have been mislead by the pictures in Leadbeater's book, *The Chakras*, and by various Hindu pictures of fanciful geometric shapes. They then mistakenly believe chakras are spinning plates with a certain number of channel branches, but consider this - how can an etheric body be powered by such things? How can they even exist?

The subtle body has organs just like your physical body *because it is an exact duplicate of your physical body*. All the higher bodies are this way. A higher body is simply a copy of a lower body at a higher stage of energy or substance. Therefore, the fanciful descriptions you read of chakras, and strange visions of chakras and Qi networks you might see, are all entirely fake. They are mara, delusions, falsities, illusions. Guess who is responsible for them? It is not you who is projecting them into your mind. You actually see these things, but they are images projected by devas and masters who have been training in visualization practice and now want to use their powers.

It is therefore very common to see such visions after a lot of mantra practice, especially visions of your bones that are becoming clean along with the attendant thought that your cultivation is working. The common vision, within dreams or during the waking state, is that your bones are somehow dirty and being cleansed through the process of mantra and/or meditation, or have already become brightened because of your cultivation efforts. The visions along these lines vary widely and are usually accompanied by unspoken thoughts such as that your body is dirty and being purified, you need to work harder at cultivation because your bones are still dirty, the color of your bones reveal the stage of your cultivation, your cultivation has reached a high stage because you can see how clean your bones have become, and so on.

Many practitioners who practice the famous white skeleton visualization technique of Buddhism may start to see images of bones within themselves or within other people and don't realize that these are also not the result of budding superpowers. They are illusory visions given by devas and masters that don't correspond to reality at all. As previously explained, many Taoists and Yoga enthusiasts often have visions of their internal organs. These visions are always due to devas projecting images into their minds.

The only reason people sometimes seem to have a ability to peer into another person's body at will is because a set of devas is constantly working on changing their Qi channels and are providing the practitioner with false visions while they are working on opening his Qi channels. If lucky, after a certain number of years (depending upon how hard they work at cultivation) the job will be done and the practitioner will attain the deva body that can leave their human frame at will. This is when they become a first stage master. Sometimes the visions provided, such as in the case of Ramakrishna, have nothing to do with other people's bodies but simply match traditional religious texts and deities.

It is also common for some spiritual practitioners to develop small superpowers – such as knowing the meaning of dreams, knowing the future, knowing what other people are thinking and so on - because that mental input is also supplied by devas. The individual does not actually have the superpower of mind reading or clairvoyance, but many fall into the misconception that they do and become proud. Some are smarter and say that they are simply "channels for God's work," but also don't know that the origins of their abilities is not "God" but some deva(s). Despite such humble words people don't know that the abilities are coming from the devas around them for a reason and not some ultimate power.

Another common vision given to people across the world concerns the existence of trolls, *dakinis*, devas, angels, elves, giants and other etheric beings. Once again, practitioners do not have spiritual powers to be able to see such things otherwise they would be able to see them constantly at will. They are fanciful visions created by the local devas who practice projecting visions into people's minds. Devas are always playful and love deceptions, so what they project is almost always misleading. The word "trickster" applies to heavenly beings.

Countless types of fictitious visions are possible. If they occur to you, do not consider them as anything of importance but simply ignore them. Just as fire is the direct cause of cooking, knowledge and analysis are the direct causes of spiritual progress and illumination rather than dreams and visions.

Dreams and Sexual Daydreams

Many of the same visions just recounted (and of course this partial list is by far non-conclusive) can appear in practitioner's dreams. You might see masters, Buddhas and saints in dreams as well as strange celestial palaces and beings such as dragons, fox spirits, protection deities and so on. All of these visionary experiences are total illusory nonsense. No one is ever given divine messages in dreams because it is an impractical way to impart information and fraught with the possibility of misinterpretation. It is true that dreams can indeed be given to you by devas and spiritual masters, but the content is normally fictitious even if what is seen seems to be perfectly real.

While in *Visualization Power* I revealed many cases where intense concentration on a problem produces a visual dream solution (such as Elias Howe's invention of the sewing machine or Kukule's discovery of the structure of the benzene ring). Typically the spiritual content of your dreams are self-induced imaginations or compensatory self-fulfillments that do not indicate any spiritual teachings at all. People who don't use discrimination (clear thinking and logic) usually fall for these things as being real or revel in them to gain self-satisfaction. Speaking frankly, the content of dreams and daydreams is usually due to subtle impressions stored in our minds that serve as the basis for our imagination.

As a related point, when young most every boy and girl has sexual fantasies that they are afraid to tell others, such as becoming younger and transforming into a member of the opposite sex. Just as fear or courage affect your Qi, these types of daydreams affect an individual's Yin Qi or Yang Qi and help open their relevant Qi channels. Along these lines men affect their Yin Qi when they imagine they are women while women cultivate their Yang Qi by imagining they are men. Sometimes young girls will dream that they become men, grow a penis, or must fight a war/demon and at that time their Yang Qi rises and starts opening the appropriate channels.

Such cases are normal and not to be taken as a calling for lesbianism just as young boys' dreams of becoming girls are not to be interpreted as a psychological call to homosexuality or transgender leanings. In no cases either are any of these things to be taken as an encouragement for transgender leanings. The role models in India of female deities also being war goddesses able to defeat demons, show that females must also cultivate Yang Qi just as men, such as Krishna or Shiva or Hercules, must also cultivate Yin Qi.

The *Vimalakirti Sutra* recounts the story of Shariputra having a vision that he was changed into a female, which refers to a type of cultivation during the twelve-year kundalini arousal where one often undergoes such illusions in order to affect their Yin Qi. Vimalakirti's ten foot square room in that sutra actually represents a practitioner's brain, and the reason all the Buddhas, Bodhisattvas and devas could fit into this small room is because astral-bodied individuals can all shrink their subtle bodies to small sizes. Thus many devas can enter the brain at the same time (where lessons are conducted) since the ability to increase or decrease the size of the subtle body is a well-recognized yogic ability mentioned in most Yoga texts.

As with the *Vimalakirti Sutra,* you can read of many cultivation tales where men became women and women became men in *Shikhandi,* by Devdutt Pattanaik, which only an enlightened master can interpret correctly for you. Of particular note is the story of the Greek Tiresias who underwent a spontaneous sex change (done by the goddess Hera) after striking two copulating snakes (symbolizing the Yin and Yang Qi of the body). Later he regained his masculinity and was given the gift of prophecy, the ability to understand bird song, and a lifespan of seven lives. Tiresias could mediate between the gods and humans, and his story with all the superpowers is essentially a Greek tale hinting at the subtle body attainment.

Along the lines of this form of cultivation, two great Hindu masters, Papaji and Ramakrishna, both wore women's clothes for a short while in order to cultivate their Yin Qi. Legends say so did Hercules, Arjuna, Thor and many other cultural heroes. This method is rarely understood but is improperly taken as homoeroticism or some other type of sexual deviancy.

Meher Baba actually explained this in his *Discourses*,

> If one is transcending sexual duality and trying to understand the experience associated with the opposite sex, sometimes one actually exhibits the traits usually associated with the opposite sex. Thus, for example, some aspirants in the male body at one phase or another actually put on the clothes of women, talk like them, feel like them, and take on their habits. But this is only a passing phase. When inner understanding of the relevant experiences is complete, they neither experience themselves as male nor as female alone but as being *beyond* the distinction of sex. The experiences connected with the male and female forms are both accessible and intelligible to the aspirants who have transcended sexual distinctions. They remain unaffected by the limitations of either, because through understanding they have freed themselves from the limiting obsessions characteristic of sex-ridden imagination.[7]

Throughout these explanations the one principle never to abandon is sexual restraint, or *brahmacharya*. For men it is the major key to spiritual progress and the most important practice of Yoga. Yoga and Vedanta consider it the foundation of life, and it is equally stressed in Buddhism, Taoism and other religions.

Lust, or sexual desire, will pursue a spiritual seeker throughout their life wearing various disguises, and you must strive to assert your independence over its pull. If a woman orgasms through sex there is little problem of Qi loss because her body will reabsorb the energy, but if a man carelessly loses his Jing and Qi time and time again, that energy will no longer be available for opening up Qi

---

[7] *Discourses*, Meher Baba (Sherira Press, South Carolina, 2000), pp. 325-326.

channels.

As the *Jnana Sankalini Tantra* wisely says, warning men how to act throughout these mentioned experiences, "A person of unbroken continence is no man but a god." This is because the restraint will accumulate Qi internally, which will then open up Qi channels and develop your deva body. One need not undergo severe sexual restraint, which is counterproductive, but one must also not be self-indulgent. Along these lines, *The Little Book of Meditation* (Bodri) offers advice and instructions.

Internal Sounds

As people make progress in meditation practice it sometimes becomes possible to hear sounds that seem to be coming from within the body. Among other possibilities, these might include the sounds of mantras, voices or even music playing over and over again. On the other hand, these can also be personal imaginations due to neurosis or too much thinking.

Some people may hear mantras while they are falling asleep or within their dreams, especially mantras that they recited while awake. Some will hear mantras inside their minds being recited automatically without their efforts. These are actually mantras being recited by devas in a playful manner and letting you hear them.

Some might hear sounds that they believe originate from the chakras. Yoga texts, such as the *Gheranda Samhita* (in the Fifth chapter) state that sounds especially arise due to the practice of pranayama. They might be similar to the sounds of crickets, thunder, cymbals, bees, the melody of bells ringing in the distance, gongs, trumpets, drums or even a flute. The school of Laya Yoga has various teachings on this.

Some people will hear voices after they start upon the road of spiritual practices and mistakenly believe they are trustworthy spirit guides. Sometimes these are devas, who are not to be trusted, and sometimes just imaginations brought forth by Qi impinging upon brain centers. The explanation is as follows.

If your Qi ascends to the back of the head, one may start to experience results related to the nerves at the back of the head, which means the optic nerves and auditory nerves on the side of the head.

When your Qi reaches the back of the head, you might hear

different types of wonderful sounds or experience a ringing or pressure in your ears. This phenomenon is produced by the Qi working to open Qi routes in the brain, especially those around the auditory nerves. The vibration or trembling of Qi will also sometimes cause some brain wave activity that will activate stored optical or auditory memories. If your intelligence is not clear and bright enough, then illusions deep inside the subconscious will result when this happens.

Someone who has deep religious beliefs may then have illusions of hearing the voice of God, Buddhas, angels, deities or other characters. Whatever is heard is actually just a big assembly; it is a mixing of previous experience - whatever has been seen, heard, thought and known before. If someone clings to the idea that these voices are real then he will fall into a state of mara or delusion and go the wrong way in their cultivation.

A person should not be puzzled or moved by this sort of reaction. Instead, he should sometimes swallow the saliva and release the feelings in his head. This requires a strong mind and persistent will to ignore the sounds and/or voices. By reciting mantras to change the sounds, and guiding the Qi downward one will pass this stage and enter the next.

On the supernatural aide, we have to honestly say that inner voices, if they are not signs of schizophrenic or psychotic delusions, may sometimes be devas misleading people (although rare), you should ignore whatever is said even if it appears incredibly accurate. Because they possess a shrinkable spirit body that can enter your brain, devas have access to all the memories stored in your neurons of everything you ever saw, heard or did in life. They practice being able to read this, which is why there is a saying in China that the Kitchen God (the protect god for a household) reports everything that happens in the family to heaven.

In short, no human secrets can be kept from higher sentient beings, especially the devas. Everything you do can be known by Heaven. No one reads an etheric "akashic chronicle" to know what has happened. Devas simply learn how to access people's memories stored in their neurons.

It is therefore easy to weave complex tales of deception by incorporating your past memories into some nonsensical dialogue they may engage in. Devas like to masquerade as famous spiritual greats or strange individuals out of play while they work on your Qi channels. In many cases they will even masquerade as demons, devils or ghosts so as to frighten a practitioner so that his Yin Qi channels can be purified.

This is one of the unfortunate horrors of the twelve years of transformation that masters must go through, and why they rarely mention the content of those years. All the devas want to practice many things, such as how to manipulate your thoughts and emotions, as they are working on cleaning out your Qi channels. Since it takes twelve years of hard work to open up all your Qi channels *after* a genuine full body kundalini awakening is initiated, why would the devas and masters bother to do so if they were not also having fun and learning through the process? The learning involves competitive games against each other seeing who has more skill in manipulating your thoughts, feelings and visions. A deva of a higher stage of attainment can win at these contests or block the skills of others. A common contest is to see who can read your memories quickest and then make connections between unconnected items within it.

Future masters (ex. Saint Anthony, Padre Pio, Upasni Maharaj, Yeshe Tsogyel, Ramakrishna, etc. before they attained enlightenment) have to suffer during the twelve years necessary to develop the *sambhogakaya* and no one, except for this book, ever tells you what went on during those years. Search the records and you will find that masters typically remain silent about their personal practices and the events that transpired during the twelve years of transformation to develop the subtle body, then Causal body and then Supra-Causal body of enlightenment.

Sometimes a practitioner might hear a singular sentence in their head, like the famous story of a Buddhist monk suffering from knee pain. At a riverbank bandaging his knee, he once heard a voice which claimed it was a ghost in his knee. The ghost said that the monk owed him from a past life, but because of his holy life he couldn't attack him to exact revenge. But now that he had become proud, he finally had his chance because the fault of that pride had given him an opening to afflict him with trouble. This was a deva, for sure, trying to help the monk become more humble and not a ghost in the slightest!

Chinese Zen master Huike is said to have heard a voice in his head when the Qi was painfully passing through his brainstem, and

Socrates said he would always hear the voice of an inner daimonion (deva). As explained, these cases are the voices of devas or a spiritual master.

All these sounds are usually caused by devas for some reason or another. Practitioners should just forget these instances and pay them no mind. By no means should a practitioner ever believe the stories devas tell that they are some spiritual great or spirit guide with fantastical information and that the individual has a destiny or is particularly great. One has these experiences due to deva training practices that have no regard for your well-being, as the *Surangama Sutra* explains, and therefore you should just ignore them.

Odors

Some spiritual practitioners become either very sensitive to odors, or can smell supernatural odors like sandalwood incense when they are meditating. Sometimes this spontaneously occurs, and sometimes this occurs because practitioners were concentrating on the tip of their nose, thus opening up the Qi channels in the nose and making it more sensitive.

Superpowers and Psychic Abilities

On the meditation trail it is common for some people to develop what they believe are personal superpowers or psychic abilities, and then get sidetracked because of these experiences. This includes the ability to know people's fortunes or feel feng shui energies without being taught. Individuals sometimes develop exceptional intuitive skills that they can't possibly have, and commonly attribute their skills to intuition, spirits, God or their own spiritual efforts.

Sometimes people seem to know the future. Some seem to develop the ability to feel inanimate objects or see/feel inside other people's bodies, sometimes psychically sensing their energy states or emotions. Sometimes they have the experience of seeing visions inside of other people's bodies, including their organs or bones. As stated, the visions of seeing other people's bones, which supposedly arises from the white skeleton meditation technique of Buddhism, are all fictitious. Sometimes people even receive visions where they temporarily seem to see spiritual beings, or celestial mansions and heavens.

Some people develop medical superpowers, such as the ability to project energy into others, know the state of someone's health, feel their Qi or know their internal health conditions. Some develop incredible healing powers but know that the powers don't come from them.

All these types of different experiences, and many more not described, make people believe they have become psychic and possess a superpower they do not actually possess. Don't ever be confused and think this. Use your powers of discriminatory thinking to consider these attainments.

Actually, these "powers" or experiences (even the power of "intuition") usually come from devas who are practicing various techniques, and the superpowers actually belong to the devas who are working through the aspirant. If the medical superpowers were yours then you could use them at will, and if knowing the future were always possible you would certainly become rich. Powers are given and taken away by devas and higher spiritual beings who use you as their conduit due to past karma.

The best way to make progress when you have these experiences is to ignore them and continue cultivating, without becoming dependent on them, by setting up a daily practice schedule of pranayama, meditation, mantra, *nei-gong* and visualization. The quicker you transform your Qi channels the easier it will be to attain the subtle body and lose your fascination with these things that really don't amount to much at all.

SUMMARY

The spiritual trail involves two aspects: (1) cultivating your mind and (2) your body. Cultivating your body involves *nei-gong* inner energy work to transform your Qi and channels because your internal subtle body is essentially energy (composed of Qi), and your physical body is actually a more solid form of condensed energy.

Cultivating your mind, on the other hand, means making it pure and free of *kleshas*. To do this you must practice meditation. Your meditation can be of either two types – with or without mental discrimination of the mind's contents.

If you only cultivate to cleanse your thought stream and neglect the cultivation of internal Qi energy, you won't attain the subtle body (astral body, ether body, *yin shen*, impure illusory body, etc.). Therefore you have to cultivate your vital life force, or Qi, on the spiritual trail. You might check out *Nyasa Yoga* for instructions.

If you only cultivate your Qi on the spiritual trail without cultivating your mind (thought and behavior), then even if you achieve the subtle body you will still be beset with problems. Perhaps you will even become an even bigger jerk than previously because now you will be able to cause trouble with your etheric spirit body. Cultivating virtue is important on the spiritual trail. You don't want to become an asshole with powers, and you also need virtue to merit the assistance from higher powers.

Only by meditating on both mind and body will you gain enlightenment; you must cultivate both your Qi and mental emptiness to become enlightened quickly. This book concentrates on emptiness meditation, or mental practice, in order to teach you how to cultivate your mind. Along this path, physical reactions corresponding to your Qi and channels are sure to definitely arise. How to cultivate those directly through inner energy work is explained in *Nyasa Yoga* and the other works that have been cited.

Vajrayana practitioners know that the first stage of the spiritual path is cultivating your mind and Qi to attain the subtle body, which happens after your kundalini arises. Because this is the sure pathway that leads to enlightenment they always pray for four things on the path of cultivation:

(1) Help in opening their Qi channels
(2) Help for making their Qi begin to circulate and for success in abandoning their violent tendencies
(3) Help so that their body becomes as soft and healthy as a baby's body so that it is not an obstacle on the cultivation path, and
(4) Help in mastering the kundalini energy so that they can reach a state of calmness, bliss and warmth.

These are all transformation achievements necessary along the way to attaining an etheric subtle body, which is the first major milestone of the spiritual path.

In *Tao and Longevity: Mind-Body Transformation,* Nan Huai-chin wrote,

> A person who says that he has an invisible and immaterial body, with or without form, that leaves and enters his physical body at will is speaking of the *yin shen* [the subtle body]. *Yin shen* is similar to those bodies appearing in dreams, but it is much clearer and more distinct than ordinary "dream" bodies. Taoists maintain that the projection of *yang shen* is the ultimate achievement of meditation and the cultivation of Tao. But if one imagines that the projection of *yin shen* is the ultimate goal of Tao, then he is either an ordinary person or in the *yin* state of a spirit or a ghost. [You must proceed higher than this attainment.]
>
> Those who meditate and cultivate the Tao will not have any difficulty projecting *yin shen* out of the body. Some may have an experience of this sort long before reaching the stage of transforming *ch'i* [Qi] into *shen* [the stage of attaining the Causal or mental body]. For example, when the connection between spirit and the body has deteriorated and grown weak, the projection of *yin shen* can occur spontaneously. This can happen to quite ordinary people who are not meditating, for it happens when one is ill, nearing death, or bordering on schizophrenia. If this can happen by itself under stressful circumstances, the student should understand that, with training, the experience will come much more easily and without the need for stress.[8]

You now know about some of the delusions that commonly appear to practitioners along this line of attainment. You can explain these things in reference to heavenly interference, such as the existence of devas, or purely go by the road of science or silence so as not to unsettle practitioners who lack wisdom or have supernatural leanings. In the next chapter we will interpret various meditation case studies solely along the lines of science, for this is what is appropriate for society and most individuals. Only top individuals can understand the Vajrayana-style teachings on the necessity of spiritual beings to

---

[8] *Tao and Longevity,* p. 108.

enter into your body, and lend you their energies to help you open up your Qi channels.

CHAPTER 5
MEDITATION CASE STUDIES

In this chapter, which is excerpted from *How to Measure and Deepen Your Spiritual Realization* (Bodri) with substantial editing, we will start to examine the experiences of various meditators and interpret them in a scientific fashion. In other words, as an alternative to supernatural explanations involving devas and spiritual masters we will only interpret various case studies using medical theories and psychological concepts.

Only an enlightened master is qualified to talk of devas and spiritual beings, so this method will offer an alternative explanation for those teachers who wish to remain centered in the ordinary world of science and help meditation practitioners without having achieved the higher ranks of spiritual achievement themselves.

No matter how seemingly profound or unusual the experiences of most meditators, the vast majority of their experiences don't go beyond simple changes in the physical body, feelings of unusual energy sensations, and superficial changes in psychological states. Therefore it is easy to interpret meditation cases along these lines. When we talk about Qi or prana, chakras, Qi channels (*nadis*, meridians, energy channels), and even kundalini (tumo, Yang Qi or shakti spiritual energy) they all refer back to changes in our inner subtle body, which is the energetic scaffolding or inner energy substrate of our physical body. This energetic double within us also affects our physical nature.

Nearly almost everyone who starts to meditate correctly will eventually feel various sensations in their body due to the movement of internal energy. This is absolutely inevitable and unavoidable. Unfortunately, many people will jump to the conclusion that these sensations are high stage enlightenment-level experiences whereas they are just the movement of internal "body wind" (superficial energy or "Fan Qi" or "wind Qi" rather than *real* kundalini Yang Qi) activated by spiritual cultivation. To understand these sensations we must clarify such situations in detail.

To be specific, we must become familiar with the broad spectrum of the initial experiences you can encounter when you first start to meditate. In this way, you will not confuse these minor events with any of the higher stages of meditation accomplishment even though there is a resemblance. Without this knowledge, people who experience this or that particular phenomenon will usually mistake it for a more advanced stage of spiritual practice because this is the natural tendency of those hoping for spiritual progress. Hence, we must analyze the common experiences of today's modern practitioners in order to put their meditation experiences into proper perspective.

To give shape to our discussion there is a marvelous book, *The Kundalini Experience* (Integral Publishing, California, 1987) by Dr. Lee Sannella, which contains an excellent collection of meditation cases that reveal a broad spectrum of experiences. I want to thank Dr. Sannella once again for his prior permission to use these cases. By examining and interpreting these cases we will be in a much better position to understand why people experience certain things due to meditation and other spiritual practices.

To understand the typical experience of a meditation practitioner as he cultivates his Qi and opens up his subtle body's energy channels, we need to match their spiritual experiences with traditional cultivation teachings. One can do so by matching the experiences with the explanations revealed within Nan Huai-Chin's *Tao and Longevity.* While the detailed descriptions in *Tao and Longevity* focus on the opening of the Qi channels in the spine, they are still sufficient to cover many of the experiences encountered by beginning cultivation practitioners.

From this book a reader will begin to understand terms such as Yin and Yang, Jing, Qi, Shen, the Qi channels (mainly the *tu mai, jen mai, zhong mai, ida, pingala* and *sushumna* channels), chakras and *gong-*

fu - all of which constitute the necessary vocabulary you must know to knowledgeably discuss meditation practices. To talk about the physical changes of cultivation in an intelligent fashion it is absolutely essential that you develop a basic fluency with these terms.

Because of this requirement, familiarity with *Tao and Longevity* is almost a prerequisite for deeply understanding the cultivation path. Meher Baba's *Discourses* and his book *God Speaks* would also be helpful in many respects as would be *A Systematic Course in the Ancient Tantric Techniques of Yoga and Kriya* by Satyananda Saraswati.

For us to be able to communicate as briefly as possible, it must be assumed that the reader already has some basic familiarity with the spiritual concepts and vocabulary within these books so that we can proceed to analyze *The Kundalini Experience* cases as succinctly as possible and without regards to any type of supernatural explanations. Without further ado, those cases and their analysis are as follows.

CASE 1: Male Professor in the Humanities

This sixty-nine-year-old man, who had many psychic experiences as a child, awoke from a nap one day in 1963 to discover a three-inch blister on his thigh where his hand had been resting. This extraordinary experience stimulated his interest in the powers of the mind. Within two years he was meditating regularly, though without expert guidance. Then, in 1967, he began formal Zen meditation.

After a few months, during a sitting, he became engulfed by a bright golden light that lasted several minutes. He had a recurrent experience a few weeks later.

During many sittings he noticed prickling and itching sensations moving up the inside of his legs to his groin, in his arms and chest, up his back and over his head to his brows. From there the sensations moved to his cheeks, the outside of his nostrils, and sometimes to his chin. Later he experienced tingling and itching in his throat during meditation. ...

Today, ten years later and several years into his retirement, the professor no longer experiences any dramatic manifestations ... He is, however, able to encourage energy flows starting in the pelvis and spreading upwards. These flows, he feels, revitalize him and have even cured him of lower back pain. Occasionally he feels an energy blockage in his throat, which is the precise location where the kundalini energy seemed to have been arrested when I first saw him.

Nevertheless, he reports many interesting physical changes in recent years. Doing only mild aerobic exercises, he feels ten years younger. His shoulders and chest have increased in size by several inches, while his waist has shrunk by as much. He is fifteen pounds lighter. His hands still get very hot at times. He hears sounds of bells, and sometimes he is awakened by a loud zzzing sound.

In analyzing this first case, the relevant question is this meditator's stage of attainment such that it has caused all these experiences.

To start, we must note that absolutely none of the phenomena reported are the results of kundalini although many people would tend to mistakenly identify them as such. None of the experiences are the manifestation of kundalini, indicative of kundalini, nor even related to kundalini.

Rather, in terms of the stages of cultivating the wind, water, earth and fire elements of the physical body (Qi, hormones, flesh and bones and warmth), these experiences are all precursors to actually cultivating the body's real Qi (kundalini). In other words, this man has not actually started to cultivate the real kundalini life force (wind element) of the physical nature, but is just beginning to activate the fringes of this energy that the Chinese Qi-gong and Tao schools call "Fan Qi (wind Qi)." When the Yuan Qi (original Qi or real kundalini energy) finally does appear, which corresponds to the genuine kundalini phenomenon of real Yang Qi, its characteristics are quite different from any of these indications. This meditator's *gong-fu* experiences are therefore only the "wind Qi" of the body whose resemblance to "real Qi" tends to cause these phenomena to be mislabeled. The experiences involve only superficial Qi energy rather than real kundalini energy.

Meditators who have a weak physical nature often easily experience sensations similar to what this professor experienced. For instance, it is especially easy to for meditators and martial artists or yoga practitioners to feel the Qi running up or down the insides of the legs to the big toes after they start to meditate. In fact, a common practice in many cultivation schools is to lightly draw the energy up from the toes along this route when you feel weak or tired, and to lightly send energy down the inner leg meridian lines to the toes when you feel you have an excess of vital energy. This is one way to help open up the inner leg channel meridians. Standing in the horse posture of martial arts, while visualizing your leg channels, is also another effective method.

From the case description provided, we can also surmise that this practitioner probably had some type of liver weakness that his meditation efforts provoked when his Qi started to push through the liver channel meridians to fully open them. If he continued meditating then this particular imbalance would have adjusted itself naturally over time. He could have also turned to nutritional supplements or herbal medicines to help strengthen his liver, and fixing this potentially debilitating problem he would have thereby improved his overall health. The point is that meditation helped him discover a problem with his liver.

If this practitioner had never started meditating this unknown problem would most likely have grown into something much more serious that may later have required drugs or surgery to correct. It is truly a blessing to discover the body's ailments through meditation and to fix them with gentle methods before they become so severe that harmful intervention is necessary. This is one of the unspoken benefits of meditation practice.

As to the sensations one sometimes feels in their legs and groin when first meditating, *Tao and Longevity* points out that

> Because the Qi cannot flow freely between the blood vessels, muscles and tendons, one sometimes experiences numbness, aches and swelling in the legs [when someone sits cross-legged and first begins to meditate]. These sensations indicate that there are obstacles in the Qi routes of Yin Ch'iao and Yang Ch'iao [two particular Qi energy meridians]. When one can no longer endure this feeling, he can loosen the legs. After awhile he will experience fresh, unfamiliar, comfortable feelings. When one has advanced to

a certain stage in meditation, no matter whether he crosses his legs or not, he will always experience these fresh and wonderful euphoric feelings. At this stage, a person will be able to cross his legs to meditate for long periods without feeling any obstructions.[9]

Explaining the importance of opening the leg meridians through meditation would require an entire chapter of explanations, but we must certainly draw attention to the fact that our life force runs through our legs as well as other appendages. For instance, when we watch infants in a crib we can see that they kick their legs much more than they wave their hands. As a child grows older they also cannot sit still. They always crawl about and then run around everywhere so as to continuously keep their legs active.

One of the reasons behind the urge for movement is because the life force is coursing through the arms and legs, and as an adult you must open up the energy meridians in the legs through a variety of practices so that Qi inside can flow freely. Meditation helps. When you finally open your leg meridians you will experience an indescribable bliss. There are an entire host of reasons why people should sit in a cross-legged position while meditating, and one of the many reasons includes the fact that it helps to force the body into opening up the leg meridians, which helps to extend one's longevity.

When we initially start practicing meditation by sitting in a cross-legged position, most people will naturally feel pain or discomfort. This is unavoidable, so don't despair when this happens even though it seems that experienced meditators are not having any problems. They went through the pain of stretching their joints too.

Despite this discomfort, it is impossible for meditation to become the cause of any type of physical sickness because meditation is simply a state of resting for the body and mind. However, when the vital energy currents of the body start circulating due to meditation and subsequently encounter obstructions, we can correctly say that meditation has revealed a latent physical weakness. Latent problems and hidden illnesses may erupt because of contact with internal vital energy activated by meditation, but meditation did not cause those pre-existing conditions. It only helps you find them so that you can take corrective action before the problems become

---

[9] *Tao and Longevity*, p. 37.

more serious.

Tao and Longevity again reminds us when this happens that, "Everyone should realize that latent diseases may be discovered, but are not actually caused by meditation. In other words, meditation increases inner vitality and begins to heal the body. By persistent meditation and appropriate medical treatment, one can recover one's health."[10]

Disease and illness are also sometimes blessings in disguise because they may cause you to rethink your life and enter into more worthwhile paths. They sometimes give you pause to reconsider and correct the way you have been living. In this way they sometimes become a great blessing. If meditation causes you to discover an unknown problem, then it too is a blessing that gives you an opportunity to fix something that might grow into an incurable condition if left unchecked.

Meditation is particularly beneficial to your health not only because the imbalances it discovers give you a chance to identify and correct any health problems before they cause major difficulties, but because it benefits your internal Qi circulation. It often alerts you to deteriorating conditions before they accumulate to cause cancer, rheumatoid arthritis, heart disease, mental illness or other serious health problems. Furthermore, meditation involves unleashing your natural vital energies and letting them flow freely throughout the body, so the path of meditation is often the actual remedial cure for many "incurable" illnesses. The fact that this meditator could have such experiences at all indicates he had achieved a degree of cultivation accomplishment in a previous life that had laid a foundation for the speedy results in this one.

Even so, we must be firm in recognizing that this man's experiences are not Tao, nor real Qi, nor the kundalini phenomenon most people commonly talk about. He simply felt sensations of minor energy currents within the body that were stirred up by meditation practice. However, if people like this practitioner know the true principles of spiritual practice they can make great progress in these directions, although they must certainly not mistake any of these experiences for the real Qi of the body.

What this man experienced were the results of internal Qi winds running along his energy meridians – just superficial streams of

---

[10] *Tao and Longevity*, pp. 45-46.

vital energy. At this level of practice it would be a gigantic mistake to conclude that the meridians had been totally cleared of obstructions. What we can say is that in cultivation a meditator first starts to superficially open their Qi channels before they can activate the true full-body kundalini phenomenon, and cultivating his Qi and Qi channels requires a good deal of time and effort that he had not yet undertaken.

As to the golden light experienced by this meditator, there are two ways we can explain it depending upon the audience. A supernatural explanation might be that this was caused by devas, but for these meditation case studies we will entirely eschew such explanations and explain the cases through science instead. The scientific explanation is that this was actually a phenomenon caused by the interaction of the meditator's Qi with his mental condition. Qi and consciousness are interrelated in the sense that your thoughts "ride" on your Qi. When the Qi impinges upon the occipital lobe or visual cortex of the brain, it is often possible from the stimulation to then see imaginary things.

With this type of explanation, we should simply say that this light manifested as a result of the friction between his physiological and psychological states and was made possible because this practitioner had made progress in his meditation practice. It was not a "light from wisdom" attainment, the "light of wisdom," "clear light" or any other type of holy light experience. Rather, it was simply a "frictional" light produced by the interaction of the energies of his body in conjunction with Qi. Whenever you concentrate on a region inside the body through mantra, visualization techniques or other cultivation methods then such things are possible due to the exerted effort. This practitioner's experiences never went beyond the skandha of form, namely the physical body.

As to our last bit analysis for this case, the reason why this practitioner's Fan Qi seemed to stop in the throat is because there were meridian channel blockages in that region. Anatomically speaking, the throat is a very complex region because of the complicated intertwining of the glands, vertebrae, muscles, nerves, veins and arteries. It is impossible to entirely open up this region of the body until one reaches very advanced stages of meditation practice that require extensive *nei-gong* exercises, such as detailed in the *Yoga Yajnavalkya* and other texts already mentioned.

As for this particular meditator, we certainly should not believe that he opened the Qi channels in his throat or that the Qi channels in his legs actually opened completely through either. When these happen there will be certain unmistakable experiences involving Qi that are far different than what this individual experienced.

CASE 2: Female High School Teacher

This middle-aged teacher of Spanish has been practicing Yoga and meditation for many years. In 1980 she started to have a variety of symptoms, such as headaches, tingling in her face and nose, pains and spasms of the throat, cardiac area, and abdomen, with popping sensations all over the body. These symptoms became accentuated whenever she would meditate. She also had sensations of emptiness and of her voice not being generated by herself.

In November 1985 a dramatic change occurred. In the midst of a thirty-day meditation period, she became aware of strong flows of energy washing over her entire body. There was also a loss of sensation, except for sensory perceptions in her head. She felt the kundalini energy pushing and pulling in her face and at the top of her head. There was a bumping, jerking sensation in the chakras of the throat, the heart, and the abdomen. These sensations were predictably intensified during the most concentrated meditations. Each area also felt greatly heated up in turn. Then she started to hear machinery-like noises in her head that became continuous over the next few weeks. With her eyes closed, she could see white light streaming from her face and head.

These symptoms subsided somewhat after three months but were triggered again after a period of intense meditation and lasted for several weeks. The kundalini energy resumed its flow up the spine and down the face and trunk. She experienced great rapture and ecstatic orgasmic sensations until she began to tire of this hyperstimulation of her nervous system.

Shortly afterward she developed laryngeal spasms, which were accompanied by the fear of choking to death.

Then the symptoms returned in full and for several weeks she experienced "heart attacks". As soon as these symptoms started to subside she began to suffer from sudden acute sciatica, which was clinically typical and later diagnosed by NMR scan as a ruptured disc pressing on the nerve. After three months of therapy, which did not alleviate her painful condition, she agreed to have surgery. By that time she had developed pronounced foot drop. There was intense pain extending from her lower back to her left big toe. She suffered from numbness of the sciatic distribution and great stiffness. Then, nearly as dramatically, there was a sudden subsidence of sciatica, and within three days she could walk with only a slight limp. Now, six months later, she only suffers a slight residual weakness of the lower left leg.

Her impression is that she must have had some weakness in her back that did not show until the intense kundalini energy became active in that area and precipitated the actual pathology. She looks upon her practically instantaneous healing as a gift of grace. All of her symptoms have disappeared, even though she continues to meditate.

As with our first meditation case study, this practitioner's experiences cannot be classified as kundalini either. These experiences do not constitute an actual kundalini awakening of any type, but once again are simply the initial manifestations of Fan Qi - the ordinary wind Qi of the body (not the real Qi) - being stimulated through meditation practice. It is unfortunate when people jump to conclusions and mistakenly take this as kundalini but that's not what most practitioners do. The characteristics of the real kundalini phenomenon are entirely different.

The reason why this woman experienced headaches due to meditation is probably because she suffered from some sort of dislocation of spinal vertebrae whose effects impinged upon her throat region. When the Qi arising due to meditation hit these problems, either the affected nerves or the energies continuing into the brain probably caused her headaches. Later she discovered that she had a disc problem in her back, confirming this diagnosis, and she decided to correct this condition through surgery.

Whenever someone's meditation reveals a problem such as this, it might be wise to first resort to acupuncture, chiropractic adjustments, various deep tissue massage or bodywork therapies (such as Rolfing, Integrative Manual Therapy, etc.) before submitting to radical, invasive surgery on the back. The general rule is to try chiropractic first and either acupuncture or bodywork massage next. In many cases a back operation never fixes the problems it is meant to solve so you can usually expect those results to be unsatisfactory. Once bones are fused because of surgical operations those results can never be undone. Chiropractic or osteopathic adjustments are usually a superior way to handle subluxations and misalignments.

Wise practitioners, when they discover they have a similar problem (revealed through their Qi cultivation), first try all sorts of noninvasive techniques before ever submitting to surgery. For instance, Asian practitioners often try a method called "shuffling the bones" that uses the body's own energy to help move the spinal bones back into their proper positions. However, to master this skill takes a lot of cultivation practice.

This practitioner was particularly perceptive in that she realized her meditation did not cause the medical problems, but simply revealed what was already there. In indicating a latent weakness, it gave her an opportunity to heal the situation before it became worse.

As *Tao and Longevity* points out,

> Meditation does not cause ... undesirable effects. They are due to old illnesses. [If for instance] the nerves and Qi routes around the renal and waist areas constitute obstacles to the Qi that is generated during meditation, ... [it must] work to open and pass these areas. If one understands this principle and has instruction from a good master about suitable remedies, these problems can all be overcome, and one will eventually recover health ...
>
> [As another example, people who are old or weak may have illnesses which] include lung disease, gastric and hepatic disorders, cardiac diseases and various other latent conditions. If a person has these diseases, at a certain stage of meditation he will feel aching and heaviness like a strong

pressure on the back, flaccidity and lack of strength or aching around the waist. Cramps or convulsive contractions may occur in the back, or congestion may occur in the shoulder, or aching may occur causing one to perspire, feel chills and fever.

If these phenomena should occur, one should understand that this trouble is not produced by meditation. The quiet in meditation is, after all, a means of rest. No one is apt to get sick from merely taking rest. One should be glad, however, because without the test of meditation, one might not have realized that one already had some sort of disease. The pains one feels show the self-healing effect of increased vitality and indicate that the disease is still curable and has not progressed to the extent that there is no remedying it. For example, a man may not initially feel any pain from a very serious wound and yet when the wound begins to heal, he will. Similarly, when a man first catches a common cold, the germs of the cold are still latent; there are no symptoms. When the symptoms of the cold are evident, the cold is already going away.

If these phenomena appear in the course of meditation practice, one should take medical treatments in addition to the healing involved in meditation. So long as one has the will to persist through these crises, the crises can lead to a healthier condition.[11]

Thus, if this woman had not discovered her spinal problem because of her meditation efforts then her condition would most likely continue to deteriorate as she got older. Who knows what other problems it was causing inside her body?

If you go to a chiropractor or osteopath and ask about the possible complications that can result from spinal misalignments (subluxations), you could sit there for hours listening to the reply. For the road of serious meditation practice it is indeed useful to have a yearly adjustment of your spinal bones and joints to make sure that your spine is straight and bones are well aligned.

It is also generally true that meditation usually makes people more sensitive to external environmental factors such as wind,

---

[11] *Tao and Longevity*, pp. 38-41.

weather, odors, people's energies, and so on. As your Qi opens up Qi channels in your brain it is easy to get headaches (the aspirin "Saridon" was my own teacher's favorite remedy) or temporarily see quick light flashes when the eyes are closed due to nerves being stimulated by Qi. Additionally, it becomes easier to catch colds due to what Chinese medicine calls "wind invasions" of the body's Qi channels that have been opening. Luckily, when spiritual cultivation practitioners get sick they know it right away and can immediately take the appropriate measures (i.e., medicine) to adjust their bodies. Ordinary people who don't meditate usually get sick without knowing it and therefore do not take any steps to heal themselves. As a result, illnesses are often given the chance to dive deeper into their bodies, quietly building strength over time that eventually erupts into cancer, arthritis and all sorts of other chronic afflictions.

When such people discover a problem it is often too late for help. They must resort to fixing matters with radical cures, such as surgery, rather than simple changes in lifestyle or the use of herbal medicines and nutriceutical supplements to fix problems. The point is that those who don't practice meditation usually do not discover the silent chronic conditions that are developing but go on compounding upon the errors that produced their condition in the first place! As they get older, people with these problems are really in a mess whereas meditation practitioners have often both prevented or cured their chronic conditions due to their practice. Meditation is a foundation of preventative as well as curative health care.

Many modern teachers do not know how to guide people through all these aberrant energy situations, but refer to them with fancy words like "kundalini" when those terms do not really apply to the situation at all. Some teachers can offer proper explanations but few know enough about anatomy, biology, psychology, science, gong-fu and medicine to be comprehensive. They are like a "blind cat bumping into a dead mouse" when they try to explain these phenomena. Some teachers label every experience as mara (delusions) so that they don't have to deal with them (due to a lack of knowledge and understanding), and then tell meditators to ignore everything that occurs when the symptoms might be indicating the need for medical intervention. It is indeed difficult to find a skilled meditation master nowadays!

Once again, this case is not indicative of the real Qi of the body, but is another example of internal wind. However, since cultivating your Qi is the very first step in the normal sequence of meditation practice it is acceptable to refer to these phenomena as "Qi" in order to simplify explanations as well as to further *encourage people in their practice efforts.*

This type of encouragement, by calling the lesser something much greater for the practitioner's benefit, is called "skillful means." When a practitioner progresses, they later awaken to the fact that what they thought was real Qi was initially just a stirring or whirling of internal wind, and they recognize that it was motivationally helpful to make this beginner's mistake of considering this as great spiritual progress.

"Wind Qi" can also be called "semblance Qi" or "semblance dharma *gong-fu*" because it appears to be the same as real Qi when you compare the descriptions, but this isn't a high stage phenomenon at all. Nevertheless, calling something "Qi" when it is only internal wind (superficial internal energy movement) is usually an excellent means to teach and motivate people in their meditation practice. It not only encourages meditators to work hard at their practice, but it enables them to better understand the meditation classics that discuss these matters in detail.

We can also use this case to comment on individuals who meditate but who also have a nervous condition. These people might experience symptoms similar to this woman's case. For these types of people, the effects arising from meditation might be the result of a mental imbalance rather than indicative of progress in spiritual *gong-fu*.

All the experiences of this female practitioner are actually manifestations of what the Chinese call "post-natal Qi," and occurred because of the interaction of the physical body with psychological states of mind. The experiences were an effect of the interaction of the four elements, so they were not the manifestation of the original Qi of the body. They absolutely were not the pre-natal Qi that the yogis of India and Tibet call kundalini. This woman was simply cultivating her body's internal wind element. Thus, we have a typical beginner's practice report that shows some of the initial results from transformations affecting the physical body.

CASE 3: Female Artist-Teacher

I first saw this forty-five-year-old woman ten years ago. At the time, she had been doing automatic paintings for fourteen years. For the past two years she has been creating spontaneous paintings of her inner states, usually foreshadowing imminent experiences.

This cycle started when she blacked out during a painting session. When she regained consciousness, she found herself lying on the floor, with her body shaking violently and filling with great energy. This condition lasted for about half an hour and recurred the next night. The blast of energy and the trembling returned the following morning while she was doing her Yoga practices. It was then that she created her first spontaneous painting.

She immediately went on to the second painting in this series. All the while she was experiencing intense waves of energy and inner heat. She was also unaware of who or where she was. She began to worry about going insane. This was followed by free-floating anxiety and headaches. Then she worked on her third spontaneous painting while hallucinating patterns of force.

It was at this point she fell apart. Depression set in, and she felt like dying. She hurt all over and cried a lot. Painting number four was created. She called it "Fractured," because it reflected her inner chaos.

Then, over a two-day period, she painted her own face with a snake encircling it. At night, on the day of completion, she awoke trembling all over. She saw a strange reddish being with an elephant face. "He" put his fingers on her forehead. Then she fell asleep again. She dreamt of painting eyes that came alive under her brush. Next morning she started work on a painting of the blue-red man. In a subsequent painting she depicted that man healing her broken head. A baby was born from that man and then grew up, which was captured in another painting.

In another crisis she did a painting of a red octopus. Then, while in an ecstatic state, she created a painting of a head superimposed on a black head. Following this painting, she felt reborn.

Her ordeal resumed with painting number thirty-three.

Overcome by a mood of depression, she felt as if she was imprisoned in a concentration camp, which is reflected in the gloomy scenes of several of her paintings. These spontaneous creations were followed by a painting of a egg with a wavy person emerging. At the end of this series, she felt alive and whole.

The next incident was fierce burning in her legs, which then spread into her chest and arms. She suffered hot and cold fevers and was unable to eat. She experienced pain on both sides of her head and behind her eyes as well as violent palpitations. Her blood pressure was found to be elevated.

Just prior to my interview with her, she experienced a cramping pain in her left big toe, as if a nail had been driven through it. My examination revealed a very red toenail, which was not due to bleeding. At this time she was also unnerved by a complete loss of hearing, which lasted for about an hour, and she believed she was going to die. She then consulted a physician, who found nothing wrong with her.

Since my interview, she has reported feeling a "throat opening" sensation, but also breathing difficulties and pressure in the head. These experiences and states seem to be associated with her Yoga practice and artistic creativity. Her teaching work seems to exert a stabilizing influence on her, and she admitted to feeling generally much better since taking it up.

This particular set of experiences is quite different from the previous two. From a cultivation standpoint, we should suspect that this practitioner was somewhat mentally unstable before she even started to meditate. From a psychological point of view, she therefore lacked the normally expected degree of mental balance at the start of her meditation practice. This possibility explains some of her mental experiences.

Many people today mistakenly believe that some people are locked away in mental hospitals because they are suffering from the kundalini experience gone astray, but this idea results from a great ignorance about the true nature of what kundalini is, namely that you have to cultivate for it to arise. Nonetheless, this case gives us pause to discuss the fact that the great diseases people will fear in the twenty-first century will be forms of mental illness rather than cancer or heart disease, and only meditation and life style changes will end up providing effective cures for these coming conditions. While this woman may not be as mentally stable as most ordinary individuals, meditation has indeed helped her to a great extent, and so is useful in the sense of serving as a helpful cure. Even so, the experiences she describes are not kundalini but once again only manifestations of ordinary Qi.

In comprehending this case, we must first understand a little of the system of psychology used in cultivation matters. Naturally, the psychological mappings used in spiritual schools differ from those employed by Freudian or Jungian psychologists, or the more modern views of Erikson and Maslow. All one has to do is peruse a book like Xuan Zang's *Doctrine of Mere Consciousness* and you will immediately notice that modern psychology is child's play compared to the mental classification schemes taught in the deeper systems of cultivation science. The psychological categories used in cultivation are extremely precise and more elaborate since realized masters, employing extremely clear discernment, have been able to map out typical thought patterns and the various machinations of consciousness.

Modern psychology and psychiatry study thoughts, but neither studies the gap between thoughts. However, it is this gap of emptiness between thoughts that is typically an initial focus on the path of meditation. If you want to truly study the mind then this gap between thoughts is what you must concentrate on observing.

The coming and going of thoughts are like the two sides of birth and death while the gap between them is like the true reality of mental formlessness (emptiness) that supports them like space. That gap between thoughts, which is a peaceful state of no-thought, shows that the mind's true nature is actually unmanifest thoughts. Someone who wants to know the true nature of the mind must come to investigate the mental quiet state between thoughts, and then extend this state until it envelops the mind in peacefulness. This is why we have discussed various forms of meditation without discrimination, or "emptiness meditations," which lack images within consciousness. You don't attain mental emptiness (formlessness) by holding onto an image but by letting go of all images, yet it helps if you first start with some image of emptiness that you can derive try to replicate before letting go of it.

Therapists today are also fond of teaching visualization methods for stress reduction and relaxation, but if you want to reduce stress then this gap between thoughts should once again become the focus of attention. In watching or witnessing meditation practice this gap becomes clearly noticeable, and then one can extend it. Watching this gap is also one of the centering awareness meditation methods within the *Vijnanabhairava*.

Individuals in relaxation classes are usually instructed to follow their breath to calm their mind, and in time it will slow down. What they actually want to reach is also a cessational gap – a respiratory pause of no breathing between the in-breath and out-breath. They want to watch their breath so that it calms down and eventually achieves a state where it seemingly halts for short periods of time, even as long as a few minutes.

During that state of respiratory cessation the true Qi of your body can begin to arise. You can prepare for this event by practicing *kumbhaka* pranayama techniques that force you to stay in a state of breath retention, and thereby gradually make the lungs more efficient so that it more easily occurs.

If modern psychiatry and psychology were built upon studying gaps like this - the gap between breaths, between thoughts and even the gap between waking and sleeping - they could help unravel many of the mysteries of the human condition.

The spiritual schools of the world are based on investigating the true fabric of the mind rather than some random temporary coloring of the mind, namely wandering thought patterns. Cultivation psychology therefore is therefore involved with realms of consciousness of which ordinary psychology is hardly aware. For example, how many psychologists have ever reached the samadhi of no-thought where the world does not even arise in the mind? Not knowing of mental experiential realms like this, they lack the full definitions by which they can determine what it truly means to be mentally healthy.

The teachings of cultivation psychology that map the mind had their first origins in the ancient Vedic cultivation schools. They later flowered under the Buddhist school of Abhidharma and then the school of Consciousness-only, whose teachings provide elaborate structural details about consciousness. The aspect of psychology we must investigate in this particular case deals with the consciousness of ordinary mentation (called the sixth consciousness in Buddhism) as opposed to the deeply embedded I-thought (called the seventh consciousness) or the universal consciousness called the *alaya*.

According to Buddhist psychology, the sixth consciousness (ordinary everyday mind of discrimination) combines together the various sense impressions (smells, sounds, etc.) and cross checks the mental images against memories and thoughts to identify objects. In other words, it enables us to know, judge and evaluate things. Since everything in existence has both a positive and negative aspect, a Yin nature and Yang nature, the sixth consciousness cannot escape this principle either. Hence it has a bright, clear side of discrimination and also a shadow side as well.

The bright or clarity side of the sixth consciousness takes in all of the information provided by the senses and makes sense of it. The Yin or shadow side of the sixth consciousness, on the other hand, operates in its own independent realm so it does not rely on the eyes, ears, nose and so on in order to operate. Since this flip side of the sixth consciousness can operate by itself, it is called the du-yin, "solitary shadow" or "solitary consciousness." It is not exactly the subconscious but shares similar characteristics.

This shadow side or Yin-aspect of the sixth consciousness is what produces the pictures that we experience within our dreams, among other things. Dreams are the operational province of the solitary consciousness as are hallucinations and the ramblings of insanity. In general, the du-yin is said to be in control of consciousness under several circumstances:

(1) During dreaming where the du-yin, free of the confines of space and time, can sometimes tap into information about the past or future.

(2) During states of sickness and mental incoherence.

(3) During states of mental illness or insanity, such as when an individual starts to ramble incoherently or takes their hallucinations as something real. Some of the mentally ill

functioning under the influence of the du-yin can even develop supernormal abilities that a normal human does not normally possess. However, this does not mean that they are more spiritually advanced since their minds are not stable, calm or clear and they do not have control over themselves.

(4) During certain stages of meditation, such as when you mistakenly believe you see the sun and moon, gods, the future, etc., or believe you have developed superpowers. This is the scientific explanation for why you might see such things rather than the supernatural explanation involving the existence of devas and higher spiritual beings projecting visions. Other cases include when you actually attain samadhi and go beyond the realms of time and space so that you are not influenced by normal sensory input, and whereby various superpowers can manifest. We can say that this is similar to insanity or mental illness, but the difference is that the individual with samadhi has complete control over their mental powers or psychic manifestations whereas the mentally ill cannot control their mental states.

Some forms of daydreaming can also be classified as the operation of the du-yin, such as when we lose ourselves inside some personal mental scenario or imagination. A perfect example of falling into a mental scenario is when we eat all the food on our plate without noticing because we are daydreaming rather than practicing concentration or clear consciousness.

Since the solitary consciousness is not restricted by space or time, sometimes mentally ill people will have the uncanny ability know certain things about us, and sometimes through the du-yin we will personally experience ESP in our dreams or exhibit superpowers as well. If we are really careful about the matter, we should also realize that ESP and superpowers in these cases have a definite connection with mental illness. Going a bit further, we can also say that if you are too intelligent or too dumb, both these extremes can be forms of mental illness so you must be careful how you interpret matters. While the workings of the du-yin can be attributed to interferences caused by devas, the introduction of the du-yin as an explanatory mechanism eliminates the need for this suggestion.

The point is that anyone who experience things like this artist will become confused when the du-yin is operating. Through lack of clarity, they will not comprehend what is really going on. Sometimes they will mistakenly believe that they know things about the future or believe they have developed various psychic abilities when their experiences are just the operation of the du-yin shadow side of the sixth consciousness. This often corresponds to the Qi not being able to pass through the hind region of the brain. In any case, this demonstrates that a person must become very aware of their own psyche no matter what school or sect they follow on the road of cultivation.

Although the following description from *Tao and Longevity* does not perfectly apply to this woman practitioner, whose mental instability had complicated matters, her case provides a perfect opportunity to introduce the special reactions which may occur when an individual's Qi, because of various sadhana, starts impinging upon the back of the brain and tries to penetrate through obstructed Qi channels in that vicinity. *Tao and Longevity* states:

> If one has enough bodily strength and the Qi ascends to the back of the head, one may notice darkness in front of the eyes when half asleep. Gradually a dreamlike state occurs, and images eventually appear. This happens because Qi affects the nerves at the back of the head, which then affects the optic nerves. Many people have dream images accompanied by feelings of love and joy or sadness and dread. These images and feelings match subconscious functions that give rise to one's mental states, thoughts and concepts. States of Mara, or demonic delusion, may occur at this stage. These states depend upon one's wisdom, thought, personality, psychological propensities, and physiological condition. They are very complicated. Without the guidance of a very perceptive master, and in the absence of self-confidence, healthy intelligence, and correct thinking, a person may be led down the wrong road.
>
> When a person understands this, he can ignore phenomena of this sort, knowing that light follows the darkness. After passing through this stage one feels somewhat more awake. Points of light, like a fluorescent

star, may appear in front of your eyes, sparkling in different shapes and colors. These colors and lights are connected with your physiology and will be discussed later in more detail. ...

When Qi reaches the back of the head, a person might hear wonderful inner sounds or experience ringing or pressure in his ears. This phenomenon is produced by Qi working to open the Qi route in the brain. The vibration or trembling of Qi causes some brain wave activity. If one's intelligence is not clear and bright enough, then illusions deep inside the subconscious will result.

One who has deep religious beliefs may have illusions of hearing the voice of God or Buddha. Often the voice will speak of the past or future, and this a priori information may be quite correct, at least in small things. Thus, one might believe he has clairaudience. Whatever is heard is actually just a big assembly; it is a mixing of previous experience - what has been seen, heard, thought and known before. This kind of clairaudience could be used to predict small matters, but it will not work on big events at all. If one clings to the idea that these voices are real, he will fall into a state of Mara, or illusion. This shows that the mind is receptive to impressions but this is not a genuine instance of clairaudience. A person should not be puzzled or moved by this reaction. Instead, he should sometimes swallow the saliva and release the feelings in his head. This requires a strong mind and persistent will. By guiding the Qi downward one will pass this stage and enter the next.

"Ideally, one should use the Taoist's internal Kung Fu, employ the special body exercises and adjustments of yoga and esoteric Buddhism and have required medical treatments when necessary.[12]

Because it is very easy to become misled by all this, the Zen masters have a saying: "For those people who practice gong-fu but do not know the theory, when they open their mouths only nonsense comes out. For those people who only know the theory but who have never had the real experience, these people are like the blind."

---

[12] *Tao and Longevity*, pp. 45-47.

To summarize, we can say that this female practitioner was not mentally stable from the start. We can phrase matters another way by saying that her nervous system was weak, which is why she was engaged in automatic painting. Her problem was not very serious, but she would definitely have benefited from some form of psychological counseling and even dietary changes. Furthermore, the description of her meditation experiences suggests that she also had an obstruction (subluxation) in the back of the neck that could have and should have been treated by one or two chiropractic adjustments.

CASE 4: Female Psychologist

As a child, following a vacation spent in a religiously oriented summer camp, this middle-aged woman experienced feelings of oneness with God and Nature for about a year. As an adult she suffered several episodes of severe depression, and was hospitalized during one of these. In 1960 and 1970, respectively, she made two attempts at suicide and was unconscious for days each time.

In 1972 she was initiated in Transcendental Meditation, which helped her bear the tragedy of her daughter's premature death. It also cured her asthma. She practiced this form of meditation for about six months and then did not meditate for a similar period of time. When she resumed her meditation practice, she switched over to the Buddhist technique of vipassana, watching her breathing, body sensations, and thoughts.

She gradually increased the time spent in meditation. By the summer of 1974, she was meditating between three and four hours daily. It was then that she found her meditations deepening. During one of her sittings she experienced a strong feeling of disorientation, of not being located in space, which instilled some fear in her. Then, without warning, there was a sudden sharp pain at the base of her left big toe, which was quickly followed by a painful ripping sensation traveling up her leg. Then her lower pelvis and perineum felt as if they were swollen. When this sensation had spread to her waist, her torso suddenly was twisted violently to the right. (She would feel the pain in her left big toe whenever a new energy center was opening up further.)

In her abdomen she distinctly felt, "I must save all sentient beings." This was followed by a cold sensation pouring down over the crown of her head, shoulders, and arms into her chest, with the accompanying words, "I am not ready yet." All this occurred about an hour into her meditation and lasted between ten and thirty minutes.

During an intensive meditation retreat several months later, she again felt her whole body being pushed and pulled by a massive energy. Then she saw/felt a fountain of light erupting from the pelvic area into her head. At the same time she had a sense that there was a wide split in the middle of her body.

In 1975 she switched to Tibetan visualization techniques to correct what a Tibetan meditation master had diagnosed as a lopsided energy flow. She started to experience closing and opening of the energy centers of her body, without reason or order. There was also a low-pitched buzzing in her head and throat during meditation and occasionally during the day. She continued to have spontaneous body movements and energy rushes and pains. However, by the end of that year she was again able to sleep three to four hours every night.

Subsequently she went to Swami Muktananda for spiritual guidance, after having seen him in dreams. He gave her a mantra and asked her to focus on her head, not her body, as in vipassana. She started to have more spontaneous body movements but the pain and fear lessened and feelings of ecstasy and bliss increased during meditation. She also experienced more tingling sensations and heat phenomena, particularly in her lower back and hands.

She began to see how there was a strong part of herself that was negative toward her own growth and spiritual maturation. But it was not until 1987 that she began to consciously work through the problems of her childhood that had proven formidable obstructions in her psyche.

In a recent follow-up interview, she reported her old kundalini headaches are persisting but the energetic disturbances have gone. She is now experiencing many spiritual connections with living and dead teachers. Psychic phenomena are occurring more frequently, and in particular she has developed the ability to heal instantly on occasion.

Let us examine how this case differs from our previous examples. For instance, there are very strong indications that this individual, who spontaneously repeated the Buddhist vows to "save all sentient beings," may have practiced spiritual cultivation in a previous life. It is unfortunate that she was unaware of the principles of practice that would have enabled her to make substantial progress in her present cultivation practice.

If this woman had known about the principle of emptiness - attaining a mental state empty of discriminative thought through the meditation practice of just letting everything go without mentally attaching to it - she could have made tremendous progress in cultivating her Qi and channels. As to her physical condition, her experiences suggest that she needed chiropractic adjustments in her neck and in the region of her pelvis.

As to the cultivation instructions given her by various teachers, let us refrain from commenting on them. Just note that the Zen school always says that there is a gate of no-gate that does not use any practice at all, so why should you put another head on top of the one you already have? It is just too bad that this practitioner did not encounter someone who could teach her about the prajna wisdom path of forgetting both mind and body.

As the text *Tao and Longevity* points out, a cultivator may sometimes

have the feeling that there is a strong force moving with difficulty along the spinal cord but is prevented from pushing upward. One may also hope that this energetic Qi force will push through the obstruction so that one can finally feel relaxed and comfortable. In Taoism, this spinal phenomenon is called the River Chariot that rolls to the location of the Chia Chih. This occurs during the process of opening the Tu Mai. This is the stage where the Qi starts to reach the Huang Yang point. If one cannot release his mind and attain the state of forgetting the body, the pressure will become stronger and stronger. Whenever this phenomenon occurs, a person's attention will automatically focus on the back and one may attempt to use the force of consciousness or imagination to push the pressure upward. Because of the concentration of attention here, the brain and stomach nerves will become tighter and tighter. The heart will contract and the uncomfortable feeling in the back will be increased.

Some schools of Taoism teach one to guide the Qi with consciousness, to push it through or to drive it. Students are to imagine the progression of the River Chariot and engage in taking deep, long, but tiny breaths (6 x 6, thirty-six deep breaths; or 9 x 9, eighty-one deep breaths) that numerically match the Big and Small circulations of heaven. Or they are to use some Taoism or yoga exercises to guide the passage of Qi through this location.

Although these direction exercises have a temporary effect and make one feel that something passes through the Chia Chih to rush up to Yu Chen (i.e., the back of the head), it is only the mental force that changes the physical feeling, but it is definitely not the phenomenon of Qi passing through the Chia Chih.

If one can attain the state of "forgetting his own body," or apply his wisdom in an attempt to forget his feelings and remain quiet without taking any mental action, then there will be a moment when suddenly, like a switch making a contact, all the tension is gone and the mind and body are loose and at ease. From this turning point one will experience the state of breadth and brightness of mind and fullness of spirit. A person whose back is humped at this stage will naturally straighten his waist and back, stretch his chest, and his breath will become smoother. For those who are born with advanced scoliosis or who have it as a result of an external wound, this is a difficult situation.

At this stage a person will be so charged that he will not fall asleep easily. Since he may be used to sleeping at a fixed time, he might assume that he has insomnia and feel frightened. It should be understood that this is not the insomnia of ordinary people. One should let nature take its course. If one cannot fall asleep, just don't go to bed.[13]

What about the practitioner who sits quietly and never has any special sensations? Not having any special reactions from meditation practice is usually due to the fact that you have not put in enough practice time or effort to stimulate your Qi. In most cases the lack of Qi sensations is due to either infrequent or improper practice because when you truly start to make progress you will usually feel the vital energy start to move in many parts of your body. Pranayama practice will help this to finally happen as well as the exercises in Nyasa Yoga. It is hard to comment on these matters and put forth general principles because each case is different.

Actually, not having any sensations is already a sensation. The *Diamond Sutra* of Buddhism says: "Whoever seeks me in appearance, or seeks me in sound is going astray and missing the Tao," Hence, there is nothing to worry about when you sit in meditation and nothing special occurs because progress is still being made even if you don't notice it. Not feeling any special sensations is also correct and what you are ultimately looking for when seeking a peaceful mind. Even so, you should also remember that you will eventually begin to feel your Qi moving inside after you start making genuine progress in igniting the vital energies of your physical nature through meditation.

CASE 5: Male Computer Scientist

This man is now in his mid-twenties. At age nine he suddenly developed shooting pains in his genitals and lower abdomen. When in bed at night, he would feel a strong force pushing its way down his throat. This was accompanied by perceptual distortions. A physician tentatively diagnosed hypoglycemia.

In his early teens, he and his friends experimented with hypnosis, and he discovered that he could easily dissociate from reality. One day, in his sixteenth year, while sitting quietly, he suddenly started to tremble uncontrollably, and his body became very hot. His abdominal pains returned with full force, accompanied by nausea. After a bowel

---

[13] *Tao and Longevity*, pp. 42-43.

movement these symptoms subsided. The next day, again while sitting quietly, he had an out-of-body experience (OBE). He had undergone a marginal OBE state when he was younger. On this occasion, however, he was able to move around the room very easily and to view his resting body very clearly. He became alarmed and by moving his arm was able to slip back into the body. For several weeks after this incident his world was collapsed and he felt he was going insane. He dissociated many times in school.

Later, during the fifth session in a Rolfing series in which his psoas muscle was being worked on, he had a strong emotional discharge, with a lot of crying and violent shaking. He felt the immediate need to ground himself. Suddenly there was a terrific energy, which felt to him like a fire hose that was being forced into his perineum and up his spine. When it reached his head there was a feeling of infinite space all around him and inside his skull. He also felt a sensation of a hole being bored into his forehead. All the while there was a display of colored lights around and inside his head. Upon the "penetration" of the forehead, he felt a great current of air rushing through the opening. This was followed by an infinite peace in infinite space.

Subsequently he suffered, as he sees it now, from the delusion that he was enlightened and that this infinite space and otherworldly focus were the only truths for him. A Zen master later told him that during that time he had been in a satori [samadhi] state.

At age eighteen he developed debilitating pains in his solar plexus. These were alleviated whenever he allowed his body to spontaneously assume various postures. Only later did he learn that these were yogic asanas. It was then that he started a program of yogic practices, including breath control, that he still follows every day for at least two hours. He was hoping all this would speed up his regaining the condition of satori. He also began to read spiritual literature.

Five years later he discovered the writings of Da Love-Ananda (Da Free John). In the midst of his study of these works he noticed a remarkable fullness in his abdomen and then his belly felt on fire for hours. To his surprise he noted that his girth had increased by four inches, without any gain in weight.

Soon afterward he became a student of Da Love-Ananda. He began to realize that his intense yogic practice was born out of the terror of dying and an attempt to remove himself from the stresses of life. He no longer suffered from the delusions of being enlightened and also saw how he had not the slightest inclination toward surrendering the stronghold of the ego, which is the single most important precondition for enlightenment.

Then he had his first formal "sitting" with Da Love-Ananda. Upon looking at his teacher, who was seated before hundreds of people, this young man was suddenly possessed by the demonic urge to utterly destroy this being. He found it incredibly difficult to restrain himself from attempting a violent assault. While he was struggling with this irrational impulse, Da Love-Ananda made eye contact with him, and he was immediately thrust into his familiar state of blissfulness and infinity. But this time he was not alone. There was a complete merging with the teacher in an enclosure of love. This was the first time he had ever had such an ecstatic experience of being in this space of love and unity with another being. At this moment the though arose in him, "I can't wait to tell my wife this." That very second it all stopped.

Gradually he became more open to this new relationship and learned to trust it. But time and again, he would rupture this by claiming credit for his condition. For a period he became acutely conscious of playing with his energy flows, as if he were masturbating with his nervous system. At other times he would enter into out-of- body states and immediately feel that this too was only an indulgence. He is now dealing with his residual resistances creatively, always reminding himself to return to the naturalness of the spiritual relationship with the teacher. Occasionally his old fears arise, but they are no longer as severe, and he is now more capable of allowing them while simultaneously locating within himself the bliss and equanimity that lies beyond fear.

This particular individual represents a great advance in spiritual progress over the previous four cases. This cultivator's foundation, perhaps due to cultivation work done in a previous life, is much stronger than the others. In fact, this is the first case in which we encounter anything similar to the real kundalini phenomenon. However, it still does not describe the true kundalini Yang Qi.

The active nature of this practitioner's vitality was the reason why he felt pains in his genitals at age nine, and is the reason he could have various unusual experiences by age sixteen. It is most probable that much of this progress was due to the fact that he was a "chaste youth" who rarely lost his semen through wet dreams or masturbation.

The cultivation stories of Han Shan and Ramakrishna clearly prove the standard teachings that *brachmacharya*, or "no leakage" (celibacy), is an extremely important contributing factor to progress in spiritual cultivation. When a man loses his semen and Qi through ejaculation, that Qi is no longer available to push open Qi channels yet that is what is precisely necessary for spiritual progress.

"If there is no water in the boiler there is no steam in the pipes;" without accumulating Qi you will have no energetic power within you with which to open up your internal Qi channels. Therefore the *Surangama Sutra* says, "Trying to cultivate samadhi without cutting off lust is like cooking sand trying to make rice. It cannot be done."

In regards to the doctor's diagnosis of this practitioner's cultivation experiences as hypoglycemia, which was incorrect, this mistake also demonstrates how Western medicine often misunderstands cultivation *gong-fu*. Unfortunately this lack of understanding will still hold for perhaps a hundred or more years to come.

Despite the experiences described, this individual certainly did not yet open his *jen mai* or *tu mai* (front and back) Qi channels, nor did he actually succeed in cultivating his physical Qi either. Even so, due to his strong vitality we might say that his meditative experience was close to matching the infinite space samadhi, which is a stage of mental emptiness that you were practicing to reach from the instructions in chapter three. You have already been provided with many instructions from the *Vijnanabhairava* that offer various ways you can cultivate this experiential realm. The Zen teacher whom this practitioner consulted acted in a most excellent manner by stating that his experience was not enlightenment, but was simply a particular type of samadhi. Unfortunately, this practitioner's karma with his teacher was not so good, otherwise he might have been guided to a stable stage of samadhi at an even higher stage of realization.

All the other sensations this individual experienced were undoubtedly a result of his strong vitality, which generated symptoms similar to the real kundalini phenomenon. If this meditation practitioner had enough wisdom and the proper guidance, his progress suggests that he could reach a much higher level of samadhi and possibly attain enlightenment. This is because the infinite space samadhi properly belongs to the formless realm and is very difficult to attain. Any individual who can reach this experience shows that he has strong cultivation roots and tremendous merit.

While none of these cases so far have talked about sexual behavior, this is an extremely important topic in cultivation matters. Although Westerners now teach young children that it is okay to masturbate whenever they want and thus readily lose their Jing by doing so, there is no teaching more dangerous nor destructive to either health or spiritual attainments. This is not something you want to encourage. The problem in spiritual cultivation is how to handle the impulses of sexual desire without actually losing sexual energy. You want to *conserve that energy so that it works on opening up your Qi channels*. This is the basis of a healthy life whereas dissipation is not the basis of health and longevity.

It is true that the habitual pulls of sexual desire are strong and deep, but you should not encourage the loss of energy if you want people to remain healthy or make spiritual progress. It is only when the vital energy of the body accumulates, through the practice of sexual restraint and non-leakage, that a man's Qi becomes strong enough to open up the obstructed Qi channels within the body, especially in the region of the pelvis. If a man carelessly loses his Jing and Qi through sexual activities, there will then be no pressure or force available to open the Qi channels. The properness or improperness of sexual dissipation and whether it is right or wrong has nothing to do with the naturalness of desire and release, but deals entirely with the matter of health and losing spiritual energy.

Unfortunately, ordinary people often do not know better than to squander their normal build-up of sexual energy, especially young adults who are advised to masturbate rather than transform their Jing into Qi for the benefits of health and spiritual progress. Thus, few seem to make genuine progress in spiritual cultivation these days and everyone wonders why. Even if someone were to become a monk, nun, priest or rabbi, their spiritual striving will amount to little unless they can refrain from losing their Jing and transform it into Qi. To do so you must cultivate mental emptiness through meditation and other spiritual practices. From the point of view of attaining spiritual progress, unless you can accomplish this necessary transformation of Jing to Qi by cultivating mental emptiness, then celibacy for spiritual purposes is practically useless although there are great health benefits.

There is also an interesting point to note from this case which keeps popping up time and time again, which is the fact that several practitioners have felt sensations in their left big toe that often manifested as pain or swelling. Shakyamuni Buddha commented on this phenomenon thousands of years ago. He told people performing visualization practices of their skeleton they should always start their visualization concentrations by focusing on the left big toe (see the *Chan Mi Yaofa Jing* or *Discourse on the Essential Secrets of Meditation*). If you are doing fire visualization practices then Hindu yogis sometimes say to start with your right big toe as explained in *Nyasa Yoga*.

The Qi routes running down the insides of the legs and reaching to the toes are some of the most important Qi channel meridians to open within the body. The legs in total are particularly difficult to transform. Opening the channels in all the tissues of the legs requires special exercises to stretch muscle fibers, visualization for the bones, and extra cultivation effort. You can only generate a subtle deva body if you open up all the Qi channels everywhere in the body, and thus because the legs and feet channels are so difficult to open many cultivation practices start with a lower body focus so that this difficult area always receives attention with every practice session. The Yoga schools even talk about leg chakras, which denote sections of the lower body involving the calves and legs, to remind people that they must work on opening/transforming these areas too instead of just the spine upwards.

Now when a practitioner feels that a particular chakra or

energy center is opening this conclusion is normally due to feeling the sensation of Qi moving in the vicinity. It is not an actual opening of the chakras or region. A meditator typically just feels the Qi stirring in a particular region of the body and then immediately jumps to extraordinary conclusions that this means something more than it really is.

When the elements of the physical body are not properly attuned or the body is not in good shape, it is normal for the body's Qi channels to shake or become warm when Qi starts to course through them and encounters obstructions. Some people may experience spontaneous movements, or may want to cough or burp to release their discomfort as the Qi opens up obstructed passageways. Sometimes people with internal diseases or great obstructions experience large reactions while people who are healthier might experience no reactions at all.

The *Hatha Yoga Pradipika* tried to summarize these matters by describing what often happens as the Qi starts penetrating obstructed Qi channels, "At the first stage perspiration breaks out, at the second stage the body trembles, and at the third stage the prana reaches the head." Of course the process is more complicated than this, and there are many variations of this general sequence as explained in *Tao and Longevity*, but generally speaking you can see how this information sheds light on the experiences being discussed.

You experience these things because the body is trying to clear blockages and internal obstructions to the flow of vital energy in your tissues. This isn't just happening along acupuncture meridians but within all the tissues of the body, which is why Yoga and other forms of stretching, which eliminate tissue knots, help in spiritual cultivation.

The more you let go of the body rather than resist change and try to block your Qi when it starts to move through areas, the quicker the job will finish and then these phenomena will disappear. Once again, stretching and *nei-gong* work, or even Nyasa Yoga practice, can help also. A typical rule for Qi transformations is that if you ignore your body when these events happen then the phenomena will arise and then depart quicker than if you held onto them. Working to transform that section of the body will also speed the rejuvenation possibilities of Qi passing through all the tissues. After the channels in all body tissues are opened your Qi will then circulate everywhere unopposed, and such experiences will disappear entirely. At the higher stages of transformation, such as during the twelve year period that most masters go through, your leg and knee muscles might even become stiffer and tighten as they are being transformed, which is why exercise to stretch your muscles is very important for the road of spiritual cultivation.

When the body's Qi channels start to open it is usually accompanied by discomfort. This is because we accumulate countless poisons in our bodies as we age, as well as knots and obstructions in our tissues and muscle fibers, and the strong force that is required to push through obstructions and eject poisons out of system causes frictional discomfort during the stage of Qi purification.

This is why yearly detoxification efforts always help spiritual aspirants, and it also explains the great pain genuine cultivators feel when their channels and chakras finally start to truly open on the spiritual path. For instance, when the heart chakra is opening up you might even feel like you are having palpitations or a heart attack, or your might simply become angry when the Qi starts passing through your liver meridians trying to open them.

Ancient spiritual masters lived in an era where natural foods were the norm. They did not have artificial chemicals, pesticides, herbicides or food additives in their diets and *yet they still had to go through the intensive detoxification-purification reactions of spiritual cultivation involving painful eliminations.* Therefore, do not believe that eating organic produce will prevent these problems. They are unavoidable. Even babies born to organic-eating vegetarian parents will have accumulated poisons and Qi channel obstructions within their bodies. Everyone must go through this elimination, detoxification, purification, or transformation process so that Qi channel obstructions are eliminated. This is how you eventually create a deva body of subtle energy.

The process of clearing the Qi channels therefore arises for everyone. We must exercise, practice pranayama breathing practices, ingest certain internal detoxification and cleansing supplements, mantra, practice visualization *nei-gong* exercises, and use meditation to help transform and purify our physical bodies. Every little bit helps. *Nyasa Yoga* and *Look Younger, Live Longer* teach how to do this as a set.

The vital force that arises to clear obstructions in the body does not come from biochemical reactions, but is generated naturally when we accumulate our Jing and Qi. A practitioner can try to mentally guide his Qi but sometimes you need to just forget the body entirely and then things will proceed naturally without need of outside interference or intercession. However, when you feel that you need to guide internal energy because of the discomfort then do so. This is the basis of *nei-gong* work or Nyasa Yoga.

The force necessary to clear any obstructions will, because of cultivating a detachment to discriminative thought, usually arise naturally over time and then act on its own. All we need to do is have faith in the process. Nature is not wrong in what it tries to accomplish, especially when the Buddhas and Bodhisattvas are helping us.

Another common misconception is that the real kundalini energy is hot like fire whereas it feels like blissful, peaceful warmth in each and every cell. Thus the genuine kundalini phenomenon can be compared to the natural warmth of a healthy young baby. When you feel that your Qi is hot this is partially due to the fact that your Yang Qi is naturally warm, but the extra degree of hotness represents a frictional force involving blockages in your energy meridians. Hence, when you read stories of meditators getting very hot, in most cases this is not the real kundalini phenomenon but just the frictional heat generated as your Qi struggles to push through internal obstructions in the channels.

Indian yogis sometimes eat bitter herbs during their cultivation practice because this helps to cool down the heat generated by their use of forceful techniques to ignite the Qi energies of the physical nature. Several Christian mystics were also known to use buckets of water in order to cool themselves from the results of their spiritual practice because the transformations of *incendium amoris*, which is the Christian term for kundalini, can really be that heating.

Swami Narayanananda once explained that there are four classical characteristics of kundalini, the first of which includes heat:

(1) There is a strong burning, first along the back and then over the whole body.
(2) The kundalini's entrance into the central spinal canal, called *sushumna*, is attendant with pain. However, this and any of the other disturbing phenomena should not be taken as a sign of disease.

(3) When the kundalini reaches the heart, one may experience palpitations.

(4) One feels a creeping sensation from the toes, and sometimes the whole body starts to shake. The rising sensation may feel like an ant crawling slowly up the body toward the head, a snake wiggling along, a bird hopping from place to place, like a fish darting through calm water, or like a monkey leaping to far branch.

These classical descriptions are very incomplete. According to Chinese Taoism and school of Esoteric Buddhism, an actual kundalini arousal can be of two types - a Yin type or Yang type. The correct Yang type of kundalini phenomenon, which is born from emptiness, feels warm and peaceful. The Yin type, which produces burning sensations, is usually due to abnormal awakenings that are forced and is not necessarily connected with mental emptiness. For instance, Chinese medicine refers to fevers as internal Yin fire, which accounts for some types of kundalini experience. Similarly, Chinese culture calls the Emperor a "Yang fire" while his officials are called "Yin fire," meaning that Yin fire experiences are not the real kundalini phenomenon either.

Generally speaking, people who meditate are usually playing with thoughts and mentally entertaining some sort of scenario in their minds. Therefore they usually only experience the Yin type of awakening. The Yang type of experience can be identified when every cell of the body feels as if you were experiencing a warm, cozy summer day. This is the correct and genuine kundalini phenomenon. Therefore, it is incorrect to say that kundalini arousal will always be hot or be accompanied by burning sensations because in most cases this is just your latent vitality working to clear the Qi channels of their obstructions. As usual, the hotness is just a sign of friction from internal blockages. Even the Tibetans have contributed to this mistaken notion by translating the term for kundalini using the term "fire" rather than "warmth," so this is a common mistake that people have been making for ages. Because of this mistranslation, many people misunderstand the nature of this phenomenon entirely.

Most people who cultivate have been influenced by Yoga school teachings and therefore try to raise their kundalini by forcing its initiation by using *kumbhaka* pranayama techniques. They do not choose the path of emptiness meditation and prajna wisdom analysis, whereby it will arise naturally in time. They cultivate forceful techniques, from force they get friction, and from friction they experience heat rather than comfort and bliss. This is an acceptable road of practice too, but you must know the result you will get.

Technically speaking, we must also note that the kundalini phenomenon does not originate from the back of the spine, but rather from the region of the perineum and pelvis. To think that cultivation *gong-fu* originates from the head rather than from below, as is claimed by Anthroposophy, is also just plain nonsense. In *The Journey to the West*, Sun Wukong retrieves his powerful staff, representing his Qi, from the bottom of the ocean to denote the fact that your Yang Qi arises from your perineum. In *Nyasa Yoga* you will find descriptions of the pelvic chakras and the reasons why it is difficult to open up the Qi channels in this region. It requires sexual restraint and many types of stretching exercises that you're your body convert Jing to Qi.

Cultivation *gong-fu* can be compared to the circular weather rejuvenation cycle through the following analogy: the sun shines on a body of still water, the water evaporates and ascends into the sky forming clouds, the clouds mass together and form rain, and the rain water falls and returns to its original home. Thus, we have Jing transforming into Qi, the Qi ascending through the *tu mai* spinal channels to reach the brain, hormones and Qi now descend through the front *jen mai* energy channel downwards, and the pattern repeats all over again. This is the nature of the Qi cycle within the body and you can clearly see that it does not start in the head.

Pain will usually accompany the progression of the Qi as it initially enters and starts to clear any of the Qi channels that are most responsible for spiritual progress, such as the central, left, right, front and back Qi channels. When the Qi actually progresses enough to reach the center of the heart chakra, an individual will typically feel anxious or nervous and the heart may experience palpitations. The vibrations or pain we feel from this type of progress occur because our Qi channels are not yet purified through the "fire of yoga," so before the central channel opens we will normally feel aching and discomfort as various poisons and blockages are removed. As previously mentioned, Buddhism describes eight major sensations that can arise from the movements of Qi including pain, itching, coldness, warmth, weightlessness, heaviness, roughness and smoothness. These eight are not all-inclusive descriptions, but rather just general guidelines for the many types of sensations that can occur.

Low-stage and high-stage meditation practitioners often deceive themselves when experiencing all these sorts of experiences, mistaking them for something higher than they actually are, and it is almost impossible to convince the stubborn or ignorant that their conclusions are incorrect. If you tell someone who has been working hard at cultivation and who fervently desires progress that their experiences are not what they imagine, you are only going to be met with denial, disbelief, deafness and even hatred. If you tell people they are mistaken they will often dig in and cling to incorrect notions with even stronger zeal. Even experienced Zen masters experience troubles like this when teaching talented students, although talented students will usually thank their masters later for being so frank after they finally recognize their mistakes.

When someone reads the description of a particular stage of cultivation, they will usually try to match the symptoms reported with their own experiences. If many characteristics match they will then conclude they have attained that same stage when they usually have only achieved a "semblance dharma" – a small achievement that looks like something more profound but isn't. This is like the experience of young doctors and psychologists-to-be who are studying the descriptions of various illnesses in medical school. Sometimes students will match these descriptions with their personal experiences and then mistakenly fear they have contracted some terrible disease themselves.

Thus, there are countless people who think they have cleared their Qi channels, opened the supreme bliss chakra at the top of the head, activated their kundalini, achieved the Taoist *yin shen* transformation-body or even attained enlightenment when they have achieved nothing of the sort. People can mistakenly believe they have attained all sorts of high cultivation states when they have no level of attainment whatsoever! This has been seen time and time again. I cannot even begin to count how many people believe that they have opened their head chakra or "third eye" and become enlightened. They haven't even attained the deva body, so how would this be possible? If you don't have a deva body you are not enlightened. This is a rule.

Unfortunately, most of these individuals are only cheating themselves because they are experiencing superficial sensations of wind Qi coupled together with great hopes and self-delusion. Many people even employ the proper cultivation terminology within this net of self-delusion because they have studied the right information, and this helps them to validate their wrong conclusions. One of the reasons for this book is to help clear up these misconceptions.

In a case of semblance *gong-fu*, an individual's personal experiences will closely resemble an actual stage of cultivation accomplishment although they are not the genuine phenomenon in question. The most that can be said is that with a great deal of wisdom, merit and continued effort, the experiences of the practitioner will serve as a precursor to the actual attainment that will manifest in time. Thus, there are many continual "refinings" of a particular *gong-fu* experience that must be experienced over and over again before the genuine stage of accomplishment is finally achieved. However, a practitioner's hard work and merit will earn them an analogous taste, or semblance, of the final experience ahead of time.

Generally speaking, there are a variety of different Qi sensations you can experience through meditation. Some practitioners will feel coolness coming out of their body, and some might feel warmth being issued. All these reactions can be understood by studying Chinese medicine.

The reactions of meditation can also cause you to feel hot, bloated, itchy, or smooth. Sometimes you can feel soreness and sometimes tingling, lightness (such as the sensation of floating), or even heaviness. As the body starts to adjust itself to a state of more optimum health, some people can even have the experience of feeling like they are getting bigger or smaller. When you are expelling sickness Qi then those with stomach, intestinal or liver problems may often burp or feel nauseous, while lung and throat problems will sometimes give rise to coughing as they are being corrected.

To understand these various interactions you really must understand the interrelationship of Qi and physical states outlined in Chinese medicine because it was developed based on an investigation of Qi. For a first attempt at this goal, *The Yellow Emperor's Classic of Internal Medicine* will prove especially helpful. Indian Ayurvedic medicine may also provide some helpful insights, but Chinese medicine's usefulness seems foremost in this particular arena.

Hearing sounds in the head, as we have seen in several cases so far, is explained very clearly in various texts of Taoism. When the Qi wind starts going through the head channels it is common to hear these sounds as the Qi channels clear themselves of obstructions. The *Hatharatnavali* says that after certain pranayama exercises one might hear internal sounds like that of crickets, a flute, thunder, cymbals, a black bee, bell, gong, trumpet, or drum. Therefore we know that the wind Qi inside the ear Qi channels can make all sorts of sounds. This short list of sounds is simply indicative but not comprehensive.

Some people concentrate on these sounds, believing they are meaningful in some way. However, this is mistaken. For instance, there is a famous story of a practitioner who become so absorbed in an uninterrupted sound of "Om" that he heard in his head. He thought it was due to spiritual progress without realizing that it was actually due to the steady humming of a nearby refrigerator. As *Tao and Longevity* explains,

> when the Qi is really passing through the head there will be sounds like "Pi Pi Pai Pai" in the head. This is the reaction of the nerves induced by the Qi working to open up the paths. The sound is nothing strange; it is like the sound one hears when he covers his ears with his palms and hears his own heart and the circulation of blood. However, if one's attention is absorbed by these sounds or if there is some latent disease in [the] Upper Warmer, then one will want to shake his head quite often. If a person does not know the treatment for this, or if he cannot deflect his attention from it, it will become a kind of sick state. On the other hand, if the meditator knows how to be calm and quiet and can ignore this feeling, then he will naturally attain [the state of] Ching An [which is a stage of lightness and calm which precursors the onset of samadhi] ... There are some people who experience this phenomenon in their youth without practicing meditation. One might think of it as a kind of neurosis but if it is not stimulated by other factors, it is not a disease.[14]

---

[14] *Tao and Longevity*, p. 51.

The various phenomena which practitioners experience due to meditation always have a scientific basis behind them. They just seem strange experiences because people are not familiar with them. We know, for instance, that when people become really frightened that their hair can stand on end or even turn white. Although this rarely happens, we are not mystified if it occurs because it is known to be possible. Cultivation *gong-fu* is no different in that there is always a scientific explanation behind the manifestation of various spiritual phenomena. While science explains things in terms of blood, hormones or internal biochemistry, cultivators must also add to this list an understanding in terms of Jing, Qi, Shen, Qi channels and mental states.

Thus, when we read of the famous story of the demon of lust that attacked St. Francis of Assisi during the winter, knowing of cultivation theory we can surmise a scientific reason behind the eventual departure of his sexual desires. St. Francis cured his lust by going out into the cold and making "wife" and "children" snowmen. He then stood in the cold pointing to the snowmen, and started talking to himself about all the problems that would arise if he took a family. When his lust finally abated, he felt it was because his conversation had befuddled the lust demon so that it departed. In actual fact, it abated because his exposure to the cold had chilled his body and thus affected his Qi channels. The effect was just like the strategy of "taking a cold shower" that men sometimes use to put the cool on sexual desire. If you understand cultivation matters and the science involved, you can easily understand such stories and develop the type of understanding behind Jing, Qi, channels and chakras that we need today.

You can often match present day scientific knowledge with insights about spiritual *gong-fu* in order to gain some inkling about the workings of superpowers too. For instance, there is the famous story of a mantrayana practitioner in India who stopped a raging elephant in its tracks by reciting mantras over some herbs while blowing over them pointed toward the elephant's direction. If one recognizes that certain plant substances can cause drowsiness and that certain mantras can supposedly magnify the etheric Qi of plants, you would immediately surmise that the master was holding poppy leaves in his hands. The mantras amplified the etheric potency of the poppies which caused the elephant to get sleepy.

Similarly, certain mantras in India supposedly prevent death by snakebite. One day a smart individual recognized that they probably thinned the blood to prevent coagulation and thus learned how to use them to treat heart attacks.

CASE 6: Female Artist

This woman, now in her late fifties, had practiced Transcendental Meditation for five years when she began to experience occasional tingling in her arms and heat in her hands. Next she was unable to sleep for days, with energy surging through her whole body. She also had several dreams of having her consciousness separated from her body. A continuous loud sound started to appear inside her head. Soon there were cramps in her big toes, followed by vibratory sensations in her legs. Overnight, her big toenails darkened, as if hit by a hammer, and eventually partially separated from the flesh. The tissue in her legs felt torn by vibratory sensations. The vibrations spread to her lower back and from there swept over her body up to her head, causing a sensation of a band around her head, just above the eyebrows. Then her head started to move spontaneously. Later her whole body would move sinuously, and her tongue would automatically press against the roof of her mouth.

Both phenomena are well known in yogic circles. The cleaving of the tongue against the palate is counted among the most secret practices of Yoga. It bears the technical designation of khecari-mudra or the "space-walking gesture." The "space" here is the inner space (kha) of consciousness. All kinds of psychic powers are attributed to yogis who have mastered this technique. In the case of this woman, the mudra or "gesture" of inverting the tongue occurred involuntarily.

She would also sense a strong sounding of "om" - the most sacred syllable in the Hindu tradition emanating from within her head. The tingling sensations spread to her neck, upward over the head, down to the forehead and face. Both nostrils were stimulated, causing a feeling of elongation of the nose. At times her eyes seemed to move separately, and the pupils felt like holes that bored into her head and met in the center. Then she felt tremendous pressure at the back of her head, at the crown, and across the forehead. This pressure would become especially severe during reading, resulting in acute discomfort around the eyes and in a pulsing sensation at the top of the head.

This was followed by the experience of a brilliant light and of bliss and laughter.

The tingling sensation spread further down to the mouth and chin. It was then that she began to have dreams of heavenly music. Then the sensations traveled to her throat, chest and abdomen, and eventually she felt as if there was a closing of the circuit in the shape of an egg: The energy was moving up through the spine and down through the front of the body. As it developed, the circuit activated particular energy centers on its way - starting in the lower abdomen and proceeding to the navel, the solar plexus, the heart, the head, and finally the throat. After this closure she experienced a continuous feeling of energy pouring into her body through the navel area. This feeling stopped after the circuit was completed. The whole experience had strong sexual overtones. It was also accompanied by spontaneous yogic breathing (faint and controlled).

The greater part of this kundalini activity occurred over several months. Subsequently she experienced only occasional kundalini phenomena, mostly during meditation or when relaxing in bed. Throughout the protracted experience, this woman understood that she was undergoing a kundalini awakening, since she had read about this phenomenon before. In the beginning she felt relaxed about what was happening to her and simply allowed the process to unfold as it might. But eventually she became perturbed and had difficulty integrating her experiences with her daily activities. The inflow of energy prevented normal sleep for months, and, since it continued during the day as well, she found herself incapable of efficient work. She felt herself thrown into the position of a detached observer of her own activities. In due course she brought the situation under control.

The general effect of this kundalini arousal was positive. There has been steady progress toward an ever greater sense of connectedness with what this woman calls her "higher self" - a sense of being in touch with an unshakeable core, a center, that is unaffected by all the ups and downs of everyday life. In my follow-up interview with her, she remarked ... that, with the exception of pressure in the head, all physical sensations have ceased.

This artist is different from our previous case in that she has experienced the correct awakening of the Qi and partially opened the *tu mai* and *jen mai* (back and front) Qi channel energy meridians. However, this woman's central channel has still not opened yet. She did not open the crown chakra on the top of her head either, which actually means the brain, which is why she felt the sensation of pressure in the head.

A relevant passage from *Tao and Longevity*, which provides some insight into this case, runs as follows:

Taoists call the top of the head Ni Huang Palace and yogis call it The Crown. Some Taoists believe that this is the phenomenon of opening up the Tu Mai completely. But, this is not the case. These are merely changes along the Tu Mai that accompany the initial opening of the central nervous system. This is followed by stimulating the function of the top of the head to enhance the uniform distribution of endocrine secretions. However, at this step some people will have temporary pain or a heavy sensation at the top of the head, as though it were being pressed by something, or they may feel extreme tightness. This is due to the fact that the Qi route in the head is not completely open, or because one's attention is unduly attracted to feelings and sensations and one is preoccupied with them. If one can divert his attention and forget his head and let it be natural, then a very comfortable and refreshing feeling will gradually be generated and will move downward from the top of the head.[15]

The fact that this woman could not sleep, an affliction we have encountered previously, is actually a good sign of progress. This is because when you commit yourself to spiritual practice you want to lessen the desire for sex and sleep. The five barriers to attaining Tao include fortune, wealth, name (fame), sleep and sex. People all say they want to become free of these factors, but when they start to lose a single one they become frightened and lose their composure.

This particular meditator did not need much sleep anymore because she had reached the stage where her Qi was actually starting to transform into Shen (mental energy, which is a higher form of Qi). As Chinese Taoism says, "When one is full of Shen there is little desire for sleep," so this is a positive phenomenon one should not fear. This is what was actually happening in this case.

Taoism has many sayings that summarize the general sequence of cultivation progress. Most of these sayings actually refer to attainments (transformations) within the form and sensation skandhas, namely the physical and subtle bodies of the practitioner. For instance, Taoism says that cultivation will cause your Jing to transform into Qi, Qi into Shen, Shen into Emptiness and you must then let go of the Emptiness to attain the Tao.

This refers to the generation/development of the subtle body, made of Qi, out of the physical body composed of Jing. Next, the Causal body develops out of cultivation work on your subtle body, the Supra-Causal body is generated out of the Causal body, and the perfect *sambhogakaya* or Immanence body is created out of the Supra-Causal body. The Supra-Causal, Dharma or Clear Light body corresponds to the stage of initial enlightenment (*nirvana* with remainder) that is the precursor to the stage of complete and perfect enlightenment.

All of these bodies form as a result of transformations you bring about in the lower level body due to your cultivation work. Hence, the successive body attainments are the physical body, subtle body, Causal body, Supra-Causal body and then completed *sambhogakaya* (Immanence body). When you attain a new body it is always attached to your other bodies that you can use independently like appendages.

These bodies are already within one another, or you can say

---

[15] *Tao and Longevity*, p. 50.

that the energies for developing these bodies are within each other. They permeate one another and you have to distill them out into a new body through spiritual practice. On the road of spiritual cultivation, you simply cultivate the energies so that each body can emerge from the previous, lower (more condensed or denser) substrate and survive as an independent life on its own.

We also have three other famous phrases from Taoism that deal with more mundane accomplishments:

When you are full of Jing, there is no desire for sex.
When you are full of Qi, there is no desire for food.
When you are full of Shen, there is no desire for sleep.

Accordingly, this female artist actually experienced a bit of Shen fullness whereas non-cultivators usually experience sleep problems due to stress or because their bodies are very weak. As the Chinese medical text *The Classic of Difficulties* states, "Old people suffer from a debilitation of their blood and Qi, and their passageways for their flows are rough and choppy. Therefore during the day they are not sharp while at night they do not sleep. Thus you should understand why the elderly cannot sleep."

As to various other points in this case study, we once again discover the importance of the big toes as well as sensations on the inside of the legs where major Qi channels run to the feet. This woman's spontaneous body movements indicate that her Qi was encountering obstructions to its circulation, and these reactions manifested as it worked to clear her Qi channels of blockages. After a while this practitioner (and any other) would certainly rid herself of any hidden illnesses and extend her normal life span.

When taken in conjunction with the other phenomena, the fact that her tongue started naturally curling backwards during meditation indicated that her *jen mai* was being opened. This is a practice, well-known in the yoga schools, which is said to help prolong a person's longevity. If the front *jen mai* channel (the Taoists call the "red sparrow") opens all the way then the tongue will curl back even farther and sometimes even recede into the throat a bit.

Why did this practitioner feel she was a separate consciousness? This experience resembles one of the first stages of the Tao where you feel that you are separate from the physical body, which is a stage of learning how to detach from the physical body. At an even higher stage of attainment you might feel like you have no body at all. Any familiarity you develop with this experience can prepare you to cultivate during the transitional period of dying, which is the basis of Tibetan bardo yoga teachings. Unfortunately, this practitioner's wisdom/understanding was not high enough and due to lack of teachings she was unaware of the correct principles and theory of cultivation practice. Otherwise, she could have used that auspicious timing to make much more progress with her cultivation attainments.

Naturally, it took her some time to become accustomed to these physical and mental changes just as it takes some time to get used to living in a new home or apartment. In time all the various sensations ceased as expected since obstructions in the Qi channels always eventually clear out as long as Qi keeps passing through them.

The physical benefits to this practitioner, at just this early stage of cultivation, certainly include a longer life, a more beautiful figure and complexion, and freedom from certain illnesses that were destined to erupt with age. Spiritually, if this woman were to keep working hard it is probable from this case description that she could definitely achieve some measure of spiritual attainment.

CASE 7: Male Scientist

This person, now in his sixties, began Transcendental Meditation in 1967. After about five years he suddenly started to have gross thrashing body movements during meditation and at night in bed. After a few weeks these involuntary movements subsided. Several months later, on going to bed, he felt a tingling sensation in his lower legs, followed by cramping in his big toes. The cramping extended to other muscles before it gradually faded. The tingling sensation spread to his lower back, and he "saw" a reddish light there. The light solidified into a rod, which he then sensed and "saw" being pushed up his spine. Next it extended forward to the umbilical area, accompanied by many tingling, vibrating sensations. Step by step it moved up the spine to the level of the heart and then extended forward to stimulate the cardiac plexus.

When it reached his head, he "saw" floods of white light, as if his skull were lit up from inside. Then the light seemed to sprout out the top of his head as a solid beam. Some time later he felt a vibration in his right arm and wrist and also in his left leg. As soon as he attended to these sensations, they disappeared. He also experienced energy currents running through his shoulders and arms in waves of three or four per second, later increasing to seven and more per second. At one time, when he focused on the center in his head, violent and uncontrollable spasms occurred.

At various times this kundalini activity was accompanied by a variety of internal sounds, mostly high-pitched whistling and hissing. At other times, he heard flutelike musical tones. Frequently he would experience peace and bliss.

Then his sleep began to be disturbed again by automatic movements of the body. Sometimes he would awaken to find himself doing spontaneous yogic breathing and assuming a variety of Hatha Yoga postures. After several nights of this, the tingling sensation traveled to his forehead, nostrils, cheeks, mouth, and chin. This whole process was accompanied by ecstatic feelings, and he experienced sexual arousal when the activity centered in the pelvic area. Then all these effects ceased, returning only from time to time when he relaxed at night in bed, and he could shut these off by turning on his side.

About a year later, pressure developed in his head at night and started to move downward. Simultaneously, a tingling sensation moved upward from the stomach. He experienced all this activity as if from a distance. The two stimuli met at the throat, and he felt as if a hole appeared where they joined. He further experienced, still from a detached witnessing disposition, all manner of purely spontaneous sounds being emitted from that hole in the throat. Approximately six months later, the stimulus moved down from the throat to the abdomen, where it remained for a few months before moving down into the pelvic area.

This scientist had an inherently sensitive nervous

system. Yet his awareness that he was undergoing a kundalini arousal and his knowledge of what to expect, together with the stabilizing effect of a meditative discipline, made him less susceptible to the disorganizing aspects of the kundalini cycle ... and so he was not beset by anxiety during the process.

This case contains the typical experiences one would expect of an ordinary meditation practitioner. As already revealed, the vibrations in the body (such as feelings along the spine) and the sounds in the head originate when the Qi starts strongly passing through and then encountering obstructions within those regions of the body. These obstacles make it impossible for the body's ascending Qi to complete a full circuit and return to its origins.

This individual could hear high-pitched noises during meditation because his Qi could not fully penetrate through the small *nadi* channels located around the region of the ear. People who catch a cold or "get wind in the head" might sometimes experience this same phenomenon.

When meditators start to hear sounds in the head we have to remember that it is usually nothing supernatural. This is what we should tell people otherwise they will become mentally imbalanced and go down the road of supernatural misconceptions. Most of the strange sounds you hear are due to Qi working to open up obstructed passageways along the nerves, or in the auditory centers of the brain, which causes vibrations that affect consciousness. Since Qi and consciousness are linked, there is an interaction between the activity of Qi opening up channels in the body and the mental state.

Why did this man feel that various activities seemed as if they were happening from a distance? This was not unusual considering his advanced age, which means that he had probably lost most of his Jing over the years due to sexual activities. This feeling of being far away is a Qi phenomenon already mentioned in our extensive list of such sensations provided by Buddhism.

From the description of his experiences, it would seem that this meditator was experiencing all the Yin characteristics of his stage of accomplishment and none of the positive Yang experiences. This is something you would expect in a case of decreased vitality. To make progress in his cultivation at this point in time it would be essential, imperative in fact, that he first restore his lost vitality through herbal medicine, meditation and self-restraint before he can achieve higher states of attainment. Meditation along with sexual self-restraint will never fail to restore a man's lost vitality.

As regards the factor of his yogic sleeping postures, you must remember that many of the original yoga postures in India (asanas) were positions people naturally found themselves assuming without being taught when Qi started coursing through the muscles. Others were developed for the purposes of stretching. Later all these positions (asanas) were formulated into the classical standardized teachings. This man's body discovered these postures naturally just as a cat naturally discovers how it should stretch its own muscles for maximum benefit without ever being taught. Thus, these postures are not a past life legacy nor do they constitute anything particularly mysterious. These reactions to the Qi movements inside him were completely natural, like yawning or stretching, and did not constitute anything that should have provoked worry or concern.

In the fifth and sixth meditation cases we reviewed, we can say that the practitioners had very good *gong-fu* but would have benefitted even more had they understood the spiritual teachings on emptiness and prajna wisdom so as to be able to skillfully apply them. Nonetheless, overall these various experiences are some of the initial phenomena you might naturally encounter when you start upon the path of meditation. It is wrong to think you absolutely must experience these same phenomena, but it is perfectly proper and natural if they do occur. Therefore, they are nothing to fear when or if they happen.

CASE 8: Actress

This woman, now in her early forties, had many psychic experiences in her childhood. As an adolescent she suffered from recurring migraine headaches, mental disorganization, and impulsive disruptive behavior. She received psychotherapy for these symptoms for several years, was diagnosed schizophrenic, but was never hospitalized. When she was twenty-four years old she began to meditate, using various techniques. About a year later, her headaches became worse. But then, within a few weeks, her head pains, mental disorganization, and disruptive behavior suddenly ceased.

Within a year, tingling sensations started in her legs, then spread to her arms and chest. After a few weeks they extended to her neck and the back of her head, and soon down to her forehead. They were more noticeable during meditation. At intervals her entire body, but especially her hands, would become very hot. During meditation she was troubled by swaying and jerking of her body, and by anxiety. ...

Sometime later the physio-kundalini cycle started again. During one long meditation she became aware of her throat in a new way. She felt as if her head had become separated and floated above her trunk; her throat started to produce sounds on its own, and she became aware of a separate observer-self. Most of her kundalini symptoms ceased after this experience, which was a typical "throat opening."

Since then her meditations have been quiet and peaceful. She reports that her productivity and contentment have greatly increased.

In this connection it is helpful to recall the experience of the British psychic Matthew Manning (1975), who was plagued by poltergeist phenomena from an early age. These persisted until he discovered that he could do automatic writing. Soon he found that he could paint in the style of several great painters, completing a work in ten to twenty minutes. This then turned out to be his most fruitful channel of expression. Once the bulk of his energy could be thus expressed, the poltergeist activities ceased.

To understand this particular case we must recognize that this girl was initially sick; pre-existing internal illness explains many of her case symptoms. It would have been best if she had gone to a naturopathic, Ayurvedic or Chinese doctor who might diagnose any internal organ imbalances and treat them with relevant adjustments. From the description it is quite probable that she suffered from some type of chronic infection or had experienced past problems (which never really healed) involving her lungs and bronchial tubes.

With regards to her specific experiences, the reason this

practitioner felt she was floating in the sky was because her Qi was stuck in the region of the neck. It could neither ascend nor descend, easily move up or down, because those Qi channels were not yet fully opened. Many people sometimes dream at night they are flying, which often happens when some Qi ascends into your head during sleep. If you practice sending Qi into your brain before you sleep (by inhaling a lot of air into your lungs and then slowly releasing it while feeling the energy enter into your brain) you will eventually increase the frequency and vividness of your dreams. In any case, ascending Qi within the body can cause the flying sensation.

As to poltergeist phenomena, in many cases when Qi externally manifests this accounts for poltergeist experiences. When adolescents have frequent and sudden mood swings, in special cases this can cause Qi fluctuations that have a tie-in with various poltergeist phenomena. There are indeed some cases where the poltergeist phenomena are genuinely connected with external entities, but these are very rare. In the USA there are many more cases of poltergeists than in Asia because of the nature of America's climate, geographical magnetism, electrical surroundings and other Qi related environmental issues. From a scientific standpoint, such phenomena are often related to the electrical conditions in an area.

We can also guess from Matthew Manning's case that his visual cortex, located in the back of the skull near the "jade pillow" region of the hindbrain, probably had some channel blockages. However, when this man took up painting, which shunted more energy to different areas of the brain, he probably alleviated some of this problem.

CASE 9: Female Psychologist

In 1973 this woman, then in her forty-first year, noted the onset of heat in her head and chest, with tingling sensations over her body and head during meditation. She had been engaged in various intensive group and meditation disciplines for a number of years. Another curious phenomenon occurred during that time. Whenever she would do the tongue-and-palate exercise she had been taught during a meditation retreat, she would experience orgasm like waves rippling through her body.

She felt hot much of the time, particularly in her chest and throat, yet sensations of coldness were mixed in. She felt shaped like an egg, and her whole being felt unified. Vibrations started in the pelvic area and from there moved up her back to her neck. Her chest felt soft and open. She heard brilliant bird song inside her head and felt a tingling in her throat. Once, three years earlier, she had felt like a giant heart while meditating. At the time, she experienced a prickly itching heat all over her body, but she was not troubled because she believed that these sensations indicated successful and centered meditations and a flow between herself and others. She assumed that she was experiencing a kundalini awakening, which she believed to be dangerous unless the "higher mind" was in control.

A few months after the kundalini symptoms started in 1973, she felt, during meditation, as if she were two feet taller than her normal self and as if her eyes were looking out from above her head. At this time she was sure that she knew what people were thinking, and many of her impressions were confirmed.

Soon after this, her feet began to hurt and headaches started. The headaches grew worse whenever she attempted to stop the rippling sensations she was experiencing in her body. She noted that the headaches came when she tried to regulate the rush of energy passing through her. Massage helped the pain in her feet, but it was still so severe that she could walk only with difficulty and was unable to drive. She ate very little, her sleep was fitful, and she suffered some nausea. It was hard for her to talk with people. At times, she questioned the reality of her experiences, wondering if they were just a crazy episode.

She felt heat on one side of her back and was convinced that, unless it spread to both sides, she would be in danger. Once she succeeded in spreading it, this crisis passed. Then a tingling sensation started to move from her pelvis up her back and to her neck. She began to see light inside her skull. She was amazed to find that she could see this light all the way down her spine as well. The energy and tingling moved over her forehead and became focused under her chin. She felt as if there were a hole in the top of her head. Sleep became very difficult for her, and for the next six weeks, meditation was the only thing that helped her. She felt that if she did not meditate, the heat flowing in her body would grow so intense as to damage her system. Other people could feel excessive heat when they touched her lower back.

Although she felt "strange" at times, she was determined to avoid psychiatric help during her trouble, because she feared that she would be labeled and treated as insane. When her symptoms were more than she could bear alone, she worked with various meditation teachers.

Then she began to experience rippling sensations and shaking of her body, and she felt as though she was being cleansed and balanced. Shortly afterward, she felt a prickling in her cheeks and under her chin. Then all unpleasant phenomena ceased, and she had no further difficulty, although she continued her meditation practice. She underwent this physio-kundalini cycle in the span of a year. She later started a successful center for personal growth and was able to help others who experienced difficulties in the kundalini process.

Most of the comments we can make about this case have been previously stated. A review of previous explanations should therefore enable you to understand the origin of many of this woman's experiences. In particular, there are three new points that we should note:

(1) From the Chinese medical point of view, this woman's physical body can be classified as having internal dampness (wet), which is the reason she experienced so many of the various heat phenomena. Chinese medicine has a medical diagnosis of internal dampness or heat-damp and her description fits this classification.

(2) This woman had studied psychology, and so she had developed the tendency to over-analyze situations. People who continually use their minds (such as PhD's, scholars,

intellectuals and so on) tend to keep on using it during their cultivation practice, and this tendency toward mentation definitely contributed to this woman's symptoms. We can also say that this practitioner tended to be a nervous, anxious type and that this natural tendency had also biased her experiences. People who use their minds too much tend to bias themselves toward this nature.

(3) This practitioner actually generated many of these phenomena through the use of her own mind, and then guided herself accordingly. In other words, because of her own subconscious thinking and planning she created many of the external phenomena herself (such as the big heart, egg, etc.), which she then used to help guide herself to make further progress in practice.

As with Chinese medical diagnosis, when you analyze someone's cultivation experiences you must take into account a variety of factors such as the individual's age, gender, living conditions, education, occupation, whether or not they are sexually active and so on. While the transformations due to cultivation follow a general form and pattern, the pattern will be influenced by all of these attendant factors. Just as with medical diagnosis, only when you take into account these other factors will you be qualified to understand an individual's cultivation situation.

A last point to note is the fact that this woman had an experience where she once felt two feet taller. This was due to the normal opening, purification or cleansing transformations in her Qi and channels that generated this illusory feeling. Some people may actually feel they are smaller or larger, sometimes even as large as the universe, due to meditation practice. Naturally, these are imaginary feelings due to Qi flows rather than reality and do not correspond to any esoteric truth in the literal sense.

Such feelings are always due to Qi movements and transformations of the Qi channels, along with their interactions with consciousness, and must not be confused with genuine samadhi attainments. In other words, in this practitioner's particular case the feelings were entirely illusory.

CASE 10: Female Librarian

This woman, now in her mid-fifties, had been a meditator in her own style for many years. One day, in 1968, she lost awareness while meditating with her hands on a table. She awoke to find char marks on the table corresponding to her hand prints. She had the table refinished before I could examine it. No heat manifestation of any kind ever happened again. Because she did not show a regular progression of symptoms, I regarded her as a possible case of arrested physio-kundalini.

The most unusual aspect of this case is the char marks, which some people might mistakenly assume are a manifestation of kundalini heat. Actually, the reason this individual could generate char marks on the table is because (using Traditional Chinese Medicine classifications) her internal physical body could be classified as subject to "damp heat." As a result of this excessive internal dampness, a problem often addressed in Chinese medicine with herbal remedies, this individual might already be suffering from types of "wet" diseases such as arthritis or rheumatism or will suffer so in the future.

Sometimes meditation will generate a Yin feeling of coolness or cold rather than a Yang feeling of heat or warmth in the body. No matter what sensations develop, all of these sensations depend upon the interaction of the four elements within the body and eventually pass away due to further meditation progress. While meditation is a cure for many ills, the availability of Traditional Chinese Medicine, Ayurvedic or naturopathic herbal remedies is also a real help to quicken the balancing process that must occur in spiritual practice.

CASE 11: Housewife

In 1972 this woman, who was then in her mid-fifties, experienced the onset of an intense and disturbing process. She suddenly felt that something was descending over her head. Indira Devi (see Roy and Devi 1974) described in almost identical words this experience, which happened during her first meditation and which was soon followed by a spontaneous kundalini awakening. In the case of our woman, this feeling or sensation was followed by a fainting spell. This pattern recurred several times. Remarkably, she was never groggy after regaining awareness, as might be expected with a convulsive disorder. Physicians were unable to give her any relief.

Then, one time, she heard a voice saying inside her head: "Are you ready?" Later she heard internal music. One day she was feeling well until late in the afternoon when the base of her left big toe started to ache. Soon the pain extended up her shin, and she could feel the working of her knee joint. The pain was intermittent but disabling. She spent a few days in bed, where she spontaneously assumed many yogic poses.

Several days later her body felt "worked on" from the toes up to the back in segments. This process was accompanied by pain on both sides of her nose and by waves of energy and tingling sensations up her neck and down her face. There was also the sensation of intense heat in her back, and she experienced severe viselike pressure around her head. During some of these energy flows she was forced to breathe in a sighing manner. Occasionally there were torsional whipping movements of her head and neck, and once the energy moved down into her head, causing her scalp to get cold and her face to get hot.

Over a period of about three years, she slowly became convinced that she had been selected by God to be born anew as an advanced human being. Thus, she yielded to the tendency that Jung (1975) had warned against: that of claiming this impersonal force as her own ego creation and, as a result, of falling into the trap of ego inflation and false superiority. She expected others to understand exactly what she was speaking about and to accept her word unquestioningly, and she grew distrustful of anyone who disagreed with her interpretations.

This is a very simple case to analyze. First we must note the likelihood that some of this woman's neck vertebrae were misaligned, which accounted for her various head movements such as the swaying. The way to fix this problem, as commonly mentioned, would be to go to a chiropractor or osteopath for spinal adjustments. Chiropractic adjustments are useful for all spiritual practitioners and must be thought of as a proper way to adjust the spinal vertebrae. If the spine is misaligned it will often feel uncomfortable during meditation practice. Sometimes you may even develop a fever if the spinal vertebrae are misaligned and your Qi starts to hit those misalignments as it ascends. If the neck vertebrae are dislocated it is easy to develop headaches.

Secondly, this women's older age bears a factor on this case. She had probably already gone through menopause or was going through it. When women go through menopause their personalities can change greatly. Oriental medicine and Chinese Taoism tell us that female bodies change in seven-year cycles while male bodies change in eight-year cycles. Therefore, a woman typically experiences her first menstruation around age fourteen (2 x 7 years) and experiences menopause at around age forty-nine (7 x 7 years). Of course, the increasing prevalence of pseudo-estrogens in the environment (from plastics, pesticides and pollution) means that some women may experience their first menstruation earlier than fourteen years of age because of estrogen overload. In fact, Shakyamuni Buddha had predicted long ago that the childbearing age on earth would eventually drop down to around five years of age. The age of first menses has already dropped precipitously in tune with these predictions.

Men start to experience their manhood at around sixteen years old (2 x 8 years) and by age fifty-six (7 x 8 years) their prenatal Qi has gradually become exhausted. According to Taoist principles, reaching each of these ages marks the beginning of a new life. Reaching age fifty-six does not mean you are declining, but people often associate this age with deterioration and decline. The real problem is that ordinary people do not know how to rejuvenate themselves when they get older.

At this age, one can still indeed attain a subtle body and enlightenment but you must proceed in practice as follows: if you are a woman and are practicing before menopause then you must attain a stage where your menstrual period stops, called "returning to the state of a virgin." Then she has to continue cultivating hard so that it returns again. If a woman starts her cultivation practice after the onset of menopause she must first practice well enough so that her menstrual period returns. This indicates hormonal rejuvenation and a return of youthful vitality. Afterwards she must work even harder so that it stops once again.

In other words, you must work a little harder at your cultivation than those who are younger, but you can still succeed. In fact, at this stage in life you will generally have far less distractions and more time available to devote yourself to this effort. Therefore your chances of success can be higher than for those much younger. Physically speaking, getting older is the beginning of a new life, but people do not realize this and develop problems in their psychological outlook.

Surprisingly enough, a naturally calm and quiet person such as this housewife can spontaneously exhibit all these symptoms after menopause without meditating at all. In fact, these phenomena can occur much more readily than before menopause! Her symptoms are similar to a kundalini awakening, but many were actually natural reactions due to the Qi phenomena that relate to a quiet mind. This is why some older people can have "spontaneous" spiritual experiences.

The point is that the phenomena in this case constitute a natural reaction that sometimes spontaneously occurs to people of a calmer quiet nature, and they can occur more readily after menopause. Unfortunately, this woman combined her experiences with delusional concepts of religion and God and thus diverted her own spiritual progress. This is an unfortunate deviation due to delusive self-deception, and it is a pity to see because it represents an obstacle on the path.

As to the separate issue of hearing a voice inside her head saying, "Are you ready?" this was most probably a Bodhisattva or deva playfully talking into her brain, as they sometimes do before a group of helpful devas goes about working on opening up her Qi channels via their own energy work.

CASE 12: Male Psychiatrist

This colleague of mine, now in his early forties, had been meditating regularly for three years and also had served as a subject in our research with the magnetic stimulator when, in 1975, he experienced a kundalini awakening. It is worth noting that he was born with a spinal defect for which he had surgery that left him with chronic lower back pain since his teens.

In December 1975 this psychiatrist attended a weekend at the school of the late Swami Muktananda in Oakland, California. Upon being touched by the Swami, he went into a deep meditation. Within ten minutes, his mouth automatically opened widely, and his tongue protruded. After a few minutes, he experienced a blissful calm and many inner visions, in which Swami Muktananda appeared to him and helped him experience a fusion with the guru. A few minutes later, he "saw" the interior of his abdomen, chest and throat light up with a golden energy. Then his lower back began to ache severely. At the onset of the pain, a white light in his head became more and more intense. The back pain disappeared toward the end of the meditation and did not return. Following this remarkable experience, his meditations at home became very productive. Emotional problems and unfinished incidents seemed to find solutions very rapidly and at great depth during his meditations.

Then, in the middle of January 1976, he developed a rash that formed a curved line. It began at his lower back, crossed his spine twice, and veered off to his left shoulder. He was wondering whether it might have a symbolic significance, rather like the stigmata of some Christian mystics. At about this time, he also noticed a return of the high-pitched sounds and scratching noises during meditation that he had experienced earlier, after being stimulated many times over a period of several months with the magnetic device.

In January he participated in a second weekend intensive during which he was again touched by Swami Muktananda. Immediately he felt painful tingling and hot and cold sensations spreading over his upper back and neck. His throat burned, and there were automatic movements of head and neck. Then he felt inner peace and blissfulness. Later his head started to spin, and he felt vibrations in his hands. Next his knees began to burn and he felt a buzzing up his spine that ended in feelings of light and energy in his head. Throughout these experiences his breathing was irregular - at times rapid and shallow, at other times slow and deep. Everything seemed to be breaking loose inside him, and he felt as though he were in labor.

Toward the end of this meditation, he experienced great inner peace and a deep knowing of his inmost self, followed by a total sense of freedom and of "coming home." The next day he had difficulty returning to his usual state. He was uncoordinated and unable to concentrate. For several days he felt physically exhausted.

His meditation, however, continued to deepen. Then, for a few days, he experienced intense pain in his left big toe and left foot, which spread to his lower leg. He also had an ache on the left side of the back of his head. The pain extended to his left eye, which would occasionally close automatically. After a few days, this intermittent pain disappeared. The pain in his leg, which had resisted all treatment, cleared at about the same time.

In his day-to-day life, family and friends experienced him as more relaxed. A physical therapist, whom he saw regularly, confirmed that my friend felt more relaxed and integrated since this kundalini awakening. His sense of having "come home" grew into a feeling of at-oneness with the world.

Then, during meditation, itching developed on his forehead and occasionally on his cheeks, indicating a further progression of the physio-kundalini cycle.

Toward the end of 1976, he visited Swami Muktananda's hermitage in Ganeshpuri, India. He meditated three times a day for a total of four hours. Another two to three hours were spent chanting. During most of his meditations, he experienced ecstatic love-bliss, and he would frequently "merge with the blue light of consciousness." This intense spiritual discipline stimulated the kundalini energy in the region of the first and second chakras. As a result he experienced powerful surges of energy that sent his uro-genital system into orgiastic spasms. He felt his semen flow upward through the body's central channel (traditionally known as sushumna-nadi).

He later understood that this experience was associated with the "piercing of the first knot." He spontaneously entered a period of complete celibacy. He witnessed the baby toenails on both his feet falling off the same night.

After his return from India, he spent several years integrating his spiritual experiences with the practicalities of daily life, achieving a rare attunement and balance. Other meditative experiences followed, indicating the "piercing of the second knot." During one of his evening meditations, back again at the Ganeshpuri ashram, the kundalini energy became intensely focused in the subtle center between the eyebrows. Swami Muktananda spontaneously walked over to him and immediately began to work his fingers over the space between the sixth center and the center at the crown of the head. Streams of kundalini energy started to flow in a V-shaped pattern toward the crown center. Since that time, he reports, the kundalini energy has rarely left the crown center.

In this meditator's case there are lots of physical feelings and sensations being reported, but none of them are due to the attainment of samadhi. For instance, this man felt that his vital energy had reached his generative organs and he describes symptoms similar to Taoism's categorization of Jing transforming into Qi. Whether he actually achieved this transformation or not is something we cannot comment on because there simply is not enough information presented here to make a conclusion. However, this practitioner definitely did not reach the stage of transforming his Qi to Shen.

As to his belief that he opened the central channel of the body, which the Hindus call the *sushumna nadi* and the Chinese call the *zhong mai*, he actually experienced an opening of the *jen mai* channels in the front of the body instead. In their cultivation and medical schools the Hindus tend to emphasize the central, right and left energy channels in the spine whereas the Chinese emphasize the front and back channels (*tu mai* and *jen mai*) of the body. Naturally the Chinese also recognize the existence of the left and right channels although Chinese cultivation schools state they will open naturally once the *tu mai* channel is opened since that is effectively the spine.

The *jen mai* and *tu mai* channels open automatically when someone cultivates emptiness of mind or matches their thoughts with their breath, whereas most yoga school exercises are designed to forcibly open the Qi channels through the efforts of pranayama exertion. If a practitioner is not sufficiently prepared this can then cause all sorts of problems.

This practitioner has worked hard at their cultivation, but mistakenly assumed that they had opened the central channel when they were quite far from this stage of accomplishment. When one really opens the central channel all sorts of experiences are possible due to the Qi entering the brain. One possibility is that you might see a dark blue light comparable to the color of the sky at twilight. When someone attains samadhi, the practitioner will also feel like they can see all the stars, moon and planets even with their eyes closed. However, when this practitioner saw the "blue light of consciousness" this visionary experience was the result of imagination rather than a real thing.

As to the strange rash, which zigged and zagged across the practitioner's back, this was stimulated by a problem in the neck bones and spinal vertebrae. The reason the back pain eventually subsided is not because the Qi actually penetrated through the troubled areas but because it found an alternate route around the problem. As we have recommended before, this person should also visit a chiropractor, osteopath or other type of bone-setting professional to determine whether any spinal manipulations can help, and should also visit deep tissue massage or physical therapists. At times, such adjustments will not only improve a practitioner's health but also the quality of their meditation as well.

SUMMARY

Thus ends our brief analysis of twelve ordinary meditation practitioners. If we had been able to meet these individuals in person then we could have added much more to our commentary, but this is a good level of analysis given the available case information.

In reviewing these cases, the first point to note is that while everyone thinks that the various *gong-fu* phenomena they experience is indicative of kundalini, none of these practitioners had reached the level of cultivating the real kundalini Qi of the body. Furthermore, none of our case study practitioners have exhibited the ability to reach any level of stable samadhi either. The vast majority of sensations we have encountered result from the initial reaction of the Qi wind as it excited or made its way through the inside of the body's tiny Qi channels. In other words, most of what we have reviewed are physiological reactions to Qi arousals that occur naturally due to quiet psychological states.

When the real Qi phenomenon is finally experienced, it will manifest itself quite differently from internal wind Qi. True Qi produces a flood of warm fullness that will be experienced in every cell of the body at once. This produces a state of physical bliss which is peaceful and calm, and much more full and enjoyable than sexual orgasm. But to get to this stage you must meditate often, must not let your Jing or Qi leak, must allow your Jing to transform into Qi by engaging in emptiness meditation and must cultivate merit. The books *Twenty-Five Doors to Meditation, The Little Book of Meditation, Nyasa Yoga* and *Meditation and Its Practices* details many of the methods one can use on this road of practice.

From these cases we have also discovered that lot of people have unfortunate experiences due to the fact that their bodies need some type of physical adjustments. Sometimes these experiences appear due to latent illnesses, weaknesses in the internal organs, or from an internal imbalance of some type, all of which can often be adjusted or eliminated through Chinese herbal, Indian Ayurvedic or naturopathic medicine. On this note we can once again reference Nan Huai-Chin's *Tao and Longevity*, which notes that the colors meditators see often reveal where a health problem may lie:

> Seeing uncertain and changing colors, either in visions or dreams, may be due to latent disease in the viscera. If the kidneys and related genital nerves deteriorate or are weakened and diseased, this will be reflected by the phenomena of light seen in the form of black points or solid black. If the liver is diseased, the color will appear to be blue; if the heart is diseased, the color seen will be red; if the lungs are not healthy, the color one sees will be white; if the spleen or stomach are diseased, the color seen will be yellow; if the gallbladder is diseased the color seen will be green.

From the standpoint of Chinese mystics, seeing black in dreams, visions or hallucinations usually indicates trouble and disaster. The color blue indicates sadness, grief or sorrow, and green indicates hindrance from hallucinations, or Mara. Red indicates inauspiciousness. Yellow and white are auspicious, indicating calm persons and smooth situations. However, these are not fixed rules.[16]

Meditation can therefore be considered a type of super X-raying process that is more efficient than MRIs, PETs or CT scans. This is because it often reveals hidden illnesses that will only worsen in time if they remain uncorrected. Meditation is often our best diagnostic vehicle for discovering subclinical conditions as well as a method to help bring about the necessary healing.

As science will later prove, resting the body and mind through meditation is certain to contribute towards healing and optimum health. At the lowest stages of practice it is sure to improve your health and longevity, and at the higher stages of practice it can lead to a deva body attainment and eventually enlightenment. The deva or subtle body attainment is the first step towards the *sambhogakaya* attainment mentioned in Buddhism.

In meditation practice the typical practice is to let go of any thoughts and sensations that arise, which is "cultivating detachment" and also "emptiness" since they will eventually depart. In this book we have not covered the *nei-gong* practices where people subject themselves to the mental "pushing" of their Qi and try to force Qi channel openings. *Nyasa Yoga* and the other tantric yoga texts cited deal with this topic, but more gentle methods are found in *Visualization Power* and *Look Younger, Live Longer.*

The famous story of Japanese Zen adept Hakuin, found in *A Second Zen Reader* (retitled *The Tiger's Cave*) by Trevor Leggett, illustrates the type of gentle inner energy exercises that meditators can use to balance the Qi energy within their body when it produces symptoms as seen with these twelve practitioners. As a Zen student, Hakuin over-exerted himself in strenuous and scattered cultivation exercises and found himself in dire straights. His forceful meditation style resulted in the Qi ascending to his head so that his ears constantly heard a rushing sound, his lungs felt as if they were on fire,

---

[16] *Tao and Longevity*, pp.48-49.

and his legs felt as cold as ice.

No matter which remedy Hakuin tried in order to solve his self-induced ills, and no matter which meditation master he consulted, no one could explain or cure his ailments. This would also be the case today if he were to visit various doctors. As we have seen in several much simpler cases, misdiagnosis would be the inevitable result.

Searching everywhere for a cure, Hakuin was lucky enough to hear of a Taoist mountain hermit, Master Hakuyu. Hakuyu taught Hakuin the following internal energy remedy which people can use to help cure Qi imbalances within their physical nature. He said:

> Your condition is pitiable. By contemplating on truth too strenuously, you have lost the rhythm of spiritual advance, and that has finally brought on a grievous malady. And it is something very hard to cure, this Zen illness of yours [caused by over-exerted concentration on a koan]. Though the sages of medicine frown over your case and put forth all their skill with needle and cautery and drugs, yet would they be helpless. ...
>
> From the mounting of the heart-fire your grievous illness has arisen. If you do not take it down you will never recover, though you learn and practice all the healing remedies human and divine. Now it may be that as my outward appearance is that of a Taoist, you fancy that my teaching is far from Buddhism. But this is Zen. One day, when you break through, you will see how laughable were your former ideas.
>
> This contemplation attains right contemplation by no-contemplation. Many-pointed contemplation is wrong contemplation. Hitherto your contemplation has been many- pointed and so you have contracted this grave malady. Is it not then proper to cure it by no-contemplation? If you now control the fire of heart and will and put it in the Tanden [tan-tien] and right down to the soles of the feet, your breast will of itself become cool, without a thought of calculation, without a ripple of passion. This is true contemplation, pure contemplation. Do not call it dropping your Zen contemplation, for the

Buddha himself says: "Hold your heart [mind] down in the soles of the feet and you heal a hundred and one ills." Further the Agama scriptures speak of the use of the So cream in curing mental exhaustion. The Tendai [Tien-tai school] meditation classic called "Stopping and Contemplation" deals in detail with illnesses and their causes, and describes the methods of treatment. It gives twelve different ways of breathing to cure various forms of illness, and it prescribes the method of visualizing a bean at the navel. The main point is always that the heart-fire must be taken down and kept at the Tanden and down to the soles, and this not only cures illness but very much helps Zen contemplation. ...

If the student finds in his meditation that the four great elements are out of harmony, and body and mind are fatigued, he should rouse himself and make this meditation. Let him visualize placed on the crown of his head that celestial So ointment, about as much as a duck's egg, pure in color and fragrance. Let him feel its exquisite essence and flavor melting and filtering down through his head, its flow permeating downwards, slowly laving the shoulders and elbows, the sides of the breast and within the chest, the lungs, liver, stomach and internal organs, the back and spine and hip bones. All the old ailments and adhesions and pains in the five organs and six auxiliaries follow the mind downwards. There is a sound as of the trickling of water. Percolating through the whole body, the flow goes gently down the legs, stopping at the soles of the feet.

Then let him make this meditation: that the elixir having permeated and filtered down through him, its abundance fills up the lower half of his body. It becomes warm, and he is saturated in it. Just as a skillful physician collects herbs of rare fragrance and puts them in a pan to boil, so the student feels that from the navel down he is simmering in the So elixir. When this meditation is being done there will be psychological experiences, of a sudden indescribable fragrance at the nose-tip, of a gentle and exquisite sensation in the body. Mind and body become harmonized and far surpass their condition at the peak of youth. Adhesions and obstructions are cleared away, the organs are tranquilized and insensibly the skin begins to glow. If the practice is carried on without relapse, what illness will not be healed, what power will not be acquired, what perfection will not be attained, what Way will not be fulfilled? The arrival of the result depends only on how the student performs the practices.[17]

This is actually a Taoist-style technique for cultivating the physical body, but it does not lead to enlightenment. It simply works on adjusting the Qi imbalances within the physical body, and aims to bring about corrections in mental and physical health. If you are following a road of practice and find you need it, then by all means use it or the other gentle practices cited in the books recommended. Unfortunately we must keep citing these books because you cannot put all these teachings and exercises in one volume.

On the road of spiritual practice there are no denominations and you must use any remedy that works, whether it comes from a particular nation such as the USA, Germany, or Russia; whether it comes from a particular religion like Buddhism, Taoism, Hinduism, or Christianity; whether it comes from a particular civilization or race like the Chinese, Indian or Tibetan; or whether it comes from a particular gender (male or female) or any other classification. This is the rule of discipline in cultivation: do not worry about the origins of a technique and sectarian claims of ownership, but as long as it is virtuous and not harmful you should simply use what works!

The cultivators who are not likely to succeed in their practice are those who are afraid to borrow from different religious schools and traditions or try new things. These are the people who are already firmly stuck in dogma and who tend to cling to claims of religious pre-eminence. You should only care about the effectiveness and veracity of various teachings and techniques. This is the right way to practice in our tremendous universe of innumerable beings and teachings. This is also a "scientific" attitude in that it focuses on producing the results of spiritual cultivation without a sectarian bias.

Hence, this "So Cream Meditation" is a powerful *non-denominational* technique that can successfully help many severe

---

[17] *The Tiger's Cave and Translations of Other Zen Writings*, Trevor Leggett, (Charles E Tuttle, Vermont, 1995), pp. 144-154.

illnesses such as arthritis, cancer and even tumors. It can also help eliminate imbalances within your body that result in cold and clammy hands, skin problems, and other related conditions. This method has such a wide variety of effective uses, such as extending one's longevity and banishing illness. Hakuin employed this method until his death. In fact, he attributed his great vitality and longevity to the daily use of this gentle practice. It is something we can all imitate and I highly advise it.

We have also discovered from these cases that many ancient cultivation traditions have correctly categorized various stages and aspects of cultivation, as we found by recalling that Shakyamuni Buddha emphasized the left big toe and many meditators had problems in this area. Many practitioners independently verified various cultivation teachings through their own personal experiences. If you cultivate correctly, that is what will always happen because spiritual cultivation is a science whose results can be anticipated.

CHAPTER 6
STATES OF DELUSION THAT COMMONLY AFFLICT SPIRITUAL PRACTITIONERS

On the spiritual trail you are bound to experience various delusional states, many of which have been explained in the *Surangama Sutra*. Due to these states of delusion you may think you are becoming more psychic, more spiritual or even going crazy. Most of these states are delusions caused by the devas and masters working on transforming your Qi channels for the attainment of the subtle body, which takes years of cultivation efforts on your part. These delusive experiences can be understood a little if we pull together several seemingly unrelated stories.

For instance, in *Kundalini: The Secret of Life*, Swami Muktananda wrote:

> There is a state called tandra, which you spontaneously slip into under the inspiration of Kundalini. In tandra you have visions of mountains, river, deities, saints and even other worlds. Tandra resembles the state of sleep, but it is quite different from the dream state. The visions you have in tandra are not like hallucinations or dreams but are as real as the sights you see with your physical eyes. Often you have visions of events in the outer world, which turn out to be true. In fact, you are able to see the entire universe in the

state of tandra while sitting in one place with closed eyes. At times, you may see the whole system of nerves, veins, and arteries, and the digestive and eliminative tracts in the body in a multicolored light, which spreads through all the nadis. You can even see the prana flowing through them with increasing intensity as the purification of the body continues. …

There are more subtle experiences which can come to a meditator as the Kundalini rises through the sushumna. Not every meditator will have all these experiences, for experience varies according to one's temperament and the intensity of one's faith and devotion.[18]

It is well-known that the Hindus sage Ramakrishna experienced many types of visions during his years of cultivation prior to enlightenment. In *The Visions of Ramakrishna*, it is explained that:

Most of his visions, especially of the Mother, were of great beauty. Swami Saradananda tells us that Sri Ramakrishna saw at this time limitless forms of the Devi, from the two-armed to the ten-armed. The Master himself speaks of meditating under the tree when 'Sin' appeared before him and tempted him in various ways. It came in the form of an English soldier (pointed symbolism!) wanting to give wealth, honour, sex pleasure, occult powers, etc. 'I began to pray to the Divine Mother!' I still remember that form of the Mother, Her world-bewitching beauty. She came to me taking the form of Krishnamayi, but it was as if Her glance moved the world.' The most beautiful of all these visions, he said, was that of Raja-rajesvari, 'Queen of queens,' one of the traditional ten forms of the Divine Mother, who is also known as Sodasi. 'It looked,' he said, trying to put this into language, 'as if the beauty of the person of Sodasi had got melted, spread all around, and was illumining the universe in all directions.' …

In this period, the close of Tantric sadhana, the Master

---

[18] *Kundalini: The Secret of Life*, Swami Muktananda, (SYDA Foundation, New York, 1994), pp. 32-34.

had visions also of various male figures such Bhairava, companion of Siva; under the vilva-tree where most of these practices were undertaken, he had many 'flaming visions' and other mystical experiences the contents of which he was not able to reveal.

'There were then so many extraordinary visions and experiences in the Master's life day after day,' says Swami Saradananda, 'that it is beyond the power of man to mention all of them.'[19]

One of the best selling business books of all times is *Think and Grow Rich*, by Napoleon Hill. As a result of his mental mind training practices, Hill reported the following experience:

Long before I had ever written a line for publication, or endeavored to deliver a speech in public, I followed the habit of reshaping my character by trying to imitate the nine men whose lives and life-works had been most impressive to me. These nine men were Emerson, Paine, Edison, Darwin, Lincoln, Burbank, Napoleon, Ford, and Carnegie. Every night over a long period of years, I held an imaginary council meeting with this group whom I called my "Invisible Counselors.

The procedure was this. Just before going to sleep at night, I would shut my eyes, and see, in my imagination, this group of men seated with me around my council table. Here I had not only an opportunity to sit among those whom I considered to be great, but I actually dominated the group, by serving as the chairman.

I had a very definite purpose in indulging my imagination through these nightly meetings. My purpose was to rebuild my own character so it would represent a composite of the characters of my imaginary counselers. Realizing, as I did, early in life, that I had to overcome the handicap of birth in an environment of ignorance and superstition, I deliberately assigned myself the task of voluntary rebirth through the method I have described

---

[19] *The Visions of Sri Ramakrishna*, Swami Yogeshananda, (Sri Ramakrishna Math, Chennai: India), pp. 43-45-

above.

I knew, of course, that all men have become what they are because of their dominating thoughts and desires. I knew that every deeply seated desire has he effect of causing one to seek outward expression through which that desire may be transmuted into reality. I knew that self-suggestion is a powerful factor in building character, that it is, in fact, the sole principle through character is built. …

My method of addressing he members of the imaginary cabinet would vary, according to the traits of character which I was, for the moment, most interested in acquiring. I studied the records of their lives with painstaking care. After some months of this nightly procedure, I was astounded by the discovery that these imaginary figures became apparently real.

Each of these nine men developed individual characteristics, which surprised me. For example, Lincoln developed the habit of always being late, then walking round in solemn parade. He always wore an expression of seriousness upon his face. Rarely did I see him smile.

That was not true of the others. Burbank and Paine often indulged in witty repartee which seemed, at times, to shock the pother members of the cabinet. On one occasion Burbank was late. When he came, he was excited with enthusiasm, and explained that he had been late because of an experiment he was making, through which he hoped to be able to grow apples on any sort of tree. Paine chided him by reminding him that it was an apple which started all the trouble between man and woman. Darwin chuckled heartily as he suggested that Paine should watch out for little serpents, when he went into the forest to gather apples, as they had the habit of growing into big snakes. Emerson observed – "No serpents, no apples," and Napoleon remarked, "No apples, no state!"

These meetings became so realistic that I became fearful of their consequences, and discontinued them for several months. The experiences were so uncanny, I was afraid if I continued them I would lose sight of the fact that the meetings were purely *experiences of my imagination.*[20]

One of the most famous Tibetan cultivators of all time (other than Milarepa, Gampopa, Naropa and Marpa) was the female yogi Yeshe Tsogyel. In her autobiography, she wrote of many strange experiences she had to go through before becoming enlightened, including the following:

Then in the extremely isolated meditation cave of Nering Senge Dzong and other places, after I had sworn an immutable commitment, I continued my physical austerity. I sat in mute *samadhi*, never relaxing the important points of posture, sitting immovable in lotus posture, my eyes set in a fixed gaze. The malicious local gods and demons, however, could not endure my *samadhi's* glory, and created magical illusions, threatening me with seductive and fierce, embodied and disembodied, phantoms. First they projected themselves as various delectable foods, and repeatedly appeared in front of me. Then they transformed themselves into all manner of material objects, clothes, horses, oxen and every possible necessity and luxury that this world can offer. I overcame all these temptations with my *samadhi's* radiance. Through my insight into the nature of the world as illusion, inasmuch as I felt profound disgust for attachment to worldly things, some of these phantoms dissolved; by changing earth and stone into dung by the power of my *samadhi* I rendered some repulsive; and some vanished after my wish that they became that district's future store of food and wealth was fulfilled.

On another occasion these demons projected themselves as charming youths, handsome, with fine complexions, smelling sweetly, glowing with desire, strong and capable, young men at whom a girl need only glance to feel excited. They would begin by addressing me respectfully, but they soon became familiar, relating obscene stories and making lewd suggestions. Sometimes they would play games with me: gradually they would expose their sexual organs, whispering, "Would you like

---

[20] *Think and Grow Rich*, Napoleon Hill, (Ballantine Publishing Group, New York, 1960), pp. 195-197.

this, sweetheart?" and "Would you like to milk me, darling?" and other such importunities, all the time embracing me, rubbing my breasts, fondling my vagina, kissing me, and trying all kinds of seductive foreplay. Overcome by the splendour of my *samadhi*, some of them vanished immediately; some I reduced to petty frauds by insight into all appearances as illusion; by means of the Bodhisattva's meditation that produces revulsion, I transformed some into black corpses, some into bent and frail geriatrics, some into lepers, some into blind, deformed, dumb or ugly creatures, and without exception they all vanished.

Then these malicious gods and demons demonstrated their violent devices. The earth moved beneath me, shaking and quaking, emitting an empty roar louder than the bellow of a thousand dragons, with the intolerable banging of black lightning, the roaring of white lightning, the swishing of red lightning, the knocking of yellow lightning, the baying of blue lightning, the shimmering of iridescent lightning, and the blazing of the light of the sky. Likewise, I was threatened by a terrific display of weapons, various knives, sharp-pointed daggers and spears, all glistening steel-blue, bristling menacingly, jostling for space. I dissolved these apparitions with my *samadhi* of divine assurance.

Another day I was besieged by phantom herds of ferocious beasts. Tigers, leopards, bears, yetis and other carnivores appeared, roaring above and outside the cave entrance. From my right and left, animals attacked from every direction, howling in their various styles, their mouths gaping ravenously, snarling in rage, beating their tails, their paws scratching at me, shaking their bodies, hackles risen, hair bristling. From the assurance I had gained from abandoning attachment to my body and love of myself, arose compassion for all these beasts, and they vanished. Then, leaving me with no respite, a vast arm of billions of different insects and worms led by spiders, scorpions and snakes inundated the area. Some slipped through my sensory doors, some bit me, some stung me, some scratched me, some climbed over me, some jumped on me, some fought each other, ate each other and left piles of carcasses scattered about. There was no trick that these insects failed to use to frighten me. I shuddered a little, yet I found pity in my heart, but the insects became increasingly terrifying and loathsome. 'Since I have often vowed that I will in no way be attached to any form of body, speech or mind,' I thought to myself, 'why should I now be afraid of such illusory tricks of spirits, the activity of sentient beings – insects – that is karmic manifestation? Because all behavior is determined by positive or negative concepts, I should understand that whatever occurs, good or bad, is a mental construct, and so keep a level head.' ... I [then] entered the samadhi of universal identity in which there is no discrimination of evaluation, and the apparitions vanished.

Again a variety of shapes and forms appeared. Many limbs without bodies hung in space before me. Many exceedingly repulsive forms flashed in and out of my vision, writhing around in spectral configurations in space. An enormous head without a body, its upper jaw lost in the clouds and its lower jaw resting on the ground with its tongue lolling in between, its fangs gleaming white, appeared closer and closer. Other violent forms also appeared: within a castle the size of a mustard seed many men struggled and fought, fires blazed, floods poured forth, landslides hurtled down, trees fell, gales blew, etc., but always I would sit unmoving in *vajra*-like *samadhi*, and the forms would vanish.

'We are the legions of gods and demons, Khatra and Kangtra, come hither from the southern lands lying between E in Nepal and Ja in Bhutan,' pronounced a voice, and these demons proceeded to threaten me with various sounds. Some wept, some raged, some wailed and some roared. Then thunderbolts fell from above, fire blazed up from below, and in between rivers flowed backwards. Blizzards of various weapons swirled about me. In this manner they strove to obstruct my meditation. ...

Not long after, led by devils, local demons and *nagas*, all the gods and demons who had previously threatened me with their illusions came to offer their lives to me. The devils, local demons and *nagas* in particular, vowed to protect my *dharma*.[21]

In the Taoist story of the ten trials of the sage Lu Dongbin (similar to the Twelve great tests of Naropa or Twelve Labors of Hercules), which refers to the time period prior to his enlightenment, at one time he was alone reading a book in his room when (like Yeshe Tsogyel) countless ghosts, demons and monsters suddenly came from every corner of the world to attack and slay him.

Lu Dongbin was not the slightest bit fearful but kept on doing his chores without paying them any attention, ignoring them entirely. One of the monsters yelled that Lu Dongbin had wronged him in a past life and now needed to sacrifice his life. Without any fear Lu said, "Go ahead and take my life since I took yours in a past life. This is fair." All of a sudden Lu heard the clapping of hands, a shout in the air, and then the sky turned blue and all the ghosts and devils vanished. Standing there was his master Han Zhongli who had been looking and laughing at him while all these events were happening.

The Christian Saint Padre Pio of Pietrelcina, when going through the twelve-year period of transformation leading to enlightenment, would also commonly see apparitions of demons and devils coming to attack him. Padre Augostino reported that Padre Pio said the Devil appeared to him under many different forms: "The Devil appeared as young girls that danced naked, as a crucifix, as a young friend of the monks, as the Spiritual Father or as the Provincial Father; as Pope Pius X, a Guardian Angel, as St. Francis and as Our Lady."

Padre Pio said that the Devil also appeared in many other horrible forms too with an army of infernal spirits or without any apparition. Furthermore, Padre Pio was often troubled with deafening noises. Nevertheless he passed through these experiences and later in life he demonstrated many miracles and superpowers. He had become capable of developing these abilities because he had gone through all the difficulties of generating a subtle deva body and then higher attainments.

---

[21] *Sky Dancer*, Keith Dowman, (Snow Lion Publications, Ithaca: NY, 1996), pp. 77-84.

The mystics St. John Vianney, St. Teresa of Avila, Venerable Anne Catherine Emmerich, St. Joseph of Copertino, St. Paul of the Cross, and St. Dominic are just some of the few Christian saints who also experienced such visions. Proof that they successfully completed their period of purification that generated the deva body, if they really did go through it, includes the fact that they could later demonstrate various superpowers such as the ability to read minds, control the elements, heal the sick, or know the future. These powers all become possible after one attains the subtle, Causal or Supra-Causal bodies. In fact, the only reason these individuals became saints was because they went through this troublesome process that occurs when your real kundalini finally awakens and a twelve-year period commences that finally produces the deva body.

One of the most famous Christian saints who also demonstrated miraculous abilities (just like other well-recognized Hindu, Buddhist, Taoist, Sufi and Jewish masters), and who also suffered from such visions, was St. Anthony the Great. According to Athanasius's *Life of Saint Antony*, written in 357, when St. Anthony the Great was a simple monk cultivating in the desert he also he underwent great trials "caused by the devil," who afflicted him with phantom images of naked women that he overcame by the power of prayer. As with Yeshe Tsogyel, later phantoms (visions) appeared in the form of all kinds of monstrous beasts and hideous reptiles including lions, bears, leopards, bulls, wolves, asps, and scorpions that seemed as if they were about to attack him or cut him into pieces.

St. Athanasius wrote: "The demons made such a racket that the whole place was shaken, knocking over the four walls of the tomb; they came in droves, taking the form of all kinds of monstrous beasts and hideous reptiles. And the whole place was filled with lions, bears, leopards, bulls, wolves, asps, scorpions. The lions roared, ready to attack; bulls seemed to threaten him with their horns; snakes advanced, crawling on the ground, seeking a place of attack, and wolves prowled around him. They all were making a terrible noise. Groaning in pain, St. Anthony faced the demons, laughing: 'If you had any power, only one of you would be enough to kill me; but the Lord has taken away your strength, so you want to frighten me by your number. The proof of your powerlessness is that you are reduced to taking the form of senseless animals. If you have any power against me, come on, attack me! But if you cannot do anything, why torment yourselves unnecessarily? My faith in God is my defense against you.' Hearing this they left him in peace.

Later in life St. Anthony also demonstrated many miracles due to his superpowers because he had undergone the twelve years of Qi and Qi channel purification transformations necessary to create the subtle body, Causal body and higher. This story proves he went through the process.

Switching to ancient Greece, in Plato's *Apology* Socrates claimed to have a daimonion (divine spirit) that frequently warned him - in the form of a "voice" - against mistakes, but never told him what to do. In other words, he heard voices in his head. Until today, no one has ever been able to interpret this correctly saying whether this was a psychotic tendency, the result of disease or an artful story.

Turning to China, in the Chinese story *Journey to the West*, the protagonist monkey Sun Wukong meets his match when he encounters a Six Eared Macaque monkey, who disguises himself as Sun Wukong, knocks the monk Tang Sanzang unconscious and steals his baggage. He fights with the real Sun Wukong and neither of them is able to overcome the other. No one is able to differentiate between the real and the fake Sun Wukong until the two appear before the Buddha.

These stories do not seem at all connected, but they are all related to the spiritual path of cultivation. Here is the meaning of these tales.

If you are meditating well and your Qi channels are opening, this is always accomplished through the help of spiritual beings which various schools call heavenly devas, *dakinis*, angels and so on. When a good person dies they become just this – a deva or angel, namely a being made of Qi rather than physical flesh and blood. Devas also include the students of masters who achieved the subtle body, which is the Buddhist stage of at least a *Srotapanna* (Stream Enterer). Devas are people like you and me who attain the subtle body, also known as the *yin shen*, impure illusory body, deity body or deva body. The term Buddha or Bodhisattva refers to attainees of the Supra-Causal body and higher.

After the real kundalini arises, you will normally go through twelve years of hellish experiences where your Qi and Qi channels of your subtle body are being purified. This is when you will usually experience all sorts of delusive visions, like those just recounted, until you finally attain the deva body or *yin shen* body made of Qi, which is the foundational stage for attaining the final *sambhogakaya* of Buddhism. In order to attain the next higher body on the spiritual trail, which is the Causal body, devas themselves (who have bodies made of Qi) need merit and the way they obtain that merit is by doing the hard work of helping you open up your Qi channels under the direction of their teacher. They usually give you mara delusions during the process, and all sorts of other troubles, simply because they want to test out their powers. No one gets twelve years of work for free.

When people are at the foundational stage of having their Qi channels start to open, masters and devas will therefore typically cause you to experience all sorts of visions as well as thoughts and emotions to affect your Yin Qi and Yang Qi. If they want your Yin Qi to arise they will frighten you through mara visions (illusions) of ghosts and evil things so that you are frightened into believing you are haunted or being attacked by demons. Naturally these appear as real experiences to the practitioner, but they are actually just fictitious illusions – mara delusions. This explains why these saints and sages all went through these frightening experiences. They were not *real* attacks by devils and demons but just illusions projected into their brains by devas practicing their skills.

If they want your Yang Qi to arise then the devas will provoke you with different visions such as of naked women to draw forth sexual desire. Anger is another emotion evoked so that your Yang Qi will arise. They might also cause other Yang stirring emotions to arise such as feelings of pride, courage, over-confidence or superiority. Along these lines, Shakyamuni Buddha explained that a practitioner might be manipulated into becoming "swollen with a sense of pride, wrongly convinced they have become equal with Vairocana Tathagata." Self-satisfaction might be provoked along with feelings of superiority.

All throughout these stimulated emotions and visions the Buddhas and Bodhisattvas are actually controlling your emotions. The thoughts you think are your own are not your own at all but are caused to arise for a purpose whose reasons you will never be able to fathom. The devas will never tell you what is going on or why but will always mislead you. That is the rule: they will always mislead you with lies and misdirection. The name "trickster" applies as a definition for their behavior. They will always be laughing throughout the process, since they seek entertainment throughout this process, which is another reason cultivators mistakenly take them as devils and demons while they mentally suffer. The laughter is due to them battling one another to see whose skill level is higher in getting you to have the thoughts they want.

While doing all this work on your Qi and channels, the devas are also being taught how to give people thoughts, and so they will practice giving you particular ideas and battle with one another in contests to see who is stronger with these abilities. You have to suffer while they undertake these battles. A common battle is "speed memory read" where they test to see who can read your memories quickest (stored in neurons) and then make connections.

A particularly popular battle is when two masters, each with several bodies, battle to see who is better at controlling all their bodies. Using their subtle bodies they will battle to see who wins at giving you a particular thought while with their Causal (Mental) bodies they will battle to give you a different thought and with other bodies they will battle to see who can win over the other in giving you thoughts and emotions. This is all done simultaneously to see who has better control over all their bodies. Since at the level of the Supra-Causal body they can emanate lighter etheric versions of this body, called *nirmanakaya*, they also project these from far away distances on the spur of the moment and battle with thee emanation bodies too in order to see who has better abilities. As you can surmise, the major way in which Buddhas help people is simply by giving them thoughts and ideas. Sometimes this is the only way to help improve circumstances.

A common demonstration is by great masters who have a subtle body, Causal body, Supra-Causal body and others and can use them all independently with skill to both control your thoughts and those of the audience. Sometimes you will receive multiple levels of thoughts which are due to a master using three of his independent bodies to give you three separate types of thoughts or knowledge simultaneously. While it may seem like the thoughts are coming from different devas, they are all coming from just one individual even though they seem entirely independent and unlinked to one another. Since a master will develop many bodies, they must learn how to use them independently and often demonstrate this skill to the devas using you as the demonstration tool.

A higher body can override the thoughts of a lower body, which is why it is said that a master at a higher stage of attainment can "take away," meaning block or suppress, the superpowers of someone at a lower stage of attainment. This is because all such powers are due to thinking which can be overridden through a higher level body or stage of attainment.

You are the guinea pig for contests and testing because later, as a superior level deva yourself (since you went through this process of cultivation), you will be using similar skills within the minds of people to help them. They will also do the same for emotions. All of these battles involve the brain stem, which is the seat of intentional thinking in the brain, as well as other special brain areas. The brain stem is divided into two parts, one Yin and Yang, and you are supposed to cultivate the Qi going through it on the spiritual path.

Furthermore, having access to every memory you ever had because they are all stored in your brain's neurons, the devas will have contests to see who can find information quickest within your neurons. They will also pull forth into present consciousness every "sin," wrongdoing, crime, mistake or embarrassment you ever performed in the past to yourself or others, no matter how small. They may bit by bit work at making you hate your teacher. Sometimes they will lead your thoughts into some crazy "mission impossible" scenario so they can watch the mental processes as you try to mentally ponder some sort of solution to the impossible. Shakyamuni Buddha called this "indulging in unremitting deep reflection (analysis)."

Usually what devas do is just pull information from whatever is already stored in the brain's neuronal memories to create dialogue, especially things you have forgotten. Enlightened masters aren't restricted to this during the rules of training because Buddhas commonly give you entirely new thoughts that have nothing to do with whatever you have in your memories. Since devas practice visualization skills, they will also typically practice giving you visions and auditory experiences, both good and bad. At a higher stage they will practice giving you dreams. Because they have little concern for you and just want to test their skills against each other in battles, a future master going through the twelve-year period of transformation goes through hell. Later they don't want to frighten people about what they went through so no one ever talks about all these experiences. They don't want to scare away adherents from the spiritual path but this is what you have to go through in this world to generate the subtle body.

In this light, and in conjunction with the subsequent chapter on mara spiritual delusions from the *Surangama Sutra* that explains these teachings, and which follows, some of these cited stories can be easily explained. I hope that practitioners passing through these experiences, and the previous ones mentioned in chapters four and five, can view them in this light so as not to cause harm to themselves or fall victim to the belief they are losing their sanity.

There are two categories of practitioners who experience these things. The first belong to future spiritual masters who will undergo at least twelve years of such things. The future masters will, at the minimum, develop a *yin shen*, deva body, astral body or subtle body called the initial fruit of the spiritual path during these twelve years, and perhaps higher bodies depending upon how hard they keep working during this time. The second are regular people who will only occasionally undergo just minor experiences along these lines, and those already mentioned, but who cannot explain them. These people don't have to worry about the trials and tribulations that future masters normally go through because it only happens if you go through a true kundalini awakening, which is rare.

How do we know it takes twelve years to complete the set of Qi and Qi channel transformations (kundalini awakening) necessary for building the foundation of the *sambhogakaya*?

Ramana Maharshi said, "The sastras say one must serve a guru twelve years for enlightenment." Sai Baba of Shirdi also said, "I stayed with my master for twelve years." The sage Matsyendranath, the traditional founder of Hatha Yoga, is said to have cultivated within a fish's belly and then emerged after twelve years of practice. Mahavira, the founder of Jainism, meditated as an ascetic for twelve years and then attained enlightenment. Upakoshala, practicing *bramacharya*, tended his teacher's sacred fires for twelve years. Vardhamana Mahavira, the 24th Tirthankara who founded Jainism, undertook ascetic practices for twelve years before becoming enlightened. Shivabalayogi attained self-realization after twelve years of arduous cultivation practice. Swami Sivanandaji Maharaj did vigorous cultivation work for twelve years in order to attain enlightenment. Ramakrishna spent twelve years in practice and Asanga spent twelve years meditating in his cave. The Vajrayana master Naropa is said to have endured twelve hardships in order to meet his teacher Tilopa. Many more accounts of the twelve-year period are found in my book *Nyasa Yoga*.

In *The Truth Is*, the Hindu sage Papaji explained, "Kundalini is lying dormant in everybody in the muladhara chakra of the astral body which is in the heart of the physical body. This energy is sleeping and you give rise to it by concentrating on different chakras one after the other. ... focusing on the chakras will cause the energy to start traveling upward through all the chakras. Finally, it reaches the top and then you will feel that you are not the body, but that you are out of the body. This is a difficult process and takes at least twelve years in a quiet place with a good teacher."[22]

Now for some other explanations. In Muktananda's explanation of tandra, what you are seeing are samples of the fake visions normally given to people by devas. His synopsis of these visions, which are only indicative of what is possible, is essentially the same as the first ten delusional meditation states mentioned in the *Surangama Sutra*, which follows. As previously stated, if you think you see inside your body or inside other people's body, this type of false vision is one of many types already mentioned in the *Surangama Sutra*.

In Ramakrishna's case, most of the glorious visions were due to various masters practicing their visualization skills because he was a high stage master reborn, so he had less of the negative Yin Qi visions. This is also due to the fact that he had already used other methods to extensively cultivate his Yin Qi, such as dressing as a woman and identifying with female deities, and therefore didn't need as many fearful Yin Qi provoking visions to arise. Many of his vision types are also explained in the *Surangama Sutra*.

In the case of Napoleon Hill, who was performing visualization practice (see my book *Visualization Power* for instructions), some devas caught on that he was doing this and started playing around with his visualizations to test their powers. As tricksters, they always have fun with people, cheating them in various ways, when they do this. Hill's cultivation had finally reached a sufficient stage where a spiritual master and his students had started

[22] *The Truth Is*, H. W. L. Poonja, (Weiser Books, York Beach: Maine, 2000), p. 447.

working on his Qi channels, and they took the opportunity to practice their own mental skills by possession of his thoughts at those moments.

Devas will set up the delusion of an entire world of fake gods and goddesses in our brain for their own amusement, in order to sharpen their skills, as they work on opening someone's Qi channels, but in this case they simply hijacked the daily visualization that Hill was already employing. With a sense of humor, because they are always laughing with joy, they basically hijacked the mental training he was using. Then they started causing trouble.

Basically, at times enlightened masters will create an entirely fictitious, false, make-believe world of gods, goddesses *or other circumstances* to teach deva students how they can slowly control someone's mind to do whatever they want. Such an event, called a "miar" (rhyming with liar), is not something you can break free of just as it is difficult to break free of astrological influences. It is like a gigantic hallucination where all your thoughts make sense, but the story you cumulatively build out of these thoughts is preposterous. In other words, it is like a bog of lies you cannot escape. During a miar you can be made to believe in almost anything. The only thing you can do is wait until it is over, never acting in the real world against common sense and never being taken in by the miar.

The *Surangama Sutra's* section of mara delusional states pertaining to the conception skandha (which are the thirty-first to fortieth delusions) gives a small idea of the type of mental projections that are possible. Another story within Buddhism tells of an asura king who vowed to kill many people, and so to prevent this fifty Arhats got together and with their "dhyana powers" made this powerful king afraid even of his own shadow. This too was an example of a miar, or the ability of enlightened beings to shape someone's thoughts to what they want.

Of course, it is nearly impossible to resist a miar as the imaginative scenario built up is entirely fictitious but "owns you," for when it occurs it is like you are possessed. You are stuck in the mud of a pile of delusions. Once within a miar your reasoning will be subverted and you won't be able to think clearly. Your thoughts will be twisted this way and that. During a miar you can therefore be brought to think anything.

For instance, when you read the Biblical story of Abraham

almost sacrificing his son on an altar, this unreasonable act of almost insanity was no doubt one of the initial miars that Abraham (who certainly achieved enlightenment otherwise he would not have become the Father of the Jewish tradition) went through at the start of the twelve-year period of kundalini transformations. Who was the one who told him to sacrifice his son and why would he actually believe he should do this? Would you believe a human stranger who told you to do so? Only someone in a miar, thinking he is dealing with angels or some other type of higher beings, would believe such a thing.

At the commencement of the kundalini awakening, at least during the first one hundred days, the miars you go through are severe and follow the exact type of pattern that Abraham went through with his son. The overlap of descriptions is unmistakable. In particular, you have to be brought to emotionally extreme states of fear and also sexual desire in order to raise your Qin Qi and Yang Qi at the appropriate times so that certain Qi channels can be worked on to help open them fully.

The temptations of Buddha and Jesus were also stories representative of these types of experiences. While the Buddhist and Christian stories suggest that Buddha's testing and Jesus' temptation happened in one day, the stories were actually just shortened representatives of what goes on during this twelve-year period.

Only by sticking to the standard societal rules of behavior can you avoid ruin during the onslaught of a miar, which is why typically only monks and nuns or sadhus are usually put through this since they have little or nothing to lose when they act incorrectly because of its influence. Most of the people who go through this become the enlightened saints, sages and religious greats of their traditions, but few want to talk about it so as not to frighten you.

The miar is one reason why Hindu tantric practitioners are told never to undertake various strange mantra and ceremonial sadhanas without a master's permission. Such sadhanas, hundreds or thousands of years old, are each administered (you might say owned or protected) by a spiritual master who will use that opportunity to teach his deva students how to do certain things, which will upset the aspirant's mind. Chaos usually results because few people can handle the onslaught of devas playing with their conscious thoughts. It is not that the aspirant is in some way impure that he cannot resist the attack. It is just that the devas have no discipline or restraint, and so are said to "consume" the practitioner with their excesses of thought-play. They don't usually practice their mental skills on ordinary people, so someone undertaking the sadhana represents a rare opportunity to learn skills they desire for affecting people's minds. As Shakyamuni Buddha explains in the *Surangama Sutra*, they will often torment a practitioner with visions causing him to do wrong and after hurting him, simply laugh and leave.

In the story of Yeshe Tsogyel, she reported many visions of being attacked by demons, which were entirely fictitious illusions created by the enlightened masters of her tradition and devas meant to scare her to affect her Yin Qi. This is the exact same thing that happened to the Christian saints. Whenever you become scared your Yin Qi arises, which then becomes a chance to open up your Yin Qi channels. Later Yeshe Tsogyel was shown visions of attractive men in order to prompt her sexual desire, which was meant to raise her Yang Qi so that the Qi could be used to help open up her Yang Qi channels. In the case of the Christian monks, they were shown visions of beautiful naked women.

In the stories of Lu Dong Bin, Padre Pio and St. Anthony of the Desert, the same pattern follows that scary visions were used by angelic devas in order to frighten the practitioners so that their Yin Qi might arise. That is the only way to open up Yin Qi channels unless you have undertaken various severe Yin Qi exercises, such as those specified in *Nyasa Yoga*. Even if you do those exercises you will still have to go through this type of experience, but always understand that the visions are fake illusions projected into your brain by spiritual beings in order to help you transform your Qi and channels, and teach devas how to also do this and similar things.

As to Socrates hearing voices, this was the case of a deva or devas talking to him; Socrates was not being entirely honest when he said that the deva(s) would only tell him certain things and not others. This was basically a lie he created to let other adherents later know that he had passed through this stage. When going through this process you will always have devas talking to you and pretending they are personages or spiritual beings they are not. They revel in cheating people and practicing deception. Some will try to frighten you and others will pretend to be your friend until you finally attain the deva body that escapes the physical shell. With that new body your Qi will have many powers available, and you will be able to use it to open up other people's Qi channels too. The subtle deva body is the foundational start of the purified *sambhogakaya* attainment.

Devas are mischief makers throughout all parts of this process of Qi channel transformation, so always the information they provide is undependable, inaccurate and to be ignored. Like the CIA offering disinformation packaged together with good information, they can suck you into believing falsities because they must create games for themselves to keep themselves going through twelve years of work required for transforming your Qi channels. Often they go too far in creating visions that attack people, which makes some people break down or want to commit suicide. On the other hand, they will also control your thoughts through the process so that you don't do this, but mistakes happen.

Because of the dangers of attempted suicide, at the start of the period the masters overseeing the process will first mentally check how you might commit suicide if you were so disposed, and set up mental tripwires that would notify them if you ever considered hurting yourself as this can happen if the devas go too far. Devas, even though angels, have absolutely no discipline or self-restraint going throughout this process of working on your channels because they don't get hurt themselves, and they can easily leave if things go wrong. The Stanford prison experiment, which shows that people with power tend to abuse others, is an apt description of the behavior of devas throughout this process. The Stanley Milgram experiment also comes to mind.

At times during this transformation process you will have thoughts where the actual thinker is not you, but just seems to be you. This was represented in the story of the Monkey King and the competing Six Eared Macaque monkey who disguised himself as Sun Wukong. The thinker is actually an enlightened master or higher stage deva who has hijacked your thinking process to alter your thoughts, replacing them with his or her own, but uses your voice internally. It is actually a type of possession because during this time the master is using his subtle Qi body or Shen body or yet higher body (sometimes *simultaneously* using his subtle body, Causal body and Supra-Causal bodies, etc.) to control your thinking as well as move your own. This is the only way to transform your channels.

Therefore the voice you use in your head when thinking still appears to be you, but the thoughts are not really yours although it sounds like it is you. You cannot distinguish between you and the actual talker/thinker spiritual being who is masquerading as you, but you will now seem to be able to flip all arguments to their opposite when dealing with devas and your intelligence and wittiness will seem to have increased tremendously. These are explanations I am adding to those given by Shakyamuni Buddha in the *Surangama Sutra*.

The purpose behind all this is that it takes a period of many years and the committed help of thousands of devas to continuously work at transforming your Qi and channels. You have to have tremendous merit to deserve this work, and so religious texts say you will be tested. Normally future masters go into retreat during this long stretch of time so that they can undergo these body transformations in private without much disturbance or bother from the public. Many Christian saints would lock themselves in their cells for years during this time.

During this period, the devas helping you also use you as the vehicle for being taught how to enter someone's brain and control their thoughts because this is how devas – at their level of spiritual attainment - can intervene in human affairs to help people solve problems. Buddhas and Bodhisattvas can use even higher methods. If the devas didn't get anything in turn from working on you, then no one would bother working so hard and so long on purifying your channels. In the universe it seems that no one does work for free except for parents, yet they, too, expect to be taken care of by their children when they become old.

When you mantra for help in unfortunate situations, Buddhas and Bodhisattvas will try to affect people's thoughts in helpful ways if the karma allows, and they teach devas how to do this (according to their stage of abilities) during your twelve years of transformation. Buddhas and Bodhisattvas also help people change their fortunes by giving them thoughts that lead to actions that avoid errors. All angels (devas) are trained to affect the minds of human beings in similar ways to help them solve problems.

Why should you suffer through this? Because you will eventually be their colleague and have similar powers, and therefore you go through the hazing that everyone else went through. Going through it, as painful as it is, you will then be reticent to use your mind powers to harm people when you finally attain that ability due to possessing higher spiritual bodies. Everyone is tempted by superpowers, especially the power to control others, and by going through this pain you will be less inclined to inflict any harm or pain on others to achieve what you want. Power corrupts and absolute power corrupts absolutely, so by going through the process you will end up thing twice before making unwise interventions.

As stated, this explanation of being unaware that the internal speaker is not you is symbolized by the story in *Journey to the West* where another spiritual monkey imitates Sun Wukong and no one, except an enlightened Buddha, can tell the two apart. In this case, you will not initially be able to tell apart which thoughts are yours and which actually belong to the devas, who practice doing this so that they can help change people's thoughts in cases where they are going to do wrong and should do right instead, and *where karma permits this*. When you mantra to Buddhas for help, this is how they try to help you, namely not by creating miracles but by giving you (or others) the right thoughts on how to proceed.

This explanation is also found in the "Fifty States of Delusion Afflicting Practitioners" that appears within the *Surangama Sutra*, but in a slightly camouflaged form so as not to frighten practitioners. The first thirty delusions it mentions are relevant to our meditation case studies: the first ten deal with experiences devas give you when you are cultivating your physical body (the form skandha of Jing), the next ten deal with deeper experiences related to developing the subtle body (sensation skandha of Qi), and the next thirty deal with experiences related to developing a Causal body (the conception skandha of Shen). The next ten deal with someone who attains initial enlightenment (an Arhat who attains *nirvana* with remainder by achieving the Supra-Causal body corresponding to the volition skandha), while the fifth set of ten states deals with someone about to attain complete and perfect enlightenment (a fully enlightened Buddha).

This chapter of the *Surangama Sutra* is difficult to comprehend and may require multiple readings. However, it gives a valuable non-denominational outline of the types of events meditators will commonly experience on the spiritual path to enlightenment. Individuals from every religion going through this process need to read it whether you are Moslem, Christian, Jewish, Taoist, Buddhist, Hindu or a member of any other religion.

Here is the relevant chapter from the *Surangama Sutra*, "The 50 Delusive Mara States Afflicting Practitioners as They Make Meditation Progress," with edited commentary from my book *What is Enlightenment?*:

THE *SURANGAMA SUTRA*

Just as the Buddha was preparing to leave his dharma seat, he grasped the small inlaid table beside his lion throne. But then he changed his mind and leaned back in his seat, saying to Ananda and the great assembly: "You *sravakas* and *pratyeka-buddhas* must turn your minds to the achievement of supreme *bodhi*. I have already instructed you in the correct methods of cultivation practice, but you are not yet aware of the subtle states of maras (delusion) that occur when you practice *samatha-vipasyana* (cessation-contemplation) meditation.

When a (misleading or delusive) mara state appears before you, if you are not able to distinguish it when it occurs, and your mind is not pure and balanced, you will fall into erroneous views that are either your own skandha delusions or the mara delusions of heavenly devas, ghosts and spirits, or evil demons. When your mind is not clear, you may mistake a thief as your own son (mistake their thoughts as your own). You may regard some small cultivation progress as complete achievement like the ignorant monk who, after reaching the fourth dhyana, presumed that he had attained sainthood. No sooner had he earned his heavenly reward than the signs of his approaching fall appeared. For slandering arhatship, he created his own karmic recompense and fell into the relentless hells. You must listen carefully to what I now explain to you in detail."

Ananda rose to his feet, and together with all the others in the assembly who had more to learn, they gratefully prostrated themselves at the Buddha's feet and awaited his compassionate instruction.

The Buddha said: "You must all understand that the twelve types of beings birthed in the worlds of suffering are all endowed with a profound and basic bright *bodhi* [the absolute mind substance; life's basic mind is called *bodhi* or enlightenment—it is the thing in you that is still there when objects are cast away] that is no different from that of all the Buddhas in the ten directions. However, due to the fault of false thinking and confusion about the truth, people become ignorant and because of infatuation their delusion becomes all-pervasive. Therefore, the original, absolute void (emptiness) is ceaselessly transformed into illusion, and thus, worlds come into being. In reality, lands as numerous as motes of dust throughout *samsara* all came into being due to the stubborn false thinking of the non-enlightened. You must know that space created in your own mind is like a wisp of cloud that dots the vast sky; how much more so the worlds which are within this space. If just one among you realizes your true nature and returns to the source, then all of space in the ten directions will be obliterated. Why, then, will not all the worlds within this space be shaken and shattered?

"When you cultivate dhyana and samadhi, all the bodhisattvas and great Arhats, whose mind-essences are in perfect accord, remain unmoved, but the kings of the demons, ghosts, spirits, and lesser heavens witness the collapse of their palaces for no apparent reason, and the whole earth shakes. All the creatures of land, sea, and air take fright whereas worldly men who are deluded do not feel anything. The hosts of demons, who have acquired the five supernatural powers but have not yet achieved transcendental wisdom to break their ties with *samsara*, are still attached to the troubles of this world. How can they allow you to destroy their dwellings? This is why the ghosts and spirits, Deva Mara, and sprites and demons come to disturb you when you enter the state of samadhi.

"However, do not be concerned about the maras' enmity, for they are afflicted with worldly passions while you are in the profound state of *bodhi*. They can no more touch you than wind can blow out light or a knife can cut water. You are like boiling water and they are like solid ice that soon melts away in the presence of heat. Though they rely on their supernatural powers, these are merely externals and can only succeed in affecting your mind, which is the host of the five skandhas (of form, sensation, conception, volition, and consciousness) if you let them. If you are deluded, they will be able to do as they please. When you are in dhyana, awakened, aware and free of delusion, the maras can do nothing to you. When your skandhas are wiped out, and you enter a state of perfect clarity, it is like entering the light whereas all evils are like dark vapors. As light overcomes darkness, they will perish as soon as they approach you. How could they dare to disturb your samadhi?

"However, if you fail to awaken and are deluded by the five

skandhas, then you, Ananda, will become the offspring of Mara and aid him in his work. This is like the despicable Matangi, who used spells to try to cause you to violate one of the eighty thousand rules of the order. At that time, however, your mind was pure and you did not succumb. This was a potential threat to your precious *bodhi*-wisdom and to your very being, and you might have ended up like a minister of state who finds himself suddenly dispossessed, destitute, and hopeless."

[**Editor:** These events happen within the human body as your Qi channels open up, and obstructions within the Qi flow pathways are therefore destroyed. The Buddhist sutras say that within a Bodhisattva's body even a single pore can contain innumerable other sentient beings cultivating to enlightenment, which is simply to prepare you for the truth that other sentient beings must enter your body to transform its Qi channels at the advanced stages of the spiritual path. Obviously, most people aren't mature enough for these teachings which is why they are provided through stories and analogies. Nevertheless, Taoism also says that our internal body is like its own little world of denizens, and inhabited by spirits or "worms" that reside within the channels. The Indian tantric yoga paths also show pictures of male and female devas (Bodhisattvas) residing at each of the chakras to either open or regulate the Qi flow within the human body. They usually hold various instruments in their hands symbolizing that they help open the Qi channels using various techniques, the process producing warmth.

As the Qi channels are being opened, practitioners will often see all sorts of unusual illusory experiences through waking visions, during meditation or through dreams that are provided by such beings to symbolically indicate what is going on. Those beings (devas) are usually practicing their mental projection skills such that many of the visions carry no real meaning at all.

While the illusory visions follow no set pattern, some types of symbolic commonly appear across different traditions due to having shared concepts. However the symbolic representations are not necessarily consistent from one school, tradition, country or generation to the next. Thus a Tibetan Buddhist practitioner will usually experience different visions than a Muslim, Christian, Jew, Hindu or Taoist because of the different mental material available within the practitioner's memories. Many types of the aspirant's memories are also brought to the surface during this process in order to help the practitioner make progress.

Most individuals are too immature to handle the truth behind these events, which is that beings with bodies of subtle Qi will enter your own body (especially the brain, known as Vimalakirti's room) to help you open up Qi channels, so this true esoteric explanation is not taught to the immature or mentally unstable. Such teachings are considered "secret," which only means most people don't know them. They are not taught to cultivation practitioners who lack wisdom, maturity, merit and adequate preparation. However, cultivation artwork and stories across the world helps prepare students for this truth.

This information is also the secret basis of the heavenly *dan* (medicine) method described by Taoism where devas are asked to help you to transform your physical body quickly, and is the meaning of spiritual "blessings" within other religions.

During advanced stages of Qi transformation, such as the kundalini awakening that opens all the major meridians described in Taoism, Vajrayana or Nath Yoga, one will also experience many "Deva Mara" emotional testings. Bodhisattva devas will provoke particular emotional responses in practitioners, or produce false visions, to show other devas how this is done, especially how to create thoughts. They also want your Yin Qi or Yang Qi to arise. In this way they will see which Qi channels are open or blocked (so they can help clear obstructions).

These types of mental experience are called a "trial" or "tribulation" (sometimes even "torture" or "trickery") and the process can last for years as practitioners work to open up all their Qi channels. The process is usually overseen by the unseen masters of your tradition and other saints and sages, but it is still difficult at best because the devas cannot control themselves at times due to their joy at being able to play with your mind and test themselves against each other. Buddhism simply calls this a stage of cleansing and harmonization of the four elements of the body, which also means the opening the body's Qi channels and chakras.

This troublesome process of breaking away from attachment to the form and sensation skandhas to generate a subtle deva body (cultivating all your Qi channels to create an etheric body double of Qi called the subtle body) takes years to complete after the major Qi channels are first opened during a multi-day kundalini awakening (which usually lasts about three months or "100 days"). A person going through this, which happens past the initial kundalini awakening, will then be tested over and over again on many types of experiences (greed, lust, power, anger, fame, self-preservation, etc.) over this time to see whether they still cling to them in consciousness and to see which Qi channel circulations must still be opened to generate a deity body; different emotions give rise to different types of Qi flow within the body that must be observed.

Practitioners at these levels are often put through various visionary and auditory experiences that they will often mistakenly attribute to devils and demons (ex. common in Christianity) while they are actually helpful devas and masters in disguise. You usually need to go through this process for twelve years before a subtle body can emerge after the true kundalini awakening is first experienced, and masters never speak about the process in order not to frighten practitioners.

The Bodhisattva devas and dharma protectors helping you to attain the deva body in this way, which is the first step towards the purified *sambhogakaya* Reward body that is the fifth body in a series, are non-sectarian by nature. They equally help practitioners of all schools and religions accomplish the task of Qi channel transformations by dissolving Qi blockages and opening channels. This process is symbolized by poking instruments held in the hands of deities, such as axes, that can physically cut away at Qi channel restrictions.

As more and more Qi channels open and better Qi flow circulation through more body sections becomes established, a practitioner can achieve higher stages of mental emptiness during meditation since thoughts and Qi flow are connected. The net result of transforming the inner subtle (Qi) and physical bodies is greater mental clarity, but only if the practitioner learns to transcend any clinging identification with the coarse physical body by centering themselves in a transcending, more subtle or emptier consciousness that we refer to as emptiness. If you center yourself in an overarching bodiless consciousness like space, instead of clinging to the material body, this is one way to quickly detach from the physical body and start mastering the subtle body.

Without the helpful interventions by devas going inside you to open your Qi channels, the next best way to accomplish this progress is through advanced pranayama, Nyasa, *nei-gong*, visualization and yogic practices. Basically, any form of intensive *nei-gong* or internal energy work will help, including special forms of *sexual cultivation* to excite and then move your internal energies that will open Qi channels, but those methods are considered secret or restricted because of the potential for abuse.

The Bodhisattva devas who help in these efforts often masquerade as many types of beings when working on your channels. For instance, the battles of St. Anthony of the Desert with the "devil," the struggles of St. Seraphim of Sarov (Russian Orthodox Church), or the visions of Padre Pio where "the devil" appeared to him as young girls who danced naked, as a guardian angel, as the pope or young friend of the monks, and so on all belong to this type of deva assistance. The testing of Abraham, and the visions Master Papaji had of playing with Krishna (and Namdev playing with the Deity Vithoba) also belong to this type of interaction, as do the internal voices heard by Socrates.

The Vajrayana Buddhism visions that correspond to the opening of the chakras and channels are also fictitious illusions provided by heavenly beings too, as were *all* of the visions reported in the Old Testament. Practitioners rarely pause to realize that, lacking superpowers, they cannot actually "see" these visions from their own capabilities, but are being given the illusory (untrue) visions by the Bodhisattva devas (angels, *dakinis*, guardian spirits, dharma protectors, etc.) who are playfully testing out their powers or using them to guide and encourage people along the path. There are all sorts of reasons to give people visions. The methodology that Bodhisattvas chose to help you depends upon how much cultivation work you have done, what you have studied, what exists within your memories, your karma and your degree of merit and wisdom.

Only when someone is put through these strong emotional experiences and temptations (sensation skandha experiences which strongly move the inner subtle body of Qi) posed through various forms of testing trickery—such as being told to pluck out your eye or sacrifice your son on an altar to God (Abraham)—can heavenly beings cause your Yin Qi and Yang Qi to arise so that they can more easily go about opening your Qi channels. They often make mistakes, but the general attempt is to help practitioners open the channels in their subtle Qi body that Hindus also call the *pranayama kosha.*

When all the channels in the subtle body open this can finally result in a *yin shen* or deity body achievement where the astral spirit, or subtle body, can freely leave the physical body at will. Hence Buddhism calls it a "will-born" body as well as an "illusory body" since humans cannot see this body composed of Qi and it still isn't your true nature. This is the first initial fruit of the spiritual path, and makes you an individual with two bodies tied together – an earthly and heavenly Qi body. In Taoism the individual has become an "Immortal" while in Christianity they have now become a saint. In eastern schools they have now become a master, guru or "Arhat" at the very lowest (first) stage of spiritual attainment.

This entire channel purification process, which is only experienced by advanced kundalini practitioners, typically starts with the strongest emotional responses that are connected with survival issues, and then proceeds to more subtle emotional states. If someone has done enough bodywork or yoga such that their many muscle Qi channels have already been opened, it is much easier to attain the *yin shen* deity body when you perform spiritual energy practices on top of that. That is why yoga, Pilates and other *full body* stretching exercises are extremely helpful to spiritual cultivation. Even so, you must still work hard at cultivation practices to open up all your Qi channels.

Only by practicing mantra and meditation can you even begin to open your Qi channels. Holding onto a state of concentration, such as by cultivating the four bodiless immeasurables (a mind of infinite love, compassion, joy or equanimity) that cause you to transcend the normal attachments you make to your physical body, is another method taught in a variety of spiritual schools to help in this accomplishment, as is mantra recitation.

Devas are usually trying to help human beings open up their channels all the time, such as by helping those who are sick, but the greatest assistance is usually given to spiritual practitioners. Such assistance goes by a different name in each tradition, and the help you receive depends upon your merit, wisdom, stage of progress and your degree of practice effort.

In the fifteenth chapter of the *Lotus Sutra*, Shakyamuni Buddha even revealed countless Bodhisattvas who had been cultivating within the earth, unbeknownst to others, which symbolizes the unrecognized help devas gives us internally to open the Qi channels within our physical bodies (symbolized by the Earth). The symbol of Bodhisattvas living within the earth only becomes clear to people who are working on cultivating their internal Qi channels and who start receiving this assistance, which people pray for in various traditions.

Not much is ever explained about this topic except in the Vajrayana (Esoteric), Taoist or Nath/tantric yoga schools that focus on transforming the physical body (its chakras and Qi channels) in the quickest ways possible. What people don't normally realize is that if you only focus on transforming the body and its chakras/channels - which is the common mindset of Taoist, Nath, Kaula, Vajrayana, yoga, martial arts and other form-emphasis practitioners - then your cultivation results will be limited. However, if you focus on cultivating emptiness *along with your Qi life force and physical body* – by centering yourself in a transcending witnessing state that detaches from your body and sees thoughts without attaching to them - then you can eventually quickly clear all the obstructed Qi channels in your body and become able to attain samadhi and the Tao.

At the lower stages of the path, mind (consciousness) and Qi are linked, so the Qi energy channels have to open for you to be able to attain samadhi. At the level of the Tao (enlightenment), however, you become independent of the vibrations of the Qi energies within the channels and how they interact with thoughts. It is so hard to cultivate enlightenment that many devas, dharma protectors and Bodhisattvas have undertaken the vow to help human practitioners along these lines so that they can finally achieve enlightenment. Those are the ones normally helping you.

If you have wisdom, many of the mara states of delusion can be tests to see what you still desire within your deepest mind. As long as you do not indulge in the temptations thrust upon you, the testing can help you make progress if you transcend everything via a transcending detachment. Or, the testing can defeat you. It is good to have an enlightened master during this process - seek one so that you have someone to protect you and don't run into trouble.

It is only after enlightenment (attaining the Supra-Causal body that transcends the physical, subtle and Mental bodies) that the deva maras can trouble you no more. In other words, if you attain the Supra-Causal body, Dharma body or Clear Light body of enlightenment you can transcend all the machinations of the lower-level devas as they play with your thoughts, open your Qi channels and go about their training practices in your body. Before that accomplishment you cannot be free of their influences. You can talk about this in terms of consciousness or skandhas and bodies with the point being that you are not free of the lower skandhas or bodies until you attain the volition skandha and Supra-Causal body, which means enlightenment.

The states of illusion Buddha mentioned within the *Surangama Sutra* not only accompany the opening up of your Qi channels, but represent tests that help you to learn how to transcend your lusts and desires (predispositions). Do not drop into them with indulgence despite the provocation of devas. The stories of Jesus, Buddha, Yeshe Tsogyel and many others provide examples of the trials and tribulations (temptations caused by devas) people go through when freeing themselves from the form, sensation and conception skandhas (meaning when they are generating the subtle and Causal bodies) and subject to the influence of devas.

The Biblical story of Abraham almost sacrificing his son due to heavenly instructions, and the twelve hardships of Naropa, both illustrate the types of emotional testing experiences you might be put through during the channel purification process. During such events you don't know what's going on (a miar) and will actually believe in the illusions presented to you. What you go through only has relevance for you and nobody else, but unfortunately people interpret these experiences wrongly and some of these incorrect explanations have been made into the basis of religion and culture.

Inner deva denizens, as Indian tantric kundalini pictures illustrate, will always provide auditory and visual illusions to test practitioners while training and working on opening their Qi channels. The illusions/delusions they put you through are connected to the "testing phase" you often read about regarding the great founders of religions. They are often the reason people experience strong emotional trials, "eruptions" and temptations, or hear internal voices such as in the stories of Socrates, Huike, Yeshe Tsogyel, and Abraham.

Most individuals are entirely oblivious to the actualities of the process going on (the deva involvement) until their body is finally totally transformed by Qi and they finally can generate an independent *yin shen*, subtle body, impure illusory body, deva body or deity body. At that time there is a big party involving all the devas and Buddhas who helped you, and you are taught the reasons why for many events and sufferings you underwent.]

The Ten Mara-States of the Skandha of Form

"Ananda, you must know that when you sit in meditation your thoughts will eventually dissipate (you must sit in a place to cultivate toward enlightenment and dissolve away false thoughts). When you are free of thoughts, your mind will become clear and this state of pure clarity will be the same within movement or stillness, and remain the same whether you remember it or forget it (your mind will be clear whether thoughts are moving or not, including whether you notice this clarity or get so used to it that you forget about it). In this state as you enter meditation, you are like a man with clear eyes who is standing in the dark (and thus cannot see anything in the darkness even though your eyes are fine). Although your mind is (perfectly) clear, it is not yet awakened. This is because the skandha of form conditions your meditation. If your eyes are clear, and light shines through in all directions, you will no longer dwell in darkness. This is called 'the end of the skandha of form,' which allows you to transcend the kalpa of defilement. If we examine the cause of the form skandha, the root cause is solidified false thinking."

[**Editor:** Buddha is actually saying that our physical body of "form" or Jing is basically solidified energy, and therefore is ultimately an expression or manifestation of the highest energies that also comprise base consciousness. It is a condensation of those higher energies, which are more subtle. Because the body is essentially energy and thoughts are composed of energy, this is why thoughts can tangibly affect the body. This explains the mind-body connection; mind can affect the body since the body is also a type of condensed energy.

On the road of spiritual cultivation, you must stop identifying yourself as the physical body through a type of transcending mental detachment practice that centers you in a higher, more subtle body. You should therefore practice centering yourself in a transcending bodiless awareness. By ignoring normal mental attachments by centering yourself in a transcending bodiless mental state (called emptiness or witnessing), which creates a new habit energy so as to "dissolve attachments," your Qi channels will gradually open and your mind will eventually experience a state of empty clarity after some time.

To achieve this, you must first detach from the form skandha (your physical body). The method is meditation that doesn't grasp onto thoughts, thus inhibiting internal Qi flows since thoughts and Qi are interlinked. Your Qi will start to flow naturally, your Qi channels will then start to open whereupon the warm yang Qi will often be felt moving throughout your body. That is the first start of Qi arousal because the entire body of flesh must be transformed and not just the major channel lines.

The state of clear clarity you attain by cultivating through the form skandha via a transcending witnessing practice is often described as your mind "being bright" because wandering thoughts die down and the mental realm becomes clear and relatively empty. At this stage of cultivation, your mind still attaches to internal feeling states (sensations) and the emotions that arise when you react to circumstances around you, but you are still clear about all this because you didn't suppress thoughts. You only transcended the habit of firmly holding onto thoughts. With the volume of wandering thoughts in decline, the mind now seems brighter or more clear.

For instance, a situation arises around you and because of natural responsiveness (receptivity), emotions and feelings naturally arise within your mind and body that you know via your consciousness. This reciprocal type of reaction always happens. You typically attach to or reject those states because of liking and disliking, which is also natural. In other words, you like or dislike those emotions/sensations/desires, and so you try to hold onto them or reject them rather than just let them arise freely and cleanly leave as do the images in a clear mirror. All these emotions are felt in your inner subtle body composed of Qi, hence the attribution to the sensation skandha

When you learn how to detach from these feeling-sensation states (as well as imaginations, worries, doubts and desires) that arise, this is "cultivating through the sensation skandha." By continuously detaching from this type of response you will eventually become free of the sensation skandha, but you will not yet be free of the conception skandha (because you haven't yet cultivated a Causal or Mental body). Nevertheless, your mind will become more and more like a clean mirror and by establishing the transcending habit of witnessing, you will no longer cling to all the emotions or bodily feelings that arise "through receptivity" as explained.

When you take a further progressive step and break free of the level of "all pervading" finer thoughts that comprise the conception skandha, you will reach an even higher stage of mental emptiness and cleanliness of non-clinging. In terms of skillful teachings, the conception skandha is paired with the Causal body, Mental body or Shen body attainment; someone who possesses your body with that body attainment can give you very fine thoughts. It is said that you when you attain a Causal, Mental or Mantra body (just as you obtained a subtle deva body when you break free of the form skandha) you will still not have gotten rid of the concept of the I-self; you will still have an ego-shell mind that is not open to the transcending universal *alaya* consciousness. You will not yet have attained a Supra-Causal body.

Putting it another way, if you generate a Supra-Causal body composed of the substance that transcends the composition of all living beings (including the energy of their life-force and consciousness), it is easy to use that body to know the minds of all lower beings, and thus you can become one with or unified with universal life.

To progress further from the volition skandha type of superfine thoughts (Supra-Causal body), you must now detach from the hidden/concealed thinking that underlies the sense of self and the entire energetic net of *samsara* and the transmigration of life throughout the cosmos. This means detaching from the volition skandha that in turn means purifying the *alaya* consciousness that represents all the thoughts in your body vehicle. In terms of bodies, Shakyamuni makes the correspondence of transcending these superfine thought energies with cultivating a Supra-Causal body whose substance transcends the energies that comprise the lower planes of the physical, subtle and Causal body realms. This is just a correspondence made for teaching purposes; there is no relation to the types of thoughts you have and body attainments.

A shimmering fluctuation within consciousness can be perceived at this stage and this level of energy at the volition skandha/*alaya* level is said to be ultimately responsible for your life-force and sense perceptions. This is said to be the energy that actually builds all of the lower realms. In terms of mind, the mental task of breaking free of the volition skandha involves purifying the I-am sense, which is the "afflicted mind" (seventh consciousness) in Buddhism.

Transcending this level of "hidden" or "concealed" thinking means you will finally arrive at the consciousness skandha. In terms of a body vehicle or vessel, it means generating a new body of Immanence (the perfect *sambhogakaya*) that is even higher than the Supra-Causal body of the volitions skandha-*alaya* stage (which is then said to be "extinguished" or separated from since this new body of Immanence becomes your living vehicle).

To attain complete enlightenment (*nirvana* without remaining dependency) you must attain a Buddha body of Immanence. In terms of consciousness we say that you must detach from the type of extremely fine thinking within the *alaya* (basically the energies that produce it) that is so subtle that you don't normally see its movements, and only then can you attain to Perfect Enlightenment. Those are teachings in terms of consciousness meant to motivate you to continue meditating and producing a pure mind of clarity (while hiding the fact that it is all really about body attainments). At the level of *alaya* cultivation your consciousness seems still but is actually moving all the time, like a flowing river that seems placid on its surface. That is why you still see a world even though the mind is empty of conceptions. You have to cultivate to an even higher, transcending level to be free of the *alaya* level of thoughts.

It is said that you must now return clarity to its source nature, the absolute nature, to attain complete enlightenment. If you do not ultimately reach the root of consciousness energy which is responsible for the types of thought and individual senses then you will never be able to dissolve false thoughts entirely, and so you must reach the higher stage of the Immanence body attainment whose concomitant mind-stream is like a crystal clear realm of purity and perception. This is the stage of "no body and no mind" (although of course you will have a body and a mind). In reaching this base state, it is said that the sense consciousnesses will become interchangeable.

You must pass through these stages of development one by one in sequence, like untying knots on a string one after another, to attain the ultimate goal of perfect enlightenment and find your real ultimate self-nature, the foundational substance, energy or essence that the entire universe came from. You can describe the progress in terms of body attainments (physical, subtle, Causal, Supra-Causal, Immanence), skandhas as done here in the *Surangama Sutra*, or via descriptions of the concomitant attendant consciousness that accompanies a relevant attainment.

Body attainment descriptions are best, but since most people won't attain them this path was hidden in teachings of types of thoughts (consciousness), which are described as coarse, fine, very fine and super refined. Then this was mixed together with descriptions of skandhas that really mean bodies, but were then taken to mean types of thoughts with the insinuation that a higher body produces a finer type of thought. This type of explanation always encourages people to keep practicing, but it is difficult to invent an explanation of progress levels talking this way unless you make things up.

The skandhas/aggregates are all ultimately due to thoughts, to transformations wrought by the capabilities of the mind. They are also ultimately tied to the attainment of body vehicles/ vessels that are ranked by the etheric refinement of their compositional substance. The skandhas are another way of describing the attendant, corresponding or concomitant consciousness levels for each new spiritual body that you generate on the path, with each higher level being more pure than the lower and thus the level of thought of the more refined body being finer. Hence you can describe the path in terms of skandhas, bodies or consciousness and types of thought. These are all indexes for body attainments.

Because you always end up clinging to and identifying with

any new body attainment, you must keep cultivating through all types of thoughts (attributable to the energy level of each body) to ultimately find their original source - the energy that ultimately comprises that body structure. Then you spin a new body out of that structure and start the process once again.

That is the spiritual path to complete enlightenment, and as you can see it is non-denominational. The concomitant, or attendant physical attainment to complete and perfect enlightenment is called an Immanence or Buddha body (perfected *sambhogakaya*), but this is only a way of speaking. To attain it, the standard meditation practice is watching thoughts, namely to center consciousness in an overarching bodiless witnessing that sees strong thoughts but transcends them. You can also describe this as bodiless consciousness, formlessness or infinite consciousness. This is the cultivation path in general that will in time lead you to the highest spiritual stages. At the same time you must also cultivate your Qi and channels as well (see *Nyasa Yoga*). You have to rise above any plane of energy to create a new body, which is colloquially paired (as expedient means) with a finer type of thought or purer level of consciousness.

In terms of freeing oneself from the form skandha (physical body), which is the first step on this path that spiritual aspirants must take, many unusual experiences can arise that Buddha grouped into ten large categories. They occur because Buddhas or devas give you these experiences, or because you cultivate your Qi and channels to such a degree that you start to develop a subtle body double (deva or deity body) within your physical body and you can start to experience things of the subtle plane of Qi.

Most all of these experiences recounted by Buddha in the Surangama Sutra are false visions given by Deva Maras who enter your brain to project imaginary images and sounds when you are just an ordinary meditation practitioner on the trail, but practitioners do not realize this! If you do not take any of these experiences as enlightenment or spiritual achievement, then you have the correct view. If you take any of these experiences as what you are after, then this is an incorrect view.]

1. "Ananda, in this state of penetration and mental clarity, the four elements of the world will no longer entwine you, and after a

short time your body will become free of all hindrances (your Qi channels will all open up). This state is called 'the clear mind diffusing outwardly throughout the environment.' It is a temporary achievement resulting from your progress in meditation. It does not mean that you have reached sainthood. This stage, although it is called 'an excellent level of attainment,' should not be confused with sainthood. If you misinterpret it, you will become vulnerable to the demons of delusion.

2. "Ananda, once again, in this state of penetration and mental clarity, you might become able to (temporarily) discern internal things within your own body and may even see unusual things inside. Although you perceive your body thus, this is harmless. This state is called 'the clear mind inwardly diffusing through one's body' and is but a temporary achievement resulting from your progress in meditation. It does not mean that you have reached sainthood. This stage, although it is called 'an excellent level of attainment,' should not be confused with sainthood. If you misinterpret this, you will become vulnerable to the demons of delusion.

3. "Further, with this clear mind which penetrates both within and without, your spirit and faculties and higher and lower souls might all start to take turns as host and guest. You might also for instance suddenly hear a voice in the air preaching the dharma or proclaiming esoteric truths in the ten directions. This state is a case of 'the spirit and faculties alternatingly separating and unifying with higher and lower souls that is sowing good seeds (for the results of cultivation).' It is a temporary state and is not sainthood. This stage, although it is called 'an excellent level of attainment,' should not be confused with sainthood. If you misinterpret it, you will become vulnerable to the demons of delusion.

4. "Further, when the person's mind becomes clear, revealing, bright and penetrating, your inner mental brightness will shine and it might then seem as if everything in the ten directions is bathed with the hue of sandalwood, or that all living creatures seem as if transformed into Buddhas. Suddenly, you might see (something like) Vairocana Buddha seated on a throne of heavenly light surrounded by a thousand Buddhas, who simultaneously appear on lotus blossoms in countless lands. This is called 'the effect of the awakening of spiritual awareness,' the penetrating light of which illuminates all the worlds. However, this is a temporary stage and is

not sainthood. This stage, although it is called 'an excellent level of attainment,' should not be confused with sainthood. If you misinterpret it, you will become vulnerable to the demons of delusion.

5. "Further, if you try to continuously contemplate (practice meditation) using your clear and penetrating mind without pause, by (severely) repressing and subduing your thoughts, the (excessive) effort will produce a desire for release. Suddenly, then, the ten directions of space might appear to be filled with the (radiant) colors of seven or of a hundred precious gems. Without hindering one another, the blue, yellow, red, and white colors will each manifest in utter purity. This is called 'the effect of excessive mental repression.' This is a temporary stage and is not sainthood. This stage, although it is called 'an excellent level of attainment,' should not be confused with sainthood. If you misinterpret it, you will become vulnerable to the demons of delusion.

6. "Further, if you try to investigate this clear and penetrating mind, your inner mental clarity might become so bright (concentrated) that suddenly at midnight you might be able to see all sorts of objects in a dark room as clearly as in broad daylight. These objects might persist without disappearing. This is called 'the clarity of mental refinement penetrating obscurity.' This is a temporary stage and is not sainthood. This stage, although it is called 'an excellent level of attainment,' should not be confused with sainthood. If you misinterpret it, you will become vulnerable to the demons of delusion.

7. "As your mind merges with emptiness, suddenly your four limbs may feel like grass or trees. Even if burned by fire or cut with a knife, you might feel nothing at all. Flame might not burn you, and cutting your flesh might seem like trying to whittle wood. This (immunity from injury) is called 'the union of inner and outer worlds that eliminates the four elements as the mind merges with emptiness.' This is a temporary stage and is not sainthood. This stage, although it is called 'an excellent level of attainment,' should not be confused with sainthood. If you misinterpret it, you will become vulnerable to the demons of delusion.

8. "As your mind becomes pure and clean, when you have reached a very high level of purification, you might suddenly see all quarters of the great earth, with its mountains and rivers, transformed

into a Buddha's pure land, complete with the all-pervading radiance of the seven precious jewels. You might also see Buddhas (enlightened beings), as numerous as the sands of the Ganges, filling space, together with beautiful temples and palaces. You might be able to see hells below and celestial palaces above, all without obstruction. This is called 'the result of overly-prolonged contemplation on likes and dislikes.' However, this is not sainthood. This stage, although it is called 'an excellent level of attainment,' should not be confused with sainthood. If you misinterpret it, you will become vulnerable to the demons of delusion.

9. "As you penetrate further and deeper within your mind of clarity (cultivate a deeper stage of mental clarity), you might suddenly be able to see far away market-places, wells, streets, and lanes in the middle of the night. You might (think you) see relatives, clansman, and family members, and might even hear them speak. This is called 'remote visions due to the hard-pressed mind taking flight (the suppressed mind due to overwork escapes to see things far away).' However, this is not sainthood. This stage, although it is called 'an excellent level of attainment,' should not be confused with sainthood. If you misinterpret it, you will become vulnerable to the demons of delusion.

10. "As this mind penetrates to a further extent, you might see that the bodies of men of good wisdom (sages) seem to undergo countless changes in all sorts of ways without any reason. This is called "an improper mind that is possessed by mischievous ghosts or heavenly demons." You might experience Deva Mara (an *asura*) entering your innermost mind and then spontaneously preach the dharma and its profound meaning. This is not sainthood. Not confusing this with sainthood, Mara's influences will subside. If you misinterpret it, you will become vulnerable to the demons of delusion.

"Ananda, these ten states may occur in dhyana as the result of ones' meditative mental efforts interacting with the skandha of form. Dull and confused (ignorant and deluded) practitioners do not evaluate their own level of accomplishments. Hence, when they experience such phenomena, in their confusion they fail to recognize them and wrongly proclaim that they have become saints and are enlightened. For uttering such a great lie, they will fall into the hell of uninterrupted punishment. After my *nirvana*, in the Dharma ending age, you must proclaim these teachings so that the heavenly demons cannot take advantage of these states and so that practitioners can (be on guard to) protect themselves and realize the supreme Tao."

The Ten Mara States of the Skandha of Sensation [Generating the Subtle body also known as the Deva body, Impure Illusory Body, Astral body, Etheric body, *Yin-shen*, etc. composed of Qi/Prana]

"Ananda, when disciples practicing *samatha* (cessation or calm abiding) to realize samadhi are no longer hindered by the skandha of form, they can understand that the minds of all the Buddhas operate like reflections (objects) appearing in a clear mirror. A cultivator will then feel like as if he has obtained something but cannot make use of it [he now has a fully developed subtle body but it is stuck within the physical body and cannot yet leave]. It is still like a sleeping man having a nightmare whose mind is clear and whose limbs are free, yet who cannot move his limbs but feels paralyzed because of some deviant influence. This is 'the skandha of sensation' that (still) conditions one's meditation. If that sense of paralysis ceases, then your mind [subtle body] will be able to leave your physical body to look back at your own face, and will then be free to come and go as you please without any hindrances. This is called 'the cessation of the skandha of sensation,' and when it comes to an end the practitioner can thereby transcend the defilement of views, the cause of which is wrong understanding and erroneous thinking."

[**Editor**: "Sensations" refers to both physical bodily sensations and emotional feelings that are subjective reactions to phenomena. They arise because we *contact* phenomena and then reactive, reciprocal responses arise in the mind that we like or dislike. Next, we then strongly cling to or reject these feelings after we have instantaneously evaluated their *relatedness* to us as being pleasant or unpleasant.

When you can detach from the body and no longer cling to these sensations, emotions, impulses or desires that usually move, impel or compel you, you will experience a freedom that is described as unspeakable joy and ease. It comes from the happiness that arises from no longer mentally attaching to the coarse physical body and coarse thoughts or emotions.

To put it another way, to cultivate a higher subtle body you must stop clinging to coarse sensorial impressions that arise while still knowing them with your (discriminative) mind. When you attain the subtle body you can detach from the lower physical body with its baser nature, and will feel joyous and free.

Through cultivation of your Qi and mind you can thereby attain the first dhyana, which is called "The Joyous Ground Born of Separation" or the "*vitarka* (coarse thought) samadhi" of Hinduism and Patanjali's *Yoga Sutras.* This is essentially the attainment of the subtle deva body that can leave your physical body at will. Upon its attainment you will feel tremendous joy.

You can achieve this body because you can finally separate an inner Qi body from the physical body shell due to your cultivation work. A joyous achievement, you become able to leave the body at any time using this Qi body and can separate completely to be entirely free. The deva body is also known as the *yin shen* attainment of Taoism, *siddha deha* body of the Tamil Siddhas, and illusory (deity) body attainment of Tibetan Buddhism.

While to others you will look like an ordinary human being, because of the deva body your consciousness will now be able to perceive through the senses of that subtle body (particularly seeing, smelling and hearing). You will also become capable of small superpowers such as stopping cars, filling a dry well with water or making a dead tree blossom. You will always experience a bright/clear mind at this stage of attainment because you will now be using the higher quality deva body to control everything.

In freeing yourself from the form skandha by attaining the subtle deva body you will no longer be constrained by the coarse physical world, and in freeing yourself from the sensation skandha you will no longer be constrained by views. You will no longer be so strongly controlled by personal feelings/emotions that occur due to QI energies and are essentially just personal subjective imaginations contingent upon your own interpretations (other people may experience the same thing differently). Essentially the feelings of the sensation skandha are *personal imaginations* we construct since they are conditional judgments that apply only to us. This is one of the reasons they are called *illusory thoughts*, which also includes dreams, desires, doubts, worries and imaginations that proliferate within one's subtle body.

Deva Mara will seem to attack practitioners who are cultivating the subtle body and oppose your virtuous intents because of their training games. The only way to pass these trials is by refusing to indulge in wrong pathways they might impel.

When you finally win liberation from the form skandha by achieving the will-born body (deva body, subtle body, impure illusory body, *siddha deha*, etc.), we say you achieve the "initial fruit" of the path. You reach the stream-entrant phase of practice, called the *Srotapanna* stage of Arhatship, which is someone who has just entered the path because they generated a subtle deva body. At this first stage of accomplishment, you will thereafter no longer lack confidence in cultivation teachings or doubt they lead to enlightenment because with this attainment you will now be able to converse with heavenly beings who will provide true spiritual teachings free of religion.

By attaining a deva body you will gain access to the truth so you will have proved "the truth of the path." You will no longer subscribe to the errant Hinayana belief that purity laws and the path of religious discipline alone will lead to enlightenment because you will know this is not so. You have to generate an independent subtle body (deva body) to succeed rather than follow artificial religious traditions, rules and regulations of behavior.]

1. "Ananda, cultivators reaching this stage of practice will experience a great mental clarity (mental brightness). As a result of excessive inner pressure (self-control), they may be suddenly overwhelmed by a feeling of very great sadness or pity. As this feeling swells, (under this influence) if they for instance should see mosquitoes and gadflies they might view such things as infant children that need to be protected. With great pity in their hearts, they might find themselves spontaneously bursting into tears (under all sorts of random circumstances). This is called 'a breakdown due to an overexertion in rigorous practice.' They should understand that this is harmless. This type of experience does not denote sainthood, and they should understand that after a time it will automatically disappear. However, should they confuse this with sainthood (and thus continually allow it to go unchecked), the mara of sadness will enter their minds. Then, they might (then for instance) occasionally

feel great sadness for people (they meet) and at times spontaneously burst into uncontrolled sobbing. This abnormal reaction may cause them to lose the benefits from the dhyana so far achieved and fall into a lower state.

2. "Ananda, those disciples who practice dhyana will find that as the (influence of the) skandha of form recedes and the skandha of sensation manifests, they make more progress and might feel overwhelmingly excited and/or develop an attitude of unlimited boldness. With a fierceness of mind they might (for instance) resolve to equal all the Buddhas, or might (do something like) proclaim that they can transcend innumerable kalpas in a single moment of thought. This is called 'over-confidence arising from practice.' They should understand that this is harmless if recognized for what it is. This type of experience does not denote sainthood, and they should understand that after a time it will automatically disappear. If they confuse this state with sainthood (so as to continually allow it to go unchecked), the mara of wild nonsense (wildness or madness) will enter their minds. They might become boastful and arrogant when they meet other people. They might become extraordinarily haughty and arrogant to the extent they will not recognize both the Buddhas above and humanity below. This abnormal reaction may cause them to lose the benefits from the dhyana so far achieved and fall into a lower state.

3. "Continuing, those disciples who practice dhyana will find that as the (influence of the) skandha of form recedes and the skandha of sensation manifests, they might seem to observe no new signs of progress (no new headway) while their former attainments seem to disappear. The strength of their wisdom might diminish and they might then enter a destructive state. As they see no hope of progress ahead, they might enter a state of great mental dryness (monotony) that leads them to indulge in unremitting deep reflection. They may mistake this as a sign of diligence in practice whereas this is called 'losing oneself due to a lack of wisdom.' If they recognize this for what it is, there will be no harm. This type of experience does not denote sainthood. However, should they (misinterpret this and) confuse this with sainthood (to continually allow it unchecked), the maras of non-forgetfulness will enter their minds. Day and night they might then obsessively hold their mind fixated in one place (on particular memories or situations they rehash over and over again).

This abnormal reaction may cause them to lose the benefits from the dhyana so far achieved and fall into a lower state.

4. "Continuing, those disciples who practice dhyana will find that as the (influence of the) skandha of form recedes and the skandha of sensation manifests, their faculty of wisdom may outstrip their stage of samadhi (their understanding exceeds their stage of dhyana mental quiet). Swollen with a sense of pride, they might wrongly become convinced that they have equaled Vairocana and then become prematurely satisfied with some minor achievement that they regard as complete attainment. This is called 'the mind losing (its usual) common sense and becoming misled due to the powers of discrimination in meditation.' If they recognize this for what it is then there will be no harm, but should they (misinterpret this and) confuse this with sainthood (to continually allow it), the mara of self-satisfaction at inferior accomplishments will enter their minds, possibly causing them to announce to everyone they meet that they have reached supreme enlightenment. This abnormal reaction may cause them to lose the benefits from the dhyana so far achieved and fall into a lower state.

5. "Continuing, those disciples who practice dhyana will find that as the (influence of the) skandha of form recedes and the skandha of sensation manifests, they may find themselves not only without further progress but they may seem to have lost their previous gains. Surveying the two extremes, the situation may seem very dreadful and they may feel as if they are in great danger. Suddenly they may feel incredible anxiety and great distress such as someone would feel if they were lying on a hot iron bed or had taken poison. They might feel there is no reason to live and may even ask others to end their life so that they can thereby gain release from their torment. This is called 'cultivating without the appropriate expedient method,' and is harmless if the cause is recognized. This type of experience does not denote sainthood. However, should they (misinterpret this and) confuse this with sainthood (to continually allow it), the mara of constant anxiety will enter their minds and might cause them to (want to do things like) cut their own flesh with a sharp knife or even attempt to take their own lives. Or else, suffering prolonged anxiety (or depression) may drive them to escape to wild places and avoid contact with other human beings. This abnormal reaction may cause them to lose the benefits from the dhyana so far achieved and fall

into a lower state.

6. "Continuing, those disciples who practice dhyana may find that as the (influence of the) skandha of form recedes and the skandha of sensation manifests, they may experience a state of purity (mental emptiness) and peace (tranquility) that suddenly gives rise to a sense of boundless joy so intense they cannot contain it. This is called 'experiencing lightness and ease that is unchecked by wisdom (uncontrollable due to a lack of wisdom).' If they recognize it in time there is no harm. This type of experience does not denote sainthood. However, should they (misinterpret this and) confuse this with sainthood (to continually allow it), the mara of joyfulness will enter their minds. They might (then for instance) unexpectedly burst into laughter (without cause) when they meet people or might start singing and dancing in the streets, saying that they have attained unobstructed liberation. This abnormal reaction may cause them to lose the benefits from the dhyana so far achieved and fall into a lower state.

7. "Continuing, those disciples who practice dhyana will find that as the (influence of the) skandha of form recedes and the skandha of sensation manifests, they may feel that they have already achieved full realization. Suddenly an unjustified feeling of intense self-satisfaction might arise in them along with a feeling of superiority. They might suddenly simultaneously experience all sorts of various feelings of pride such as: although inferior they are equal to others; although equal they are superior to others; they are superior to superiors; they are not inferior to inferiors; and they are fully victorious. In their minds, they might look down on all the Buddhas and still more so as to the less advanced *sravakas* and *pratyeka-buddhas!* This is called 'viewing oneself as extraordinary (supreme) without sufficient wisdom to save oneself from pride.' If they recognize it in time this is harmless. This type of experience does not denote sainthood. However, should they (misinterpret this and) confuse this with sainthood (to continually allow it), the maras of intense arrogance will enter their minds. This will cause them to stop revering stupas and temples, to destroy sutras and images of the Buddha, and to declare to their patrons: 'These images are but gold and bronze, clay and wood; the sutras are merely paper and cloth. Your own body contains the eternal reality of Buddha-truth; to ignore this and instead worship clay and wood is truly foolish.' Those who believe them and get taken

in by their words might join them in destroying sacred images and sutras or in burying them underground. They will mislead other people and earn the retribution of the relentless hells. This abnormal reaction may cause them to lose the benefits from the dhyana so far achieved and fall into a lower state.

8. "Continuing, those disciples who practice dhyana will find that as the (influence of the) skandha of form recedes and the skandha of sensation manifests, in the midst of spiritual illumination and understanding of the truth they might experience a harmonious feeling of infinite lightness and purity. They might (therefore) think that they have achieved sainthood and feel great contentment. This is called 'lightness and purity attained due to wisdom.' If you recognize it, there is no harm. This type of experience does not denote sainthood. However, should they (misinterpret this and) confuse this with sainthood (so as to continually hold to it), the maras of craving lightness and purity will enter their minds, and they will then become self-satisfied (with their incomplete achievement) and stop seeking further progress. The majority of these will become like ignorant monks who greatly mislead people and then fall into the relentless hells. This abnormal reaction may cause them to lose the benefits from the dhyana so far achieved and fall into a lower state.

9. "Continuing, those disciples who practice dhyana may find that as the (influence of the) skandha of form recedes and the skandha of sensation manifests, they might misinterpret the clear mental emptiness they experience, suddenly giving rise to the idea of absolute extinction which discards the laws of cause and effect (the realm of interdependent causality). Cultivating emptiness, their minds may become empty to the point that they end up believing in the possibility of permanent extinction (absolute annihilation). This is harmless if they recognize that this type of experience does not denote sainthood. However, should they (misinterpret this and) confuse this with sainthood (so as to continually cultivate it as a goal), the maras of emptiness will enter their minds and cause them to ridicule the holding of precepts (rules of discipline) and criticize those who hold them as men of Hinayana. They might then also wrongly say that a bodhisattva who has realized emptiness can dispense with prohibitions (because there is no reason to hold to discipline if everything is ultimately empty). Hence, they may even indulge in drinking, meat-eating, and licentious behavior (wanton lust) in the

presence of their gullible patrons. Because of the power of this demonic influence, they will exert firm control over their followers who will fail to doubt or denounce them. As time passes, demonic possession may lead them to equally regard urine, feces, wine and meat as good for food under the rationale that everything shares the nature of emptiness. They will violate the Buddha's rules of morality and discipline and commit all sorts of sins (also misleading others into committing all sorts of offenses). This abnormal reaction may cause them to lose the benefits from the dhyana so far achieved and fall into a lower state.

10. "Continuing, those disciples who practice dhyana may find that as the (influence of the) skandha of form recedes and the skandha of sensation manifests, they might start clinging to the empty clarity which penetrates their mind and even unto their bones. Suddenly a feeling of boundless love might arise and as it grows more intense, it may drive them mad by turning into intense desire or lust. This is called 'irrational desires (lustful behavior) arising from the stillness and peace of meditation that cannot be controlled for lack of wisdom.' If they recognize it for what it is, there will be no harm. This type of experience does not denote sainthood. However, should they (misinterpret this and) confuse this with sainthood (to further allow it), the maras of desire will end up controlling their minds and they will then insist that acts of lust are the *bodhi* path. They may preach the doctrine of unhindered lust to laymen and say that practicing sexual indulgence is making them sons of the dharma (true practitioners). The power of this demonic influence will prevail during the Dharma ending age and sway hundreds, thousands, and tens of thousands of ignorant people. When the mara demon becomes weary of the cultivator's misdeeds, it will depart the victim's body, leaving them without charisma, and they will run afoul of the law of the land. For deceiving others, they will fall into the relentless hells. This abnormal reaction may cause them to lose the benefits from the dhyana so far achieved and fall into a lower state.

"Ananda, these ten states associated with the practice of dhyana all arise due to the interaction of the skandha of sensation with the meditator's mind. Ignorant and wayward practitioners do not evaluate themselves. When such reactions manifest, deluded people do not distinguish these states or reflect on them, nor are they able to understand the causes. They may wrongly claim that they have attained sainthood and falsely proclaim enlightenment. For uttering such a great lie, they will fall into the hells. After my *nirvana*, in the Dharma ending age, you must transmit this teaching so that all living beings may awaken to this message, that Deva Mara (heavenly demons) cannot take advantage of such states (to have their own way), and that practitioners can be on their guard as they strive to realize the supreme Tao."

The Ten Mara-States of the Skandha of Conception (Perception) - [Generating the Causal body also known as the Mental, Wisdom, Mantra, Vibrations, or Metaphor body composed of Shen energy]

"Ananda, for those disciples who practice samadhi and for whom the skandha of sensation is no longer a hindrance (you master the deva body), although the stream of transmigration for them has not yet ended, their mind is now able to take leave of their body the way a bird can escape from a cage. From this worldly state they now have the potential to achieve the bodhisattva's sixty stages of development towards Buddhahood, and thereby freely assume any form at will or travel anywhere without obstruction. This stage can be compared to a man who talks in his sleep, and though he does not know what he is doing, nevertheless speaks clearly intelligible sentences to those who are not asleep. This is an effect of the skandha of conception. When thoughts no longer stir in the mind and floating conceptions (superficial thoughts) are eliminated, the clear mind will be like a mirror totally free of dust and dirt and it will be able to reflect every detail of this present incarnation from beginning to end. This (achievement) marks 'the end of the skandha of conception.' At this level one can transcend the defilement of the passions (also worries and afflictions). If we examine the cause of the (conception) skandha, it comes from all-pervasive false thinking (comprehensive or interconnected false thinking which creates a web of associated relationships)."

[**Editor:** The conception skandha involves the discursive thinking processes, including the thinking that moves emotions. The conception skandha corresponds to the Mental body, Causal body, *manomaya kosha*, or apparent mind-stuff sheath of

Hinduism. It is composed of a finer level of energy than the coarser energy Qi and thus we attribute finer thoughts to this skandha than coarse emotions, which are attributed to the sensation skandha and subtle body.

It is said that cultivators who attain a Mental or Causal body as their body vehicle are sometimes unconscious of the gross and subtle planes even though all their gross and subtle actions still function. Hence they are like a person talking in his sleep who isn't consciously aware of his own speaking whereas others around him can hear him. Actually, if you attain a Mental/Causal body you live in that body vessel as your primary living vehicle and operate your subtle and physical body like appendages you use, which is a better explanation. Thus you don't always pay them full attention. You can operate them, but will not fully live in them all the time.

As practitioners progress to reach this level of achievement (especially in passing through the sensation skandha), Shakyamuni says that Deva Maras will often "oppose the practitioner with desires, doubts, worries, imaginations and delusions" and "test them with temptations," as happened with Buddha, Jesus, Yeshe Tsogyel, Saint Anthony, Padre Pio and countless other practitioners. One should not follow their deviant impulses of trickery, for the devas at times cannot control themselves and you will suffer bad consequences and destroy yourself if they are given too much leeway, so seek an enlightened master for help. With wisdom one can see through the delusions that arise within your mind because of the Maras' influences but it is very hard to ignore them.

If you practice detachment from the impulses directly projected into your mind by the Mara forces, they will eventually not be able to affect you. The negative impulses will vanish when you cultivate a clear, bright (empty) mind that is no longer sucked into impulsive attachments but transcends them. In other words, you must refrain from wrongdoing and from following their inclinations and try to cultivate a "bodiless transcending body like space" that can view the inclinations without acting on them. Empty space lets things arise within it without interference or entanglement – because thoughts cannot and should not be prevented from arising – but lets them alone and they eventually depart when they are no longer needed. Then, of course, new ones will eventually arise as needed but you remain freely detached from all mental scenarios unless you use concentration to specifically hold onto thoughts.

If you can detach from the conception skandha then you can finally attain the third dhyana, which means achieving the Mental (Causal) body attainment, but this is not *nirvana* enlightenment despite its many powers and capabilities. Stationed in your subtle body you can detach from the gross world though from all outward appearances you look like and function exactly as an ordinary man or woman. Stationed in your Causal body you can detach from your subtle body and the impulses that course within it due to its composition made of Qi. In a way we can say that the mind-stream of the Causal body is the level of the attendant conception skandha, which is a finer level transcending the physical world and subtle planes.

Adepts who reach this stage often play with their new capability of projecting thoughts in others (done by using their subtle or Causal body to enter into another person's body and then think inside their brain), which Buddha explains in the *Surangama Sutra* via several representative types of visions they often give to people. There are many more types possible than these ten types that Buddha mentioned for illustration's sake.

In freeing oneself from the conception skandha by attaining a Causal body out of the subtle body (Taoism explains it by saying that the Qi body generates a Shen body, namely "Qi transforms into Shen") you can reach a stage where thoughts stop because you can cultivate a mental emptiness like space, your Qi (which is connected to thinking) also stops rotating/flowing within your body (since it is related to the production of thoughts), and your breathing becomes extremely light or even unnoticeable. With a Causal body attainment you can cultivate the third dhyana or the samadhi of infinite space/emptiness (which is not an inert mental realm of thoughtlessness).

The second dhyana attainment called "The Joyous Ground of Giving Rise to Samadhi," which is the "*vicara* (subtle thought) samadhi" of Patanjali's *Yoga Sutras,* doesn't need a Causal body for its attainment. It can be attained by a highly purified subtle deva body, but not a coarse, unpurified deva body. Masters of the second dhyana – the *Sakadagami* (Once-returner) Arhat - can cultivate superpowers such as giving sight to the blind, restoring limbs to the crippled and sometimes raising to life small creatures who have died. These are not the big superpowers, but the *Sakadagami* can certainly experience different planes and worlds of the subtle sphere.

What is important is that the mind, once free of the influences of the form and sensation skandhas because of a Causal body attainment, will no longer cling to the coarse mental phenomena that arise within it, and so the mind will become like a bright mirror wherein images that arise within it do so without any sticking. This is another description of super fine mental clarity.

The Causal body attainment of the *Anagamin* (non-returner) transcends the purified subtle body stage of a *Sakadagami,* or Once-returner, who will have at most one more life to live as a human being due to mental (skandha) attachments still remaining. The *Sakadagami's* body is basically a higher purification stage of the subtle Qi body that *Srotapannas* have attained. A *Sakadagami* can enjoy the peace of dhyana whenever they wish, and has a higher mental emptiness realization than the *Srotapanna*, but is still restricted to the subtle plane. At this stage, however, you will be largely free of attachments to sensual desires (lust, greed, etc.), ill will (such as berating others, criticizing them or exposing them to ridicule), dreams, worries and imaginations. You will still be ruled by your ingrained habit energies, however, and the ways by which you usually react as life unfolds.]

1. "Ananda, those disciples who have purified the skandha of sensation and are no longer assailed by troublesome worries (afflictions or anxieties) may become enamored of this samadhi state of perfect clarity. In this condition, they may be tempted to concentrate on sharpening their faculties for skillfully advancing. At this time Deva Mara (a heavenly being – *asura* - who causes delusions) will exploit this situation by entering the body of a bystander, using him to preach the dharma, and unaware of his possession he will claim to have attained the supreme *nirvana*. He will approach the ambitious practitioner and assume the pulpit seat to teach (explain) the dharma. In an instant, the possessed man may enable the ambitious practitioner to see him alternately appear as a monk, as Indra, a woman or a nun, or his body might emit light in a

dark room. The practitioner will become beguiled and fooled into thinking that this man is a bodhisattva, and believe what he says. His mind will thus waver, and he will then end up breaking the monastic rules and covertly indulge in worldly desires. The man will be fond of speaking about coming calamities, fortunate events, and unusual things. He may also predict the appearance of Buddhas in certain places, and speak of catastrophic fires, strife and wars thus frightening people and causing them to ruin their family fortunes for no reason. This is the case of ghosts becoming maras in their old age and then coming to confuse and disturb (harass and trouble) practitioners. When the maras are weary of their deeds, they will abandon the victim's body, and then the ambitious practitioner and his possessed master will get into trouble with the law. You must be aware of these dangers to avoid returning to *samsara*. If you become deluded and ignorantly follow this path, you will eventually fall into the relentless hells.

[This explains that a deva enters your brain, not a bystander's body (this expedient lie was said or edited into the sutra later so as not to frighten people), and makes you see visions or gives you teachings or information about future events, causing you to mistakenly believe you are enlightened. The pulpit refers to your brain stem. If ever the onslaught of devas proves too much throughout this twelve-year process you might try reciting any special mantra given to you by your master, recite prayers asking for a bit of relief. Since devas often live in religious statues, you might also cause a bit of restraint by removing any excessive number of statue homes from your own home or by going into secluded retreat (which most masters do) whereby the only ones who will then bother to come and work on you, because of the now greater inconvenience, will be those devoted to the process.]

2. "Ananda, once again, those disciples who have purified the skandha of sensation and are no longer assailed by troublesome worries and false anxieties can now cultivate a state of perfect dhyana. In the midst of samadhi, they may feel a mental urge to roam abroad. Projecting their thoughts, they may crave new experiences (adventure). Deva Mara will take advantage of the practitioner's condition to possess an innocent bystander, using him to preach the dharma, and unaware that he is possessed he will claim that he has attained supreme *nirvana*. The possessed man will approach the

restless practitioner to teach the dharma. Without changing his own appearance, his listeners might suddenly visualize themselves as seated on precious lotus blossoms with their bodies surrounded by golden rays of light. They will gather to hear the words of the possessed man, and most of the listeners will have these extraordinary experiences so that in their ignorance they mistake him for a bodhisattva with the result that the practitioner will then give in to dissolute habits and violate the monastic rules, secretly indulging in carnal desires. The possessed man will be fond of announcing the appearance of Buddhas in the world and identify them by person and place as incarnating Buddhas and bodhisattvas. Seeing these events, the fascinated practitioner will be bewitched and succumb to perverted views, thereby destroying the seeds of enlightenment wisdom. This is a case of old drought ghosts becoming maras to confuse and disturb (harass and trouble) practitioners. When weary of their sport, the drought ghosts will depart the body of the possessed individual, and then the ambitious practitioner and his possessed master will get into trouble with the law. You must be aware of these dangers to avoid returning to *samsara*. If you become deluded and ignorantly follow this path, you will eventually fall into the relentless hells.

[This individual may be tempted into playing with the resultant mental powers he achieves from a subtle body or Causal body attainment that can give other people certain visionary experiences (images projected into their consciousness) and in so indulging turns away from the enlightenment path and pursuit of true *bodhi*.]

3. "Continuing, those disciples who have purified the skandha of sensation and are no longer assailed by troublesome worries (afflictions or anxieties) can now cultivate a state of perfect dhyana. In the midst of samadhi, they may conceive a craving for uniting with it and then concentrate all their efforts on this desire. At this time, Deva Mara will exploit this situation to possess an innocent bystander, who will begin to preach the dharma, and unaware that he is possessed, even claim to have attained supreme *nirvana*. He will approach the seeker of union, and assuming the pulpit, begin to teach the dharma. Without transforming his appearance or that of his listeners, he will be able to open the minds of his audience even before they hear him speak. Their minds may jump from internal mental experience to experience such that some will seem able to see

their former lives, know other people's thoughts, peer into hell, or know all sorts of good and evil events in the world. Some will spontaneously become able to chant verses or recite sutras. They will all become ecstatic with these new experiences and feel they have experienced something unprecedented. The practitioner in his delusion will be deceived into taking the possessed man as a bodhisattva and become enamored of him (they will become beguiled and believe all he says). He will then end up breaking the monastic rules and secretly indulging in carnal desires. The possessed man will classify the Buddhas and bodhisattvas as greater and lesser, earlier and later, real and false, and male and female. When the practitioner sees these things, he may become brainwashed and easily become a heretic. This is a case of goblins who in their old age become maras to confuse and disturb (harass and trouble) the practitioner. After the goblins tire and become weary of their sport, they will depart the possessed man's body. Then the practitioner and his possessed master will both get in trouble with the law. You must be aware of these dangers to avoid returning to *samsara*. If you become deluded and ignorantly follow this path, you will eventually fall into the relentless hells.

[Because he wants to unite with samadhi, this individual succumbs to the temptation of continually playing with some of its resultant mental powers he gains by giving people certain visionary experiences (projected images).]

4. "Continuing, those disciples who have purified the skandha of sensation and are no longer assailed by troublesome worries (afflictions or anxieties), can now cultivate a state of perfect dhyana. In the midst of samadhi, they may conceive a desire to investigate the root origin of things and their transformations from beginning to end. They may intensify the keenness of their mental investigation as they strive to analyze things in detail until satisfied. Deva Mara will take advantage of the practitioner's condition to possess an innocent bystander, who will preach the Buddha-dharma, and unaware that he is possessed, claim that he has attained supreme *nirvana*. He will approach the practitioner who seeks to know the sources of things, and assuming the pulpit, will teach the dharma. With an air of awe-inspiring authority, the possessed man will win over the seeker and gain the submission of his listeners before he even speaks a single word. He may declare to all the people that the Buddha's *nirvana*,

bodhi and *dharmakaya* are there before them in the form a physical body. He may say that their own flesh and blood bodies, transmitted father to son generation after generation, are identical with the eternal *dharmakaya* of the Buddha that is permanent and never ending. He may say that what his listeners see around them is the Buddha-land, and that there are no other pure-lands nor another golden Buddha-body. The practitioner will believe him absolutely, lose his initial faith and resolve, and submit to him body and soul, believing to have attained an unprecedented revelation. He and the other deluded listeners will mistakenly take him for a true bodhisattva. They will resultantly pursue his ideas, end up breaking the monastic rules (conduct rules of purity and discipline) and secretly indulge in carnal desires. The possessed man may be fond of saying that the eyes, ears, nose, and tongue are all pure-lands and that the sexual organs of men and women are the true abodes of *bodhi* and *nirvana*. The ignorant will believe these perverse teachings. This is a case of poisonous ghosts who in their old age become maras to confuse and disturb (harass and trouble) the practitioner. When the ghosts become weary of their sport, they depart the possessed man's body, and then disciple and his possessed master will both get in trouble with the law of the land. You must be aware of these dangers to avoid returning to *samsara*. If you become deluded and ignorantly follow this path, you will eventually fall into the relentless hells.

[Using his Causal body the practitioner wants to know the origin of things from beginning to end by investigating various planes of existence. He also knows that the ultimate root source of the human body is the absolute nature and is a *dharmakaya* manifestation in the world of phenomena, so he therefore gives himself permission to freely indulge in hedonism rather than continue to follow the rules of propriety.]

5. "Continuing, those disciples who have purified the skandha of sensation and are no longer assailed by troublesome worries (afflictions or anxieties) can now cultivate a state of perfect dhyana. In the midst of samadhi, they may conceive a desire for spiritual intercourse (discussion) with others. Their minds may then wander the universe searching and seeking for profound insights. Deva Mara will take advantage of this condition to possess an innocent bystander, who will approach the practitioner and preach the dharma, and unaware of the mara, claim that he has attained supreme *nirvana*.

He will go to the seeker of spiritual communion, and assuming the pulpit, will teach the dharma. He may cause his listeners to temporarily see him as a hundred or a thousand years old. His listeners will feel great affection for him, and becoming devoted followers, will serve him all manner of food and drink, clothing, bedding, and medicine. They will never tire of waiting on him. They will all believe that he was their former teacher and wise advisor in a previous life. They will develop a spiritual attachment to him, sticking to him like glue, and feel as if they have obtained some unprecedented experience. The practitioner in his delusion will believe him to be a bodhisattva and mistakenly follow the other's thinking so as to violate the monastic rules and secretly indulge in carnal desires. The possessed man will be given to claiming that in a previous past life and particular incarnation he saved such and such a person, or that such and such a person was a wife or brother in a past life and that he comes again to save them. He will claim that he and his followers together will later go to such and such a world to make offerings to such and such a Buddha. Or he may speak of radiant heavens where a Buddha now dwells and other Tathagatas come to for rest. The ignorant will believe this nonsense and lose their original clear minds. This is a case of pestilence ghosts becoming maras in their old age and coming to confuse and disturb (harass and trouble) the practitioner. When they become weary of their sport (misdeeds), they will abandon the victim's body and then disciple and his possessed master will both get in trouble with the law of the land. You must be aware of these dangers to avoid returning to *samsara*. If you become deluded and ignorantly follow this path, you will eventually fall into the relentless hells.

[Because he has the desire to talk about spiritual topics with others, this individual can be tempted into gathering students around himself, and due to his incomplete attainment spreads mistaken teachings.]

6. "Continuing, those disciples who have purified the skandha of sensation and are no longer assailed by troublesome worries (afflictions or anxieties) can now cultivate a state of perfect dhyana. In the midst of samadhi, they may conceive a desire for deeper absorption and want to dwell in secluded places to experience peace and quiet. Deva Mara will take advantage of the practitioner's condition to possess an innocent bystander, who will preach the

dharma, and unaware that he is possessed, claim to have attained supreme *nirvana*. He will approach the practitioner, and assuming the pulpit, teach the dharma. He will cause his listeners to each (think they) know their own karma, or he might (for instance) tell a certain man that, although he has not yet died, he is already due to become an animal. (Demonstrating his superpowers), he may then tell another to stand on the first person's 'tail,' and the first man will indeed be unable to stand up. On seeing this, his listeners will greatly admire (his supernatural powers) and submit themselves to him. If someone has a thought, the man will know it immediately. He may order them to follow intense austerities (ascetic practices) that go beyond (exceed) the Buddha's precepts, and will slander monks and curse their followers. He will expose people's private affairs, not sparing them any ridicule. He will be fond of foretelling coming good fortune or disasters, and his predictions will be accurate down to the smallest detail. This is a case of a powerful ghost who has become a mara in his old age and comes to confuse and disturb (harass and trouble) the practitioner. When the mara is weary of his sport, he will abandon the victim's body, and then both the practitioner and his possessed master will get in trouble with the law of the land. You must be aware of these dangers to avoid returning to *samsara*. If you become deluded and ignorantly follow this path, you will eventually fall into the relentless hells.

[Because he craves ascetic seclusion in order to peacefully enjoy dhyana away from the disturbances of people and society, this individual might promote excessive extremes in ascetic practices, which is something Buddha warned against, and might use his superpowers in a condescending way that disparages people (since he thinks himself better than others).]

7. "Continuing, those disciples who have purified the skandha of sensation and are no longer assailed by troublesome worries (afflictions or anxieties) can now cultivate a state of perfect dhyana. In the midst of samadhi, they may conceive a desire for deeper knowledge and understanding of their past lives. Deva Mara will take advantage of the practitioner's condition to possess an innocent bystander, who will preach the dharma, and unaware of his possession, claim that he has attained supreme *nirvana*. He will approach the place where the disciple dwells, and assuming the pulpit, begin to teach the dharma. There in the assembly, the

possessed man may (for instance) show that he unexpectedly finds a large precious pearl. Sometimes the mara will appear in the form of an animal that holds a pearl or other precious gems, heavenly documents and registers, and all manner of unusual things in its mouth. He will give these things to his listeners and afterwards again possess them. He might also attempt to deceive his listeners by burying a pearl under the ground that illuminates the surrounding area. His entire audience will consider this most extraordinary. The possessed man might eat only medicinal herbs, abstaining from food, or he may live on only a single hemp seed or grain of wheat per day, but with the sustaining help of the maras he will remain strong and healthy. He will slander the monks and curse their followers, without sparing them any ridicule. He will reveal the secret locations of treasures and the retreats of holy men. Those who go there will actually meet strange persons. This is a case of a ghost or spirit of the forests, earth, cities, rivers, or mountains becoming a mara in their old age. He may encourage licentiousness and violation of the Buddha's rules (precepts), or secretly indulge in the five desires (arising from the objects of the five senses) with followers. He may subsist on just wild vegetation alone and engage in erratic behavior in order to confuse and disturb (harass and trouble) the practitioner. When the mara is weary of his sport, he will abandon the victim's body, and then disciple and his possessed master will both get in trouble with the law of the land. You must be aware of this danger and avoid returning to the cycle of *samsara*. You must be aware of these dangers to avoid returning to *samsara*. If you become deluded and ignorantly follow this path, you will eventually fall into the relentless hells.

[Because he deeply craves knowledge of past lives and other hidden knowledge, this individual is tempted into an excessive pursuit of secret information and methods for how to do unusual things.]

8. "Continuing, those disciples who have purified the skandha of sensation and are no longer assailed by troublesome worries (afflictions or anxieties) can now cultivate a state of perfect dhyana. In the midst of samadhi, they may conceive a desire for spiritual powers and all manner of transformations, so they will seek to investigate the source of transformations in their search for supernatural powers. Deva Mara will take advantage of the practitioner's condition to possess an innocent bystander, who will

preach the dharma, unaware of his possession, and claim that he has attained supreme *nirvana*. He will approach the seeker of spiritual insight, and assuming the pulpit, teach the dharma. He may hold a flame in his hand and, grasping a portion of it, put a pinch of flame over the head of each of his listeners. The flames may be several feet high, but will not give off heat and will not burn the people. He may also walk on water just as if it were dry land, or sit motionless in midair. He may slip into a bottle or a bag, or even walk through walls without any obstacle. However, knives and weapons can affect him. He may claim to be a Buddha, and though he is a layman, dares to receive the obeisance of monks. He will slander the Buddha's rules of discipline and curse the followers. He will expose people's private affairs (shortcomings), sparing no ridicule. He will be fond of boasting of his supernatural powers and self-mastery. He may cause his listeners to see visions of Buddha-lands, which are false illusions (he creates) without any reality. He may praise acts of licentiousness (the indulgence of lust) and encourage licentious behavior (conduct) which he uses as methods for transmitting his teachings. This is a case of powerful nature spirits of the mountains, seas, winds, rivers, earth, or a demon of the plant kingdom who has evolved over countless kalpas, or a Naga, or rishi (seer) who has been reborn as a demon, or the case of a dying immortal's (seer's) incorruptible body being possessed by other ghosts who become demons in their old age, come to confuse and disturb (harass and trouble) the practitioner. When these demons become weary of their sport, they abandon their victim's body. The practitioner and his possessed master will then get into trouble with the law of the land. You must be aware of these dangers to avoid returning to *samsara*. If you become deluded and ignorantly follow this path, you will eventually fall into the relentless hells.

[Because he craves supernatural powers, this individual tries to master various functional capabilities of the mind and pursues the seat of all sorts of transformations rather than search for the essence of his mind, and thus turns away from pursuing true *bodhi* and the enlightenment path.]

9. "Continuing, those disciples who have purified the skandha of sensation and are no longer assailed by troublesome worries (afflictions or anxieties) can now cultivate a state of perfect dhyana. In the midst of samadhi, they may conceive a desire for extinction in

nirvana (they crave to experience permanent cessation), so they penetratingly investigate the nature of transformations in a search for profound emptiness. Deva Mara may take advantage of the practitioner's condition to possess an innocent bystander, who will then preach the dharma, and unaware of his possession, claim to have attained supreme *nirvana*. He will approach the practitioner, and assuming the pulpit, preach the dharma to the assembled. His physical body may suddenly disappear without any trace, and then suddenly reappear and then vanish again at will. Or he may make his body appear as transparent as crystal, or his limbs may release the fragrance of sandalwood. Or his excrement and urine may appear like rock candy. He might slander the Buddhist precepts and despise all monks and nuns. He might preach that the doctrine of causality is invalid, deny there is an afterlife and reincarnation, and deny the distinction between worldly and saintly states. Though he has realized emptiness, he secretly indulges in sexual desires and holds that followers who likewise indulge will also be able to attain emptiness wherein there is no cause and effect. This is a case of the subtle essence of an eclipse of the sun, gold, jade, and supernatural herbs, unicorns, phoenixes, turtles, and cranes, which surviving for tens of thousands of years has become a spirit, and who in its old age becomes a mara to confuse and disturb (harass and trouble) the practitioner. When they are weary of their sport, they abandon their victim. The practitioner and his possessed master will then both get into trouble with the law of the land. You must be aware of this these dangers to avoid returning to *samsara*. If you become deluded and ignorantly follow this path, you will eventually fall into the relentless hells.

[Because he craves perfect extinction, this individual tries to use emptiness as an antidote to both body and mind, and due to samadhi attainments discovers various ways to make the body become empty such as through disassembly or transparency. He turns from the pursuit of true *bodhi* and the enlightenment path.]

10. "Continuing, those disciples who have purified the skandha of sensation and are no longer assailed by troublesome worries (afflictions or anxieties) can now cultivate a state of perfect dhyana. In the midst of samadhi they may conceive a desire for longevity, and may start painstakingly investigating the subtleties of immortality, seeking to exchange the mortal state for an eternal physical life. Deva

Mara will take advantage of the practitioner's condition to possess an innocent bystander, who will preach the dharma, and unaware that he is possessed, claim that he has attained supreme *nirvana*. He will approach the disciples, and assuming the pulpit seat, and begin to teach the dharma. He may declare he can (quickly) travel to and from distant places at will, and will sometimes journey ten thousand miles and return in the blink of an eye with items fetched from those faraway regions. Or he may tell someone to run from one side of a small room to the other, and through his abilities, it will seem as if the man could not reach the opposite wall even if he ran for years. These things will inspire faith in his listeners who will mistakenly believe that he is a Buddha. He may proclaim that all living things are his children, that he gave birth to all Buddhas, that he appears in the world to save others, that he is the primal Buddha and requires no spiritual practice to be so. This Deva Mara may be a jealous female *chamunda* spirit from the Ishvara heaven, or a male 'consumer of vitality' spirit from the Four Deva Kings heaven who has come to take advantage of the practitioner's meditative state when his mind is not steadfast in order to consume his vitality. These heavenly deluders may not have to possess another man, but may appear directly to the practitioner as one wielding a vajra to bestow longevity on the practitioner or appear as a beautiful girl to seduce him and thereby exhaust his vitality before a year is out. The practitioner may then start mumbling to himself as if talking to a ghost. If he fails to recognize these demons, he will usually get in trouble with the law, and will probably die from depletion before his punishment is carried out. In this way the practitioner is harassed and even brought to the point of death. You must be aware of these dangers to avoid returning to *samsara*. If you become deluded and ignorantly follow this path, you will eventually fall into the relentless hells.

[Because he craves longevity, this individual can be tempted into a life consumed with immortality seeking, and might thus pursue methods he discovers through his research of the life (wind) element that make actions seem faster or slower (prolonged).

On a practical level, for initiates undergoing the Kundalini Awakening various devas will appear to the men and women as naked desirables, which is meant to make them give rise to sexual desire. This is done so that their Yang Qi arises to help open up Qi channels. If those practitioners give into masturbation or sexual dissipation (through regular sex) because of these visions they will lose their energy.

The devas all want to practice this type of deception on you so they will use all sorts of methods to see if they can find a practitioner who is foolish enough to let them practice sexual visions in them wherein the individual finally gives in, and then harms his own body due to excess. This will cause the practitioner to exhaust his vitality within a short period of time due to semen loss, so avoid this. There are no devas or devas that desire sex with you or are having sex with you; the imaginary karmamudras one sees are all false projections into your mind. You can certainly use sexual cultivation in the path if you have a partner of the opposite sex (sexual cultivation/intercourse is the quickest way to move your vital Qi energy in a substantial way), but only if you have an enlightened master who has sanctioned your efforts and oversees the process. This is superior to succumbing to these fake visions and engaging in masturbation, which would never end until your vitality is exhausted and you have permanently harmed your body and your cultivation.]

"Ananda, know that during the Dharma ending age that these ten mara-states may afflict the practitioners of my dharma. Some demons may possess human bodies, and some may manifest themselves in their own form. They will all claim they have already accomplished the correct all pervasive awareness and will advocate lustful desires and violate the moral precepts and rites of the Buddhist order. From demon master to demon disciple this licentiousness will be transmitted, and in this way practitioners' minds will become deluded by this type of evil influence. After a few lives or hundreds of generations, they turn even sincere practitioners entirely into followers of the demons. After they die, they are bound to end up as one of the demonic hordes, and not having true knowledge, will fall into the relentless hells.

"Ananda, there is no need for you to enter *nirvana* at this time. Although you have completed your attainment to the stage beyond study (you have reached enlightenment), you must express your compassion by being willing to reenter the world during the Dharma ending age to deliver those living beings who have the right mind and faith so that they will not be possessed by maras but will obtain proper knowledge and views. I have already rescued you from the cycle of birth and death, and by carrying out my order you will be repaying the Buddha's kindness.

"Ananda, these ten phenomena that may occur in dhyana are all the product of interactions between the skandha of conception with meditative mental efforts (they can be achieved due to a Causal body attainment that is the stage of an *Anagamin*). Ignorant and deluded practitioners are unable to evaluate their level of accomplishments. In their confusion they cannot distinguish these states (fail to recognize them) when they manifest, and then may wrongly claim that they have attained sainthood. For uttering such a great lie they will fall into the relentless hells. In the Dharma ending age, after my *nirvana*, all you disciples must transmit my teachings to all living things for the sake of their enlightenment. Do not allow Deva Mara to take advantage of you, but be on guard and strive to realize the supreme Tao."

The Ten Mara-States of the Skandha of Volition - [Generating the Supra-Causal body also known as the Dharma, Clear Light or Universal body composed of Later Heavenly Qi/Prana]

"Ananda, as the disciples cultivate samadhi and free themselves from the skandha of conception, they will become free of ordinary delusive thinking (dreamlike thoughts will have been dissolved away), and their mind will always be the same whether they are awake or asleep. Their empty mind (free of thoughts) will be as still and clear as a cloudless sky, and devoid of the shadow of coarse sense impressions. Everything in the world—the earth together with its mountains and rivers—will appear in their mind as do reflections in a bright mirror, coming without sticking and vanishing without leaving a trace. They will receive (perceive impressions) and reflect with perfect response, able to react to externals unfettered by any old habits. All there is will be a single pure essential reality.

"Now the root source of life and death will be fully revealed. They will be able to see the twelve classes of living things throughout the ten directions in all their varieties, and although they do not yet understand the source of their existence, they will see that they share a common basis of life. It is like a wavering haze (a shimmering and fluctuating mirage)—pure and transparent but whirling about—that disturbs the mind's purity and which is (also) the ultimate cause of sense perceptions (the ultimate pivot point of sense faculties and sense objects). This is called the skandha of volition (action that passes on its effects). If these mirage-like (clear but wavering) disturbances are allowed to revert to their original clarity, then once they clarify (purify) their original habits, it is like the passing of ripples that settle to leave behind clear water. This then may be called the cessation of the skandha of volition. In this way a man may transcend the defilement of sentient beings. If we examine the origin of this defilement, the root cause is subtle false thinking (very subtle, hidden false thinking)."

[**Editor:** The power of Life-Energy, which is ultimately the energy that composes your body and consciousness, animates all beings. This is ultimately the hidden creative force responsible for life and death, creation and destruction, the unfolding of fate due to karma built up in former lives, and our deep habits. The power or energy for the *alaya* Supra-Causal plane is Life-energy (Later Heavenly Qi), and it ultimately empowers the whole volition skandha process of conception, growth, birth, mental development, etc. All these forces belong to the volition skandha of influences.

The volition skandha is also called the activities, impulses, volitional tendencies, compositional factors, predispositional or mental formations skandha. It is conventionally identified as (paired with) the concomitant mental attainment of the Supra-Causal (Dharma or Clear Light) body achievement, and is also known as the *alaya* consciousness attainment. The volition skandha or *alaya* energy includes (always moving) continuous natural forces related to basic life functions such as the processes of transformation including growth and decay. It includes habitual predispositions or tendencies of thought that are the karma from previous lives, and acts of will connected with our sense of "I am-ness."

Thus the conditioning forces that shape us, the on-going forces of birth and death, and the surging forces of destiny, rebirth and transformation within the realm of *samsara* all belong to this skandha—the basic hidden formational energy of life's existence. The composite volition skandha or *alaya* energies of the Supra-Causal ("universal" or "cosmic") plane include the driving force of life itself, which is a subtle form of energy that is very hard to detect.

This very subtle energy is said to be responsible for the very subtle sense of "I am" within consciousness that embodies desire because that subtle assertion "I am" contains within it the desire to be. The impulse "I am" within awareness is therefore called Power, Life-Energy or desire and this level of energy is what is ultimately responsible for life, although there is a higher level still. That higher level is the Primal, Primordial, Original or Earlier Heavenly Qi ("wind" or energy) plane that composes the Buddha body, *sambhogakaya* Enjoyment Body, or Body of Immanence.

In detaching from the type of *concealed, hidden, or hard to perceive* thoughts that comprise the volition skandha you can reach a clarity and stillness of mind where not only can you stop the movements within your body of your Qi life force (Qi circulations still to a halt), but your pulse can stop too. The resultant state of empty calmness and stillness (clear awareness) you can reach at this attainment level is why you can finally become able to perceive this subtle wavering disturbance in the mind-stream that is the energetic source of life and sense perceptions. It is a very subtle movement of energy in consciousness that gives rise to a spontaneous feeling of "I Am" within the deepest aspects of consciousness.

In other words, energy usually moves around in your brain to create thoughts, and all thoughts have the I-thought at their center. The I-thought is a very subtle, very fine thought that you normally ignore because it is almost invisible. The energy that produces it is also therefore colloquially said to be very refined. Only at this level of attainment where the mind is quiet can you see that I-thought related energy still moving within the brain. You usually never notice your I-thought at the center of your thinking and you therefore cannot notice this energy either.

In terms of consciousness explanations, if you can detach from that motive force of energy (an unsteadiness in the *alaya* consciousness) so that it settles and returns to its clear nature, you can transcend the volition skandha type of thoughts and reach the root of the *alaya* consciousness, namely the consciousness skandha. The root energy of the *alaya* consciousness is paired with the next level up, a level of energy that forms the Buddha body of Immanence that equates with Perfect and Complete Enlightenment. Attaining this body of Immanence out of the Supra-Causal energy is called "a revolution in the basis of the *alaya*." It is phrased that way to make you think that all these spiritual attainments have to deal with clearer realms of consciousness when they actually deal with just higher body attainments.

The normal explanation is that the life-force energy in its purest form is steady and still (hence Arhats often try to cultivate the samadhi of nothingness) while its movement produces the notion of individual consciousness and thoughts. This life-force energy is (supposedly) the energy of the universal *alaya* plane of being. It is the compositional energy/substance of the Supra-Causal body that corresponds to *nirvana* with remainder. As Sadguru Siddharameshwar Maharaj said, "those who have understood Brahman exist in the form of 'Life-Energy' (Chaitanya)." In this case he was taking Brahman to represent the *alaya* rather than absolute nature.

This energy is the *kundalini-shakti* sentient life-force taught by Gorakhnath in his explanation of the manifestation/appearance of living beings who evolutionarily develop out of the original essence. This energy is higher than all the subsequent realms, and contains them as their mother evolute so is therefore considered a composite realm. In terms of Qi, it is not the "nurturing Qi" or "karmic Qi" ("reward Qi") of Esoteric Buddhism but a derivative of the fundamental or primordial Qi ("Original Heavenly Qi") of Taoism, Hinduism and the Consciousness-Only school.

Just think of the universe as composed of energies that builds planes of existence transcending our own, and because a plane of existence exists then all the bodies within that plane are composed of that substance of higher energies. The attendant consciousness of those bodies is ordinary for that body vehicle and also powered by the workings of that substance or level of energy. Since the Supra-Causal plane transcends all lower life, that plane is the closest origin of life although not the ultimate energy source of the universe. Nevertheless we call it the realm of the Life-force energy. If we are just talking about the energy that comprises this life and body, we can also take this energy to ultimately be the fundamental energy of this Supra-Causal plane of existence that is higher than the subtle or Causal plane of existence.

If we want to talk about this in terms of consciousness, we have to invent fictitious correspondences to types of thought that are fine, finer and superfine, etc. and which supposedly correspond to progressively more subtle types of energy. But think: all the thoughts a sentient being has at their level of existence are actually composed of the same energy of that level of existence. There isn't any higher types of energy producing quieter or more subtle types of thought; that is just a skillful explanation meant to help you cultivate quieter states of mind that result when your Qi channels open due to all the meditation work you undertake. In the *Surangama Sutra* we use skillful means to create a dialogue of skandhas that represent different types of thought (coarse, fine, very fine, super fine) when Buddha actually wants you to understand that progress is related to body attainments whose compositional structures are composed of coarse, more subtle, much finer energy and so on.

Our volition skandha of thoughts (which corresponds to the *vijnanamaya kosha* of Hinduism, *alaya* consciousness of Buddhism, and Supra-Causal body) is not our true self or highest body aggregate possible. Buddhism calls the subtle I-am sense that arises within the volition skandha the seventh consciousness or "afflicted mind." The I-sense is ultimately behind the power of action and will, and because it is also associated with the volitional or impulsive factors of life it is the underlying cause of transmigration in the cosmos whereby beings take on different lives in a series of births and deaths.

To transcend the influence of this skandha (energy) wins one some degree of control over that process, such as the ability to chose one's next rebirth. In addition to the forces of birth and death, this skandha or type of thought is responsible for the functions of will, motivation and intention that are linked back to the concept of being an "I."

When cultivating through the volition skandha, you must work at abandoning any clinging to the I-notion (sense of I), which requires witnessing practice once again. You can also cultivate the samadhi of infinite consciousness and infinite nothingness where no thoughts appear. For progress at this stage you must detach from the I-thought consciousness (colloquially associated with your Supra-Causal body) and then afterwards transcend the entire *alaya* consciousness of existence by developing a higher body.

Actually, you just continue doing all the Yoga you did all

along to get to this stage, but wording it this way helps to continually encourage people to practice empty mind meditation. It brings everything back to a conversation about thoughts, quieter thoughts, more invisible thoughts, more subtle thoughts etc. that implies spirituality or progress is all about cultivating more clear states of mind. Wonderful!

The *alaya* or volition skandha attainment means reaching the stage of a full Arhat, which is the initial enlightenment (*nirvana* with remainder, also called *nirvana* with remaining dependency or the fourth dhyana) corresponding to the Clear Light, Dharma or Supra-Causal body mental realm, but you are not yet at the root source of all substances and energies. To realize the source energy of *alaya* consciousness, which is matched with a spiritual body of Later Heavenly Qi that is higher than the purified Qi of the Causal body, it is said that you must transcend your sense of transciency (limited lifespan and limited life extension) since it is the opposite of the continuously changing immortal substrate of composite energy at this level that is pure (remains immaculate) within its defilements (namely the lower realms built from it). Realizing the *alaya* is attaining *nirvana* with remainder (remaining dependency), but to realize your True Self or absolute nature you must take a further step to cultivate an even higher body attainment.

When you realize that *there is no one (no sentient being) who is actually thinking but just consciousness itself automatically spinning thoughts – a body vehicle "with mental operations we call consciousness generating thoughts" that is automatically operating on its own* - that realization can help you peacefully transcend through detachment the whole process of consciousness.

To say that consciousness understands something really means that an automatic machine, not an "actual independent soul being" (although we conventionally talk that way) has developed thoughts within its body vehicle so that it can comprehend, but that comprehension has no ultimate meaning since the understandings it weaves are all relatives rather than absolutes. It is relative and conditional knowledge rather than supreme, ultimate or absolute knowledge. Some evolutionary creation of the original nature can create knowledge that it uses to exist, that's all.

Knowledge itself is then the ultimate experiencer of everything as there is no real *atman*, self or living entity that is the doer or experiencer of any thought or action! A "Knowledge machine/vehicle" is experiencing knowledge, in effect talking to itself. Knowledge is talking to itself ... how is this not delusory? All this happens automatically to a "sentient entity" that we say has consciousness, but its functioning is actually like a machine. Understanding arises within that sentient machine, but there is really no such thing as a real being, ego, or life who understands. That creation is a conditional (not absolute or permanent) construction developed out of infinite interdependence. Even that being isn't an independent entity for it is created due to the existence of everything else.

Yes, there is a person, entity, self or being who understands, but what you take this to mean is not truly so. A "living being" is just another phenomenon within the universe. It is something that has consciousness, which is the ability to know due to forming thoughts (knowledge) and understanding them because of a memory so that it has more than simplistic reactions, but from a higher vantage that ability to know is just another phenomenal function in the universe relevant to its structure, like a chemical reaction, and there is no independently existing permanent soul (*true* living being) experiencing it. That "soul" experiencing knowledge is just a conditional materialistic construction. The *Diamond Sutra* of Buddhism tells you this over and over again.

In other words, there is truly no such real thing as an independent, conscious living being. Of course that is what we conventionally call ourselves, but what are we in the ultimate sense? We are a compositional structure that has formed within the original nature. We say there is a living being and of course there is a living being, but what is it? It is a conditionally created construct linked to everything else. This one can form knowledge while others cannot. Actually it is just as much an automatic machine or process that functions according to certain laws as any other phenomenon that has developed/evolved out of the original nature, and thus there isn't really a living being in the sense that you usually assume.

There is just a particular plane of energy that has evolutionarily developed into many phenomena including a particular body vehicle/vessel entity that spins thoughts of knowledge and self-awareness. Other phenomena don't have this capability. You call that a "sentient being," but it is not an immortal soul entity. That individual of course has I-thoughts, but when you think about it deeply you can realize that the "I-self" should actually refer to the one universal fundamental energy that is the ultimate source. That plane or fundamental energy, as the foundational source, is the hidden "I" or "self" of all phenomena and "sentient beings." It is the True Self, the fundamental self-nature, the absolute source. Everything that it turns into is just a phenomenon, function or appearance. Get it?

When one normally practices meditation by letting go of thoughts and keeping away from grasping entanglements by just watching them, eventually the mind quiets and reaches a state of relative emptiness where there are no longer coarse thoughts running about any more. Energy arises that begins the reinforcement of the inner subtle body. An empty mental state can be given up but the one who gives it up (the I-thought) remains. "I" remains as a witness to the empty mental state as long as you stay awake. There is still a superfine level/type of thoughts invisibly forming an I. To get through the *alaya* consciousness you must not only sometimes cultivate a state of "nothingness" or "thoughtlessness" (where the I-thought and all knowledge disappears) but then must leave behind (transcend) this inert vacuum-like state where thoughts don't stir. You have to transcend both the state of having thoughts or not having thoughts (thoughtlessness). You must go up one plane. When consciousness teachings are used to guide people, this is cultivating the "samadhi of neither thought nor no-thought." In terms of body teachings, this corresponds to the plane of Early Heavenly Qi.

All things in the universe are impermanent. The forces of birth and death are conventionally matched with the volition skandha (although they match with every plane of existence), but we use this correspondence-making to say that the thoughts within the *alaya* consciousness are impermanent and must always come and go. However, they are sometimes said to come and go within a clear base or container (pure consciousness) that is naturally absent of modifications, which you can therefore call pure unperturbed consciousness (or emptiness). That thoughtlessness of nothingness, where there isn't even an I-thought, is colloquially said to be the pure nature of the *alaya* consciousness that you experience through the samadhi of nothingness. Of course, this is just a way of speaking since consciousness is not a substance, and thus no-thought is not that substance in a state of non-movement being pure.

To reach such high experiences, enlightened Zen masters often ask students to try to mentally fathom the state of what they were like before their parents were born, meaning before they even existed and their creation was nil. What will your mental state be if you were annihilated so as to be non-existent? Any conceptual images of emptiness or thoughtlessness you conjure up are incorrect, but often help students make progress in training how to detach from thoughts through such ponderings. You cannot blank out consciousness to reach a state of empty mind (pristine awareness) but must dissolve thoughts by transcending them and letting them die down. The corresponding type of mind is a very clear consciousness, called pristine awareness.

If you could truly reach some state of non-existence or annihilation (absolute emptiness), how did your birth and existence arise in the first place? It just did though no one can trace the full sequence of cause and effect back to the first effusions from the changeless original nature. All anyone can say is that appearances will always arise but those phenomena simply cannot be said to *truly* be real (permanent, non-changing, everlasting). There are impermanent appearances destined to decay but what appears is *not real existence* (fundamental universal energy) that itself never alters or changes its nature.

To be like the original nature you therefore have to spiritually practice by residing in a transcending bodiless purity that never changes, a bodiless infinite purity (like clear awareness or empty mind) within which thoughts appear and then depart like all impermanent phenomena. Hence you must practice pristine awareness cultivation, namely emptiness meditation that doesn't grasp onto consciousness (thoughts) but just witnesses them. *In meditation practice, consciousness is supposed to imitate the nature of the original essence that is like space in that it doesn't change, and yet which allows things to arise within it, without interference, that only temporarily last.* This is why witnessing meditation is practiced as the spiritual path.

It is hard to penetrate through the volition skandha, and not doing so represents incomplete spiritual attainment – *nirvana* <u>with</u> a remainder. The physical correlate is that you haven't yet reached the higher plane of energy (corresponding to the Immanence body) that remains.

Now it is difficult to transcend the I-thought of the volition skandha (even if you cultivate the samadhi of infinite consciousness) just as it is difficult to transcend the intense desires and emotions experienced by those attaining a Causal body. The *alaya* consciousness of an individual always gives birth to thoughts, including the I-thought, unless you cultivate an ignorant samadhi of nothingness. How do you then transcend the volition skandha? In teachings you would naturally say that you need to keep cultivating detachment, non-grasping or emptiness, right?

By working to completely pass through the sensation skandha you will attain a Causal or Mental body and be able to achieve the third dhyana, which is also called "The Wonderful Blissful Ground of Separating from Joy." It has this name because with the Causal body attainment you can detach from the coarse stimulating joyous Qi that is an energetic characteristic of the first and second dhyana, namely the subtle body energy. Then you can experience a mental bliss of peacefulness, which means an emptiness of thoughts like space, but this isn't an absolute inertness of no-thought.

With the Causal body the mind has a pristine clarity like infinite space that lets all thoughts arise and be known. Because of that mental peacefulness the third dhyana is also called the "*ananda* (bliss) samadhi" within Hinduism according to Vyasa. The Causal body is extremely difficult to reach, so this stage is said to be "extremely hard to conquer" and is still slightly connected with the physical body.

An individual who attains the Causal body corresponding to the third dhyana attainment is no longer entirely conscious of (in most part ignores) their subtle and gross bodies though he will still use the gross and subtle bodies from the mental plane. When you see him or her eating, sleeping or drinking they appear ordinary from the outside, but actually they are primarily conscious of their Causal body. This is because they are residing in their Causal body unless they withdraw all their bodies into the physical shell, at which time they will seem to be more present rather than "empty."

Past this stage you can realize the "breath of life" *prana or energy* that is responsible for life. This Later Heavenly Qi can cause all things to come alive and can create living beings out of inert matter. It corresponds to a more fundamental, foundational stage of energy that is the Supra-Causal plane, although we pair this with the *alaya* consciousness and volition skandha in order to make the teachings about consciousness and hide the body connections. It is said that a master at this stage "is as if infinite energy personified," and can raise the dead or create new forms in different worlds breathing with life. This is the Supra-Causal plane, which is sometimes called original Qi, primordial Qi, or *real* kundalini Shakti whereas those terms properly belong to the next stage up. The third dhyana, however, is the Causal body plane of energy, called Shen energy by Taoism.

If you can cultivate and maintain the third dhyana for a long period of time, you can reach the stage where your life force can destroy all sicknesses within your body through the power of your Causal body. You can reach the Arhat stage of the *Anagamin* who does not have to be reborn in the human realm after death, but is reborn only in pure abodes (heavenly realms) where they can cultivate to achieve full Arhatship.

An *Anagamin* has a higher stage of spiritual attainment than the *Srotapanna* and *Sakadagami* (*Sakridagamin*), which makes him appear peaceful, content and without desire, but nonetheless still has a subtle clinging preference for positive experiences. This is still not initial enlightenment (the fourth dhyana) but this attainment corresponds to achieving the *purified* illusory body (Causal body) that makes you capable of realizing the next up *nirvana* stage of enlightenment.]

1. "Ananda, when practitioners practice *samatha* (one-pointed concentration) to obtain correct knowledge, their minds will eventually become settled and clear and will no longer be troubled by the ten classes of heavenly maras. Now they will be able look deeply into (thoroughly investigate) the origin of living things. After the origin of each class becomes apparent, they can observe the source of that continuous subtle (hard to detect), fleeting disturbance. If they then begin to indulge in misguided speculations about its source, they may fall into error through two theories concerning the non-existence of causality.

"The first errant theory is when the practitioner concludes that life originally appears without any fundamental cause because he can find no such cause in his investigation. Why is this? At this level he has already wiped out (destroyed) the mechanism of life, and by means of the eight hundred merits of the organ of sight, he can perceive all living things during 80,000 kalpas as reincarnating over and over again. Previous to these 80,000 kalpas he can see nothing (he can only see these 80,000 kalpas), and so he comes to the conclusion that all living things within the ten directions over the 80,000 kalpas arise without any cause (spontaneously), and as a result of this speculation he misses the Buddha's pervasive universal knowledge and falls into an unorthodox path that obscures his *bodhi*-nature.

"The second case is the practitioner who also concludes that life has appeared without any fundamental cause. In this case the man has perceived the root source of life and has always seen (the causality) that human beings gave birth to human beings and birds gave birth to birds; crows have always been black and cranes always white; human beings and devas have always stood upright while animals have walked on all fours; whiteness does not come from being washed, and blackness does not come from dyeing. He reasons that for 80,000 kalpas this (type of causality) has never varied and will be so even after his present body is no more. Since in extensively surveying matters (looking for an ultimate cause) he never previously found *bodhi*-nature in the process, he wonders how it could exist. He therefore concludes that there is no (ultimate) cause for the existence of life. Because of discriminating in this manner, he misses pervasive universal knowledge and falls into an unorthodox path that obscures his *bodhi*-nature.

"These two theories of the non-existence of causality (spontaneous generation without causality) are the first heresy.

[The practitioner concludes that life originally arose from no cause, but everything must arise from prior causes except the primal original nature, so he is in error.]

2. "Ananda, in their cultivation of samadhi, practitioners' minds are now concentrated and clear (settled) and can no longer be troubled (disturbed) by maras. In deeply investigating the origin of all classes of living beings, they can observe that the continuous subtle clear disturbance operates ceaselessly. If they speculate about it, they

can fall into four errant theories concerning universal permanence.

"The first is the practitioner who looks deeply into the nature of the mind and its objects (states) and finds that both are without cause. In his meditative investigation he becomes aware that over the next 20,000 kalpas all living things within the ten directions will still experience birth and death without ever being annihilated. He then takes this to indicate that the mind (and its states) are permanent.

"The second is the practitioner who looks deeply into the four primal elements—earth, fire, water, wind—and concludes that these elements are permanent in nature. His meditative investigations enable him to know that for the next 40,000 kalpas all living things in the ten directions undergo ceaseless births and deaths but throughout the process their bodies (of form composed of the five elements) are never destroyed, and takes this to indicate permanence.

"The third is the practitioner who looks deeply into the six *indriyas*—the eyes, ear, nose, tongue, body, and mind (sixth consciousness)—and the seventh consciousness (faculty of intelligence) and retention of memories, and then concludes that the source (*alaya* origin) of consciousness is permanent (eternal). Through meditative investigations, he can see that during the next 80,000 kalpas living beings ceaselessly cycle through the rounds of transmigrations and the origin of their consciousness always remains (is never destroyed). In thinking deeply on the nature of its continuation, he takes this to indicate permanence.

"The fourth kind of practitioner has already exhausted the source of the third skandha of conception. He has cut off the flow of his life force (he can now settle the life force component of his volition skandha), and since he has (also) cut off the thinking (conceptual) mind that is the source of thoughts, there is no more reason for thoughts to arise. Therefore he naturally comes to the conclusion that this is a state of non-production and non-destruction and that it constitutes permanence. From this conception of permanence, he [stops striving further and thus] misses the Buddha's pervasive universal knowledge and falls into an unorthodox path that obscures his *bodhi*-nature.

"These four theories of wrong permanence are the second heresy.

[All these theories of permanence deal with unbroken continuity of the life force in some way, rather than deal with the absolute nature which is the only permanent essence, and hence are wrong. For instance, because one might be able to view 80,000 previous lifetimes or 40 previous eons one might make the mistake of concluding that life is therefore eternal.]

3. "Continuing, in their cultivation of samadhi, practitioners' minds are now concentrated and clear (settled) and can no longer be troubled (disturbed) by maras. If they now deeply investigate (look into) the origin of the various classes of living things and observe the source of the continuous subtle (fleeting) disturbance that operates ceaselessly, they may incorrectly speculate and fall into one of the four kinds of distorted errant views concerning permanence and impermanence.

"The first is the practitioner who observes that his own wondrous clear mind pervades the ten directions and then takes it to be his own ultimate spiritual self. In finding that his own self, which is pristine and unchanging, pervades the ten directions, but since within this luminous and immutable nominal self all living things are born and die by themselves [all beings appear within his limitless awareness but their fates of living and dying seem independent of it; the pristine awareness substance itself did not participate in the events but only provided the background within which they appeared], he therefore speculatively concludes that his mind is permanent, whereas all that which is born and dies is impermanent.

"The second type of practitioner, instead of looking into his own mind, contemplates realms in the ten directions as countless as the sands of the Ganges, and concludes that those which are destroyed in the kalpa of destruction are impermanent while those which are spared are therefore permanent.

"The third type of practitioner observes his own mind and finds it to be subtle and mysterious; it is similar to molecules that circulate everywhere in the ten directions whose own nature remains unchanged yet which can cause the body to be born and then die. He regards any indestructible nature as his permanent self, and everything subject to birth and death or which flows forth from this self he calls impermanent.

"The fourth type of practitioner realizes that the skandha of conception has been extinguished (the practitioner attains the Later Heaven body that transcends the Causal body), but observes the ceaseless flow of the volition skandha and concludes that this (continuous flow) represents permanence. Since his first three skandhas—form, sensation, and conception—have already been exhausted (transcended), he calls them impermanent.

"Because of these speculations on (differentiations between) permanence and impermanence, he falls into unorthodox paths and obscures his *bodhi*-nature.

"These four theories of wrong permanence are the third heresy.

[There are several types of errors regarding the view that the self is partially permanent (eternal) and impermanent (non-eternal) such as reasoning that matter is impermanent but consciousness is eternal, oneself is impermanent but the first being present in existence must be the Creator and thus eternal, that one is impermanent because of being corrupted by errant mental factors and so on.]

4. "Continuing, in their cultivation of samadhi, practitioners' minds are now concentrated and clear (settled) and can no longer be troubled (disturbed) by maras. They can look deeply into (investigate) the origins of living beings and in this clear state can observe the source of the subtle continuous disturbance (which is the *alaya*). If they then begin to make speculations (about it) on the basis of different distinctions, they may fall into four types of errant theories regarding the finite and infinite.

"The first is the practitioner who speculates that the origin of life (the *alaya*) flows on ceaselessly without end. He judges that the past and future (of life) are finite but the continuity of his mind (of awareness which does not cease) is infinite.

"The second is the practitioner, who contemplating an interval of 80,000 kalpas can see living things in that long period of time, but looking into the time prior to that period he cannot see or hear anything. He then speculatively concludes that the period before the 80,000 kalpas is infinite and that the time where there are living things he deems finite.

"The third practitioner speculates that his own pervasive knowing is universal (reaching everywhere) and his nature infinite. Since all other beings appear within his field of awareness, though he is not aware of their knowledge (their minds), he concludes that they do not (also) possess infinite minds but are finite in nature. [Note: Your own Self is the Self of all, but understanding that you are everywhere does not mean you obtain the magical ability to see through everyone's eyeballs.]

"The fourth practitioner looks deeply into the fourth skandha of volition to the point that it becomes empty. Based on his observation, he concludes that each living being partly exists and partly does not, and so concludes that everything in the world is half finite and half infinite.

"Thus, all of these practitioners who discriminate between the finite and the infinite fall into an unorthodox path and obscure their *bodhi*-nature.

"These four theories of finitude and infinity are the fourth heresy.

5. "Continuing, in their cultivation of samadhi, practitioners' minds are now concentrated and clear (settled) and can no longer be troubled (disturbed) by maras. If they look deeply into (deeply investigate) the origin of living things and observe the source of the continuous subtle disturbance in this clear state, by engaging in speculation on what they observe they may fall into four categories of erroneous views concerning the existence of non-dying.

"The first type of practitioner looks into the origins of the process of transformation. Where he observes change (movement) he calls that transformation, where he observes continuity he calls that constancy (preservation or sustenance), where he is able to see something appear (arise) he calls that birth (creation, manifestation or production), and when he no longer observes something he calls that destruction (death or dissolution). When something preserves its nature during the process of transformation he calls it increase (growth, preservation or sustenance); when something is discontinuous through the process of transformation he calls it decrease. Wherever creation appears (when something arises) he calls it existence; non-existence is wherever disappearance occurs. This is all the result of exercising his powers of discrimination. If someone comes seeking for the dharma and asks him for teachings, he says: 'At this moment I am simultaneously alive and dead, both existent and not existent, both increasing and decreasing.' With these kinds of wild statements he confuses his listeners.

[The practitioner essentially discovers the three *gunas* of *sattva*, *rajas* and *tamas* - the three phases of the uninterrupted flow of the process of change and transformation that rules the appearance or existence of phenomena. The three phase of beginning-intermediate-ending can also be described as (1) birth, arising, creation, appearance, production, manifestation, emanation, (2) continuance, preservation, duration, maintenance, or sustenance and (3) dissolution, cessation, death, or disappearance. These three phases are also symbolized by Brahma the creator, Vishnu the preserver and Shiva the destroyer.]

"The second type of practitioner carefully scrutinizes his mind, and finds that thoughts are (ultimately) non-existent. When people come asking for teachings, he answers with the one word 'non-existence.' [Without thoughts, nothing exists.] Apart from this, he says nothing else.

"The third type of practitioner carefully scrutinizes his mind, and finds that thoughts are existent (since their appearance can be observed). When people come asking for teachings, he answers with the one word 'existence.' [Because thoughts arise, appearance and beingness are there.] Apart from existence, he has nothing to say.

"The fourth type of practitioner perceives both existence and non-existence, but because of this duality his mind is confused. When asked to explain his viewpoint, he answers: 'Existence encompasses non-existence, but non-existence does not include existence,' and all manner of nonsense that defies reason. By discriminating in this way, he creates confusion and nonsense, and thus, falls into heresy and obscures his *bodhi*-nature.

"The fifth heresy are the four absurd notions concerning the non-dying and related false theories.

[The practitioners see that thoughts arise because life force flows through the body's thousands of cranial nerves that contain names, labels and memories and without these circuits it is just pure energy. Thus with non-knowing there is just "non-existence." That energy may be contaminated or colored by habit energies that are carried over life-to-life to produce specific neural pathways. Since the energy flows through the nerves to produce names, labels and appearances, he says there is "existence" since there is knowing.]

6. "Continuing, in their cultivation of samadhi, practitioners' minds are now concentrated and clear (settled) and can no longer be troubled (disturbed) by maras. Now, looking deeply into the origin of living things and observing the continuous subtle disturbance (life force) in this clear state, if the practitioner begins to exercise speculation on the endless flowing of life, he may fall into error through the confused idea that a bodily form remains after death.

"He may strongly identify with his body and claim that physical form is himself. Or he may perceive himself as perfectly encompassing all realms and therefore claim that he possesses (contains) form. Or he may feel that the external conditions that present themselves are contingent upon himself and therefore claim that form belongs to him. Or he may believe that he relies on (exists within) the continuous flow of *samskara* (form) and claim that he resides within form.

"All of the above arise from the belief that (whether or not he has attained the form, subtle, Causal or Supra-Causal body) some type of bodily form will still continue to exist after his death. In this way, the deluded practitioner goes round and round, postulating sixteen cases of the existence of form (due to wrong conclusions involving the first four skandhas/bodies). Then he may speculate that fundamentally afflictions and *bodhi* coexist side by side without contradiction. Because of the erroneous view that (some type of) bodily form exists after death, he falls into an unorthodox path and obscures his *bodhi*-nature.

"This is the sixth heresy, which postulates the wrong theories of the existence of (some) bodily form among the five skandhas after death.

[One mistake is taking the universal *alaya* energy as his self and associating it with any body of form, which is a limitation. The *alaya* remains even though personal form disappears; personal "form" can mean the physical body (form skandha), subtle body (sensation skandha), Causal body (conception skandha) or Supra-Causal body (volition skandha). However, in terms of our absolute nature, you are neither formless or with form. No thought remains in the absolute nature so true *bodhi* (enlightenment or *nirvana*) is called the stateless state, thoughtless thought … nothing is there otherwise something would happen there. Form and formlessness don't remain. It exists without doing anything, without any prop or support whatsoever, and is the *real* "You" or True Self.]

7. "Continuing, in their cultivation of samadhi, practitioners' minds are now concentrated and clear (settled) and can no longer be troubled (disturbed) by maras. Now, looking deeply into the origin of living things and observing the source of the continuous subtle disturbance in this clear state, if the practitioner exercises speculation upon the fact he has first eliminated the other skandhas of form,

sensation, and conception (as his self and so reasons that the fourth skandha may be extinguished/transcended in the same way as the first three before), he may fall into error believing that he will have no bodily form whatsoever after his death (since the next higher state is considered nothingness).

"Seeing that his physical body no longer had a cause when the skandha of form was extinguished; seeing that the mind had no more attachments (was free of bondage) when the skandha of conception was extinguished; and knowing that the end of the skandha of sensation resulted in there no longer being any involvements (due to the lack of contact) … Thus, although the skandhas have disappeared (because of progressively detaching in turn from each of the lower bodies as the self as a new higher body is achieved) and even though life remains, without sensation and conception it is the same as (insentient) grass and trees. If form does not even exist in the present (with the infinite *alaya* consciousness), then how can it exist after (the) death (of this stage of being)? As a result, he may speculate that there is no bodily form after death (at this stage). Reasoning in this way, he posits a theory of eight cases of the non-existence of forms. From this, he may speculate that *nirvana* does not have any cause and effect, and that everything is merely names fundamentally subject to annihilation.

"In this way, because he speculates that there is no existence after death (which is the idea of annihilation), he falls into an unorthodox path and obscures his *bodhi*-nature.

"This is the seventh heresy, which postulates wrong theories that within the realm of the five skandhas form does not exist after death.

[Sadguru Siddharameshwar Maharaj says, "You must learn to discriminate the gross, the subtle, and the steady from Parabrahman and recognize it. It is eternal. Then give up untrue form and select the only 'True Thing,' 'Paramartha.' Even after the destruction of the eight bodies, (four of the jiva and four of Ishwara) our True Form (Swaroopa) lasts forever." The four *jiva* bodies are the coarse, subtle, Causal and great-Causal bodies that refer to the form, sensation, conception and volition-consciousness skandhas. The four *Ishwara* bodies include the huge gross body (*Virat*) made up of all the five elements in the universe, the subtle body of God (*Hiranyagarbha* or Golden Womb), Causal body of God (*Avyakrut*), and great-casual body of God (the Primal Illusion, *Moolamaya* or *Moola Prakriti*).

Basically, these various theories we've been considering about the state of the self after death deal with the question of whether after death the self is both conscious and material, immaterial, both material and immaterial, neither material and immaterial, finite, infinite, both finite and infinite, neither finite nor infinite, having uniform perception, having varied perception, having limited perception, having unlimited perception, wholly blissful, wholly miserable, both blissful and miserable, or neither blissful or miserable.]

8. "Continuing, in their cultivation of samadhi, practitioners' minds are now concentrated and clear (settled) and can no longer be troubled (disturbed) by maras. Now looking deeply into the origin of all living things and observing the source of the continuous subtle disturbance in this clear state, they see that the skandha of volition still remains. Since they experienced that the (three prior) skandhas of form, sensation, and conception became extinguished (they detached from their form, subtle and Causal bodies and no longer identify with any as their self – they severed the conscious connection with these bodies so that these spheres of existence become completely excluded from the scope of consciousness), they may now speculate that there is both existence and non-existence, which is contradictory. Because of speculation, this type of practitioner may fall into errant nonsensical (contradictory) theories that imply the negation of both existence and non-existence after their death.

"When subject to the skandhas of form, sensation, and conception he previously believed they existed, but on further penetration (progress) concludes they are not reality (he no longer takes their existence as the real view of reality). Now, in the midst of the flowing stream of the skandha of volition, he sees that non-existence is not really non-existence. Considering back and forth in this way, he investigates all four skandhas and concludes there is an eightfold negation of forms in life and after death. He says that each of the skandhas can be said to be neither existent nor non-existent after death.

"Since the skandha of volition is likewise (always changing) in a state of constant flux, in a sudden flash of insight he reasons that existence and non-existence are both invalid, neither real nor unreal.

"From this, he therefore concludes that there is nothing that can be asserted about death, and that all is murky and nothing can be said of it. Thus, he falls into an unorthodox path and obscures his *bodhi*-nature.

"This is the eighth heresy which postulates that there is neither existence nor non-existence after their death (nothing can be asserted about it) within the realm of the five skandhas.

[These strange theories concern the view that the self is neither consciousness nor unconscious after death and material, immaterial, both, neither, finite, infinite, both or neither.]

9. "Continuing, in their cultivation of samadhi, practitioners' minds are now concentrated and clear (settled) and can no longer be troubled (disturbed) by maras. As they look deeply into the origins of living things and observe the source of the continuous subtle disturbance in this clear state, they may speculate that there is no existence after death (nothing exists so beingness disappears). This type of practitioner can fall into error through seven theories on the extinction of existence (cessation of beingness).

"He may conclude that when the body is ended there is cessation of existence (in the Desire Realm and Form Realm heavens); or that when desire is ended there is cessation of existence (in the first dhyana heaven); or that when suffering is ended there is cessation of existence (in the second dhyana heaven); or that when bliss is ended there is cessation of existence (in the third dhyana heaven); or that when indifference is ended there is cessation of existence (in the fourth dhyana heaven and Formless Realm). Considering back and forth in this way, he exhaustively investigates the limits of these seven states and sees they have already ceased to be and will not exist again (they are already irrevocably transcended).

"Because of his errant speculations that existence ceases after death, he falls into an unorthodox path and obscures his *bodhi*-nature.

"This then is the ninth heresy, which is the confused theory that within the five skandhas there is cessation of existence after death.

[Basically, there are many possible theories about the nihilism of post-mortem survival such as that the self is material and perishes when the body breaks up at death, or another subtler body (a Causal body, Supra-Causal or subtle body, etc.) is divine and when the body breaks up upon death it is that body which perishes.]

10. "Continuing, in their cultivation of samadhi, practitioners' minds are now concentrated and clear (settled) and can no longer be troubled (disturbed) by maras. As they look deeply into the origin of

living things and investigate the continuous, subtle disturbance in this clear state, they may speculatively conclude that there is existence after death (after the annihilation of this now attained Supra-Causal body). This type of practitioner may fall into error through five false theories of *nirvana*.

"He may conclude that the realm of desire is a true refuge because of his delight in the six devaloka heavens of sensual pleasure; or he may conclude that the first dhyana heaven is a true refuge of *nirvana* because it is free of worldly cares (trouble and anxiety); or he may conclude that the second dhyana heaven is a true refuge of *nirvana* because there his mind is free of suffering; or he may conclude that the third dhyana heaven is a true refuge of *nirvana* because it is full of bliss; or he may conclude that the fourth dhyana heaven, where both suffering and happiness are no more and one is no longer subject to birth and death in *samsara*, is a true refuge. Thus, he may mistake *samsaric* heavens (that are subject to outflows) for the fundamental state of non-action (for the unconditioned absolute nature) and then take refuge in one of these five heavens as the ultimate abode of *nirvana*. Continuing in this vein, he will conclude that these five manifestations constitute true *nirvana* and will thus fall into an unorthodox path and obscure his *bodhi*-nature.

"This tenth heresy is the theory of the five false manifestations of *nirvana* within the realm of the five skandhas.

[The false theories are that *nirvana* is here and now and can be attained by the five senses, attained by detachment from the sense-desires but with thought remaining (first dhyana), attained by cessation of discursive thought (second dhyana), attained by cessation of bliss (third dhyana) or attained by the fourth dhyana).]

"Ananda, these ten kinds of wild interpretations of dhyana are all due to the interaction of the skandha of volition with one's meditative efforts, which causes one to make these speculative conclusions (which is why these insights appear). Ignorant and deluded practitioners do not evaluate (judge) their own level of accomplishments. When they experience these phenomena, they misinterpret them and mistakenly claim to have reached sainthood (enlightenment). For violating the commandment against lying, they will fall into the relentless hells.

"You disciples must take my words, and after I pass into *nirvana*, transmit them during the Dharma ending age in order to awaken living beings to these true teachings so that the maras do not arise in their mind and lead them to self-inflicted calamities (commit grave offenses), and so that all practitioners can be vigilant (be on their guard) and wipe out wrong views. You must teach them how to discipline (train) their bodies and minds so that they awaken to the Truth and avoid straying from the supreme path. Do not let them succumb to wishful thinking or become complacent with small attainments, but act as a pure guide to supreme enlightenment."

The Ten Mara-States of the Skandha of Consciousness - [Generating the Buddha body also known as the Perfect *Sambhogakaya*, Enjoyment Body, or Body of Immanence composed of Early/Primordial Heavenly Qi/Prana]

"Ananda, as the disciples practice samadhi and the skandha of volition comes to an end (its influence is negated or extinguished because you attain and abide within a higher body), within the nature of all things in the world the subtle fleeting disturbance in a state of clearness that is the common foundation shared by all living things suddenly breaks open (explodes or crumbles away). At this point, karmic resonances in the hidden (submerged) fine network defining the various planes of rebirth and the deep channels of karmic retribution are cut off (radically suspended).

"This is the threshold of the great awakening to the enlightenment of *nirvana* (one is near to realizing *nirvana*). It is like looking eastward after the cock crows and seeing the brilliant light of dawn that is already there. The six senses are empty and still and no longer wander externally (race about) in disarray. Within and without there is only pristine perfect clarity. The individual can now profoundly comprehend the original source (root) of life for all twelve classes of living things in the ten directions (which is the *alaya* consciousness), and can contemplate the source without being drawn into any of the categories. Now he has achieved identity with all things in the universe (oneness or union). As the nature of consciousness now manifests clearly (without fading), what was hidden before is now revealed. This is 'the realm of the skandha of consciousness.'

"In the midst of the world's attractions (that call to you), you are now able to maintain a state of equanimity and balance (you are immune from external attractions because you have freed yourself from the six senses by realizing the oneness identity of mind and objects). You have dissolved away the individuality of the six gates (you obliterate the separateness of the six senses because you reach their underlying basis of consciousness; they appear as separate but in nature are not separate), which now function separately when activated or revert to unity when not in use. Your seeing and hearing become interchangeable in their purity. All the worlds of the ten directions, together with your body and mind, are clear and transparent like crystal both within and without (everything is fused together into one whole, like a crystal sphere, illuminated all the way through inside and out; the whole body suffused with pristine brightness, without any obstructions). This is called 'the end of the skandha of consciousness.' In this way, the practitioner can transcend the defilement of birth. When we observe where it all comes from, it arises from upside-down false thoughts (topsy-turvy or inverted wrong thinking)."

[**Editor:** In the *Surangama Sutra* the *alaya* consciousness is taken to represent a level of thought includes your overall consciousness of everything like emotions or conceptions, only in this case it is taken to represent ALL those types of contents that compose a mind. Furthermore, it is also used as an analogy to represent or designate the Supra-Causal body, and it also sometimes represents the plane of Later Heavenly Qi/Prana that composes the Supra-Causal body. With all these different possible meanings, discussions about it can cause confusion, especially when you try to link matters.

The *alaya* consciousness, or mind of a human, may seem still and unmoving on its surface but is actually a ceaseless flowing river of continuous transformations connected through the interdependence of co-dependent arising. That's why you can see a world in your mind without coarse thoughts. Inside are ten omnipresent types of thought always operating that produce other thoughts. This level of superfine thought is taken analogously to represent the superfine energy of the Supra-Causal body attainment.

Don't get confused and think that the concomitant mind-stream of the Supra-Causal body is the *alaya* consciousness. A

Supra-Causal body is just an exact duplicate of the human body. It has an ordinary mind with ordinary emotions and so forth. Everything is the same, except that the body lives longer, is composed of a finer, more refined energy than the human body, and the mind-stream is generally quieter because all the Qi channels were opened up in its nervous system and the rest of the body to generate it. Thus it works better, but is basically a duplicate of the human body composed of a more refined energy.

The Supra-Causal body vehicle is not the absolute Self, and the higher energy plane of the Immanence body (that we pair with the consciousness skandha as an analogy) is not the absolute self either. The plane for the *alaya* level of energy that generates both matter and mind is still a functioning of your *absolute self-nature*, the fundamental essence that we call absolute nature or True Self.

Because of *prajna* wisdom understanding (discrimination) you can realize/surmise that the pure absolute nature is the pristine, partless substance or essence transcending all bodies and their concomitant consciousnesses. Consciousness is a concocted manifestation within a body vehicle that can never fathom (form a correct image of) the original nature. Sentient beings are phenomena that have somehow appeared within that energy through a long evolution of transformations just like everything else, and their consciousness composed of thoughts is like a illusion or veil that screens its true nature.

As a teaching mechanism only, the consciousness skandha is *conventionally paired* with the energy level of the Grand Illusion that first appears upon the original nature, the first emanation or effusion out of the fundamental essence. You can also refer to the Grand Illusion as Shakti, Creation, the Hiranyagarbha golden egg of Hinduism, Tathagatagarbha womb of Buddhism or Alam-i-Yahoot, the Realm of First Manifestation in Islam since everything is constructed out of it.

As to Shakyamuni's statement that there is a dissolving away of the individuality of the senses when cultivating the *alaya* consciousness, the yoga sage Matsyendra described this by saying that the enlightened state of Kula is "the state in which mind and sight are united, the sense-organs lose their individuality, Shakti becomes identical with the Jiva (living being) and sight merges into the object to be visualized." This refers to the unification of things of the same order where the difference between the knower, knowledge and object of knowledge disappear. Meher Baba explained this saying that one does not hear, smell or see but one becomes sound, smell and sight simultaneously and is divinely conscious of it, which he explains happens when all links with the gross physical, subtle, mental (Causal) and universe (*alaya* or Supra-Causal) are snapped. Take this as guidance but not as an entirely accurate description.

Alternatively, as Hui-neng explained it the first five consciousnesses and the *alaya* are transmuted to *prajna* wisdom at the stage of Buddhahood. The sense consciousnesses therefore "become united" (you reach "oneness") when you attain and then surpass the *alaya* because their sensory result *is* an object of cognition, and that object becomes one with the knower and knowing (that are also objects of cognition). The knowledge of objects becomes absorbed into the knower as one whole, which is reaching the realization of "oneness" or "unity" claimed by many religions. This is called true form *prajna*, or direct knowing. The All melts into a single knowable whole. You eliminate the split into a perceiving subject and perceiving object that destroys the inherent natural state of the mind.

When you have been able to cultivate to the volition skandha (Supra-Causal body attainment) you can reach the fourth dhyana, which is known as "merely I-am-ness" within Hinduism (*asmita-samadhi*) and called the "Pure Ground of Renouncing Thought" in Buddhism. Your attainment stage is that of a full Arhat who has no more desire for existence in the Form Realm or Formless Realm, and who has abandoned conceit, restlessness and ignorance. If the Arhat clings to this level without progressing to the next, which is the Immanence body composed of a yet higher substance (though this is described using analogies of consciousness), it means they are still involved with subtle clinging to the *alaya* storehouse consciousness thoughts and only have attained *nirvana* with a remaining dependency. Bodywise, "remaining dependency" also means there is a higher body yet to attain.

As to this thing called consciousness—the consciousness skandha—once again it is just another automatic functioning that has developed in a body vehicle container out of the energy/power of the absolute nature, which is itself our essential essence that is also the fundamental substance of all things within the universe. It is the root substance of the Triple Realm that has developed into everything. So why do we have consciousness? It is just something that has developed as one of many developments within this All. Some phenomena have this and others do not. That's all you can say. It doesn't mean that we are special phenomena.

The Immanence body, whose compositional energies are at the level of the first plane of emanation from the original nature, is described using analogies as composed of the energy at the level of the Hiranyagarbha golden egg of Hinduism, Tathagatagarbha womb of Buddhism, the Shakti or Grand Illusion (Maya) of Hinduism and so on - and *its own ground is said to in turn be the absolute nature*. All things appear out of the First realm of manifestation, which is thus a vehicle, receptacle or container. In other words, that first energy somehow evolves, transforms or turns into all other energies, so it contains them all or develops into them all. The *alaya* level of manifestation, on the other hand, is a denser appearance within that higher plane and the lowest manifestation ground for all beings. But it is also a composite plane that is the receptacle or container of all subsequent lower planes of existence that are polluted, meaning less fine.

The root form of the *alaya* is therefore the consciousness skandha, which is one level higher. Where did that energy plane come from? It is said that an original impulse, vibration or inspiration within the pure absolute nature somehow produced, through a complex evolution of cause-and-effect transformations, an entire manifestation of universal appearances, evolutes, phenomena, appearances or functions that it contains. All things somehow originated from the original nature that never moves, changes, alters or transforms. That energy, being the ultimate foundation, never changes. Maybe the density of that energy was different in one place versus another which then caused other evolutes to be created. Who knows? Science is all fixated on a Big Bang so never looks at the possibility this way.

The Later Heavenly Qi or Life-force plane that animates living beings is not an actual being/God but is the ground for all sentient beings, and its own ground is in turn the Primordial/Earlier Heavenly Qi that corresponds to the Immanence body, and whose root is in turn the absolute nature. In terms of consciousness, we use the volition skandha and then consciousness skandha to denote these bodies or levels.

It is said that everyone's inner-mind is this one *alaya* consciousness, meaning that the inner-mind of all is composed of the same level/layer of energy we call Later Heavenly Qi. Of course people's minds are individually different. A more useful thing to say is that upon attaining a Supra-Causal body, its energy is so refined that it becomes easy to know the minds of all more denser bodied sentient beings, and by residing in a body of transcending substance thus you reach the realm of "unity consciousness" where you can know what all lower-bodied people think.

Beyond the volition skandha plane of energy (we really mean the Supra-Causal body level of energy, but Shakyamuni spoke this way in order to get people to focus on consciousness rather than bodies, hoping that this would cause people to associate finer types of thought with higher levels of energy and to therefore continue cultivating meditation when you were just a physical-bodied student) is eventually the one True Reality that *supports* all matter and minds as their fundamental substance or essence. The True Reality is the True Self. It is the stateless state where no other higher energies exist since it is the fundamental primordial one. Of course it permeates everything and is permeated by everything, but at the beginning of beginningless it was alone by Itself.

The absolute original nature was never born but is uncreated, unqualified, self-so, pure and everlasting. It is devoid of fluctuations, responses and generativity. It is eternal, changeless, blissful, peaceful and pure. No one knows how Creation came about from its substance/essence since it never alters or changes into something less pure, being ultimate, but Creation is indeed here around us. No one knows how a particle can be a wave and a wave a particle either, and yet quantum physics proves they are too. Some day science may figure out how it all happened when they eschew the Big Bang theory of Creation.

When you turn around from focusing on manifest consciousness to head for the absolute ground state energy that creates all matter, energy and consciousness, this requires you to generate a body vehicle (with attendant ordinary consciousness) of an energy/substance level transcending everything known.

Attaining a high enough body, we colloquially say that you can thereafter comprehend all dharmas because you can know the minds of all lower-bodied beings when you inject a copy of yourself into their brains to read their neurons, which is what devas train to do with each new body they develop.

The *dharmakaya* as a foundational energy is truly empty of other energies, thus transcending everything. It is brought up in cultivation dialogue to indicate the absolute nature. It is also analogously paired with empty/pure consciousness, but this is just a conventional comparison for teaching purposes. It is just a form of skillful means to encourage meditation. Why? You can never really have a mind whose concomitant consciousness is the *dharmakaya* since a body vehicle will always have a created consciousness. The emptiness or even no-thought stage of that consciousness can never correspond to the *dharmakaya* of absolute energy even when empty or non-moving. Neither can any body vehicle be composed solely of the fundamental nature energy of the universe since a body would have to have parts, which means different types or levels of energy. However, this analogy within Buddhism that you "realize the *dharmakaya*" is used to motivate people to practice empty states of mind, i.e. meditation, because that is what is necessary for spiritual development. This is excellent skillful means.

The *alaya* consciousness of your mind (which refers to the aggregate of thoughts within your brain) is not the meaning of "pure consciousness" or "pure Knowledge" either. Consciousness is not a substance, so there is no such thing as a pure substance of consciousness. There are just thoughts or no thoughts, knowledge or no knowledge. The closest thing possible is a state of no thoughts, or thoughtlessness, where consciousness isn't operating. Thoughts have stopped. However, there is no substance that is still (non-moving) in this instance although cultivation schools will use wordplay to trick you into thinking this way so that you make progress.

If we were to use that form of trickery, which even I am sometimes doing in these explanations to show you how things match, "pure consciousness" or "pure Knowledge" should actually refer to the consciousness skandha rather than the *alaya*, yet some people designate the stateless state that is the absolute nature as

Pure Consciousness too.

Calling the fundamental nature "Pure consciousness" is a popular approach in Vedanta, and is just a matter of nomenclature for instruction's sake. Calling the fundamental nature "emptiness" is probably more helpful for cultivation purposes since along the spiritual path your mind becomes progressively *emptier* or quieter along the way. Whatever is prior to Knowledge/Consciousness (the consciousness skandha) is conventionally said to be Reality or True Self so a better terminology for leading people upwards is that Pure Awareness or Pure Consciousness should be designated as the consciousness skandha since it is a construction. Pure Awareness or Pure Consciousness therefore belongs to a sentient being, although you can call the absolute nature these names for teachings purposes to lead people upwards.

Hence, sometimes people apply these terms to the original nature too. As long as you get the point it doesn't matter, which is that (1) on the spiritual path you can cultivate five different bodies, (2) each corresponds to a different energy level/plane of manifestation, (3) and each is colloquially paired with a different concomitant type of finer thoughts or consciousness that we call a skandha, but this is just a convention to help you make progress while hiding the fact that it is all a path of Yoga about cultivating bodies., (4) to cultivate a higher body you have to cultivate inner energy work and an empty state of mind via meditation practice, hence all the dialogue on emptiness, pure consciousness, thoughtlessness, no wandering thoughts, pure awareness (without thoughts), pure mind, purity of mind and so on.

Thoughts and conceptions that are conventionally matched in the *Surangama Sutra* with the conception skandha, for instance, are not powered by Shen energy. The superfine volition skandha thoughts (such as the I-thought) are not composed of Later Heavenly Qi energy either. They are generated within the human body so are composed of the same energy level that comprises the human body. Those correspondences of skandhas to bodies are just made for the purposes of skillful means to hide the fact that you are cultivating bodies, but phrasing things in terms of consciousness that then implies higher, more refined or more purified levels of thought.

In short, different types of thoughts do not match with higher planes of energy because all thoughts are created out of the same type/plane of energy that composes your body at that level of existence. In other words, the attendant consciousness for each body vessel you inhabit is powered or composed out of the same energies (energy level) that creates that body. It isn't a higher body that gives you more subtle, finer, less coarse ("thinner") thoughts.

Even if the facts within these lengthy editorial explanations are wrong (because it is hard to explain things correctly), as long as you stick to this simple explanation then I believe you will be able to guide yourself through any inadvertent errors I have made in trying to link bodies to skandhas, types of thought and energy planes of manifestation.

When you "produce a revolution in the basis of the *alaya*" this is said to mean that you let go of even the knowledge of existence/beingness - the most subtle self-notion. What it really means is that you generate an Immanence body from within the Supra-Causal body, and thus with the fifth body of the *sambhogakaya* you are done with the spiritual path of attainments (at least as far as they will tell you right now since the explanations are restricted to just the five bodies). Of course, this accomplishment is phrased in terms of consciousness with (at times) explanations that tend to confuse people, but which are meant to be helpful.

Consider this. If the I-thought disappears this produces the samadhi of nothingness that you can in a way (colloquially or as a teaching mechanism) equate with a type of Pure Consciousness or pure beingness (since it lacks thought modifications while you still exist), but this is a useless state of beingness akin to inertness. There is nothingness or thoughtlessness in that state. Even though a state of peacefulness, that is useless for existence, isn't it? That is why masters cultivate the samadhi of nothingness only temporarily as a training vehicle.

If you can cultivate an Immanence body whose compositional substance is higher than that of the Supra-Causal body, you are said to attain Complete Buddhahood. Instead of using bodies, we explain this using the terms of consciousness or skandhas or thoughts by saying that by abandoning the most subtle attachments to a self-notion of personal existence (the I-thought of the volition skandha and *alaya* consciousness), attachment then *breaks open* to win true enlightenment—the true nature of reality. All these instructions are really trying to do is get you to let go during meditation to cultivate a mind that is free of sticking to Qi, which is connected to your thoughts, so that it can begin to rotate and you can begin to generate the subtle body.

With the attainment of Complete and Perfect Enlightenment, whose concomitant level of mental purity is *conventionally* or *colloquially* said to be the original nature or *dharmakaya* (which isn't true), it is taught that no longer is the precious gemstone wrapped in layers of rags that obscure it. A true state of empty mind, which you want to cultivate in meditation, is then reached that is so pure/empty it is considered as the original nature of the mind, or original mind essence. This unknowable true mind nature, empty of everything phenomenal due to its oneness of purity, is called the void or emptiness in Buddhism because it is like empty space. You cannot actually realize the fundamental energy as your mind-stream, but you can cultivate better and better body vehicles whose minds are progressively more pristine or pure just like it. *The states of clear clarity or pristine awareness for those bodies is said to be attaining the fundamental essence of the mind.*

All such teachings are simply meant to lead you to cultivating these higher bodies with more pristine states of mental clarity (and higher abilities that let you help people) so it doesn't matter if the teachings don't exactly match up as long as they push you towards generating higher and higher bodies through any motivational explanations necessary. Most all those explanations will talk about consciousness being empty, and all the spiritual achievements will require the practice of meditation.

If we talk of the functioning of the primal absolute essence that develops into the universe, this includes many things including the level of energy that composes the Immanence body and then the volition skandha Supra-Causal plane that gives birth to all things. This plane of energy is also called Unfathomable Light (Uncreated Light) in Western religions or Clear Light energy in Vajrayana Buddhism. These terms are simply used to motivate meditators to cultivate a clear state of pristine awareness once again, i.e. empty mind. Therefore spiritual literature pairs the *alaya* energy with the "brilliance" behind the inner-mind, the light of the Self, the "Light of the World" or "Luminous One" that makes mental thoughts possible. These just refer to a state of very clear pristine awareness reached at that attainment.

Religions also sometimes call the *alaya* all-consciousness "God the Creator" because they pair it with the Supra-Causal energy level, and all lower things spring from that level of energy. The Supra-Causal level of energy isn't really the level of energy that powers *alaya* type thoughts within a human being, but that correspondence was made ages ago to help encourage a practice of emptiness meditation.

Remember that the absolute nature (fundamental energy) never changes, and therefore never generates anything. It is simply the true support or highest substance within everything without which nothing can appear. Being changeless, no one knows how It came into being or gave rise to anything else (how It developed evolutes since it remains pure as the original energy) but It did, so we just have to accept the fact.

When you recognize your true identity is the unchanging universal ground essence, this realization helps people release their grasping onto the self-notion and thereby helps them overcome all suffering and afflictions. The cultivation path to this attainment is "not dwelling" or "non-grasping" which results in freedom, liberation, salvation, spontaneity, naturalness, or "emptiness."

Non-grasping is therefore the cultivation path of Qi practice since Qi and consciousness are linked. It is also Nagarjuna's practice path of the Middle Way wherein you let consciousness arise without clinging to it and don't cling to inert emptiness either.

This is also called the practice of presence, and also the practice of witnessing. You are a living mind, so know your own mind! Don't get lost in states of stupor or ignorance where there aren't any thoughts, don't ignore cause and effect, and always choose the road of morality and virtue. Non-grasping is not only a meditation practice but an inner Qi practice because it frees your Qi so that it can move naturally without being affected/bothered by thoughts. In regards to witnessing (without entanglement) any Qi sensations that arise within your body, this is called anapana practice.

Buddhism doesn't like to call the absolute nature-essence "pure consciousness" because of the potential for mental clinging due to this term, but uses "emptiness" because It is empty of every subsequent phenomenal thing and the term implies that you should let go (non-grasping) to realize a (relatively) empty state of mind.

The terms consciousness, consciousness skandha and *alaya* consciousness are all used interchangeably in a confusing manner but the dialogues all aim at encouraging you to cultivate non-grasping, whereby thoughts die down themselves as Qi channels open, so that you can attain the deva body as the first step of spiritual attainment. After that you realize that spiritual cultivation is really just a path of Yoga practice, but that has been hidden by teachers since most people will not succeed. However, by wording it in this way they will still be working hard at cultivating clear consciousness through meditation. This is proper since there are gigantic benefits to meditation practice even if you don't succeed in attaining a deva body.

The *alaya* consciousness is a composite phenomenal construction. Everything in the mind arises within it. The corresponding energy level or compositional plane of the universe is the Later Heavenly Qi plane, which is not the *dharmakaya*. Water is the essence (substance) of ice and the *dharmakaya* is the root substance/essence/energy of all things. The consciousness of a body vehicle that comes attendant with that sentient vehicle is just another one of the infinite wondrous functions that have developed in the universe, and It is the uttermost substance or essence of the energy of consciousness and the body vehicle that gives rise tot hat consciousness. By calling it "emptiness" this motivates the practice of meditation, and provides instructions without need of saying anything else, aligning you with the path and the original nature itself.

While manifest consciousness *must ultimately have a root nature* that is of the same substance as the absolute nature, which you can easily deduce through discriminative wisdom understanding, you can never really create/generate a body vehicle out of that purest energy. You can only create one out of high evolutes of subsequent energy, but not out of one type of energy alone that is the purest and highest without any differentiation. While some schools refer to that primal essence as "pure consciousness" or "pure knowledge," I believe it is best just to refer to this ultimate substance/essence as True Self or *dharmakaya*. It is also called the "highest, purest, clearest" (which are words we can also apply to consciousness as guides to the spiritual path) and *this is what is truly real in life*.

You are this self-nature that is indwelling within all beings, permeating them bit by bit because it is their ultimate compositional energy. When any sentient beings says "I" this "I" actually refers to this original essence; using the word "I" everyone is referring to the same ultimate host nature. "I" actually refers to the fundamental essence or energy that generated the universe.

There is a co-emergent union of this unchangeable absolute energy/nature with everything since the root energy of all energies is this absolute energy substance. Thus it pervades everything. As the *Heart Sutra* says, all things are It and It is all things; all the skandhas are emptiness and emptiness (being the code word for the original nature or energy) is all things.

Your consciousness within a body of Immanence is said to resemble the purity of the absolute nature, but this is just a way of speaking. The absolute nature and the manifest consciousness of a sentient being in its body vehicle are certainly not separate from one another, and as a teaching instruction the concomitant consciousness of this body vehicle is said to be like the *dharmakaya*. Of course, this is just a manner of speaking to make resemblances so don't get confused about this.

To achieve the enlightenment of complete *nirvana* is liberation from the "shadows" of the five skandhas. You then generate and inhabit a perfected *sambhogakaya* (Immanence) body and let consciousness arise, but you are detached from these thoughts (just as you practice at each stage of the way). You are said to be free of (extinguish) attachments to even consciousness itself (the consciousness skandha) because you just let thoughts arise and depart without clinging *just as you practiced at each step of the path*. This is the Middle Way taught by Nagarjuna.

While we colloquially speak of inferior spiritual stages as enlightenment, the Immanence, *sambhogakaya* or Reward body attainment is the only true enlightenment (sometimes called the state of "no mind and no body" or "No More Learning") and there are ten stages or *bhumis* of purity which progressively rank progress towards this perfect attainment that can only be achieved with an Immanence body attainment. You can cultivate all sorts of samadhi-dhyana and yet, if you don't achieve "entry into," awakening to, or "returning to" the root source nature that is described as the apex of all religious paths ("God"), you will still not be fully enlightened. If you want enlightenment, you should try to attain the whole thing.

As my teacher once wrote [*Working Toward Enlightenment*, pp. 255-256] on the attainment of Tien Wang-Wu, "At most he had attained the *dharmakaya*, but he had not yet transformed the *sambhogakaya* and *nirmanakaya*. Therefore those who study Consciousness-only must realize, as the Sixth Patriarch said, 'The Sixth and seventh consciousnesses are transformed at the level of cause. The first five consciousnesses and the eighth consciousness are transformed at the level of effect.' The sixth and seventh consciousnesses are easy to transform. Once thoughts are empty, and past, present, and future are emptied out, the sixth is transformed into a pure illuminated realm of immediate awareness. If your meditation work advances further, the seventh consciousness can also be emptied out, and one can attain initial enlightenment. This is transformation (achievement) at the level of the causal basis. Many people who cultivate practice reach at most to the station of bodhisattvas at the level of the causal basis. Transformation at the level of effect is difficult. The first five sense consciousnesses associated with the eyes, ears, nose, tongue and body, encompass this physical body. The eighth consciousness, the *alaya* consciousness, encompasses not only the physical body, but the whole material world. The first five and the eighth consciousness can be transformed only when the level of effect is complete, only when you have realized the level of the fruit of enlightenment. How can this be called easy? So if you want cultivation, cultivate the whole thing. If you only cultivate half, all you can do is come again in future births. If you have enough time, the best to do is complete the whole project in this lifetime."

This discussion on the "transformation of the sense consciousnesses at the level of effect" pertains to reaching the stage mentioned where the sense consciousnesses become interchangeable, and is only achievable at the upper enlightenment *bhumis*.]

1. "Ananda, you must know that as the disciples come to thoroughly perceive that the skandha of volition is empty, it will

return to its source, which is the skandha of consciousness. Although they have then wiped out birth and death, they have not yet achieved the pure and profound perfection of *nirvana*. Nevertheless, they are now able to unify the functions of the six sense faculties. They have a pervasive awareness of all living beings in the ten directions and know they are emanations of consciousness. They can enter the source of perfection, but if in reverting to it they take it as the cause of true permanence, and regard this as correct, they will fall into error and become an adherent of the Kapila doctrine which holds undifferentiated consciousness (primordial obscurity without layers of emanations – the consciousness skandha or first emanate) as the origin of reality, and thus, miss the true *bodhi* of the Buddha-nature and lose correct knowledge and understanding.

"This is called the first false condition of the skandha of consciousness, which holds that the consciousness (mind) thus realized is the ultimate attainment (a place to which to return). In this way one strays far from perfect enlightenment, turns one's back on *nirvana*, and sows the seeds of heresy.

2. "Ananda, progressing further, as the disciples come to thoroughly perceive the emptiness of the skandha of volition, they are then able to wipe out birth and death. However, before realizing the perfection of *nirvana*, they may regard pure consciousness as their substance (ultimate essence), and then insist that the twelve classes of living things throughout boundless space all flow from it (as the ultimate source). In this way (by believing they are the ultimate subjective creator) they will fall into the error of believing that they have an ability they do not really have (they believe that they create what they do not in reality create), and thus, become an adherent of the deva Maheshwara, who appears in a limitless body. Thus, they will miss the true *bodhi* of the Buddha-nature and lose correct knowledge and understanding.

"This is called the second false condition of the skandha of consciousness, which holds that consciousness is the ultimate creator and that this is the highest attainment. In this way, one strays far from enlightenment, turns one's back on *nirvana*, and sows the seeds of great arrogance for asserting an omnipresent (all pervading) self.

[There is no will behind the creation of sentient beings. Their existence is just an anthropomorphic happening. They aren't even sentient beings; they are only the creation of energy in a certain form and the foundational root of that energy is higher than pure consciousness, the samadhi of nothingness or the consciousness skandha.]

3. "Continuing, as the disciples come to thoroughly perceive that the skandha of volition is empty, they are then able to wipe out birth and death but have not yet realized the perfection of *nirvana*. If they cling to the skandha of consciousness as their refuge (final abode), they may assume that both the body and mind and all things within boundless space in the ten directions spring forth from there as well. Then they will wrongly insist that the realm from which all of this issues forth (emanates or arises) is the truly permanent body, which is not subject to birth and death. Because of this misinterpretation of consciousness as permanent (indestructible), they will understand neither the Uncreated as well as creation and destruction (the realm of interdependent origination - *samsara*). Because of this deluded interpretation, they will fall into error by taking what is not permanent as permanent and become adherents of Ishvaradeva (the divine creator of all things). Thus, they will miss the true *bodhi* of the Buddha-nature (enlightenment) and lose correct knowledge and understanding.

"This is called the third false condition of the skandha of consciousness, which sets up the causal mind (*alaya* consciousness) as the ultimate attainment (as the final refuge), and therefore produces an erroneous conclusion. In this way one strays far from enlightenment, turns one's back on *nirvana*, and sows the seeds of a distorted view of perfection.

[The practitioner should not mistakenly take the *alaya* consciousness as the Self or consciousness skandha. The four Mahakavyas of Hinduism, when wrongly interpreted ("I am Brahman," "The Self is Brahman," and so forth) lead one to the mistake of equating the manifestation of the *alaya* consciousness as the absolute nature, Parabrahman or True Self. Sometimes the *alaya* is equated with the consciousness skandha and in some schools the consciousness skandha is considered higher. In both cases, neither is the Self.]

4. "Continuing, as the disciples come to thoroughly perceive that the skandha of volition is empty, they are now able to wipe out birth and death but have not yet realized *nirvana*. Based on their idea that there is universal awareness (consciousness), they may formulate an

interpretation that even plants are sentient and do not differ from men, and so after death men can return as plants. If they regard this indiscriminate idea of unrestricted universal consciousness to be true, they fall into attributing knowledge (knowing) to where there is no knowledge (knowing) and become adherents of the doctrine of Vasistha and Sani, who held that everything is sentient. Thus, they miss the true *bodhi* of the Buddha-nature and lose correct knowledge and understanding.

"This then is called the fourth false condition of the skandha of consciousness, which incorrectly concludes that the knowing mind is the ultimate attainment. In this way one strays far from enlightenment, turns one's back on *nirvana*, and sows the seeds of a distorted view of awareness.

[The practitioner is one who does not thoroughly penetrate through the *alaya* consciousness to realize the absolute nature, which is the ultimate root source and true nature of manifest consciousness, awareness or knowing. Through a wrong understanding they take consciousness as the host rather than guest. Awareness, consciousness or knowing is a function of the absolute nature but they take it as the ultimate, and incorrectly attribute ultimate causality to it, thus missing *nirvana*. Consciousness or awareness itself should be taken as the guest rather than the host, but the opposite mistake is made in several of these ten roads of error.]

5. "Continuing, as the disciples come to thoroughly perceive that the skandha of volition is empty, they are able to wipe out birth and death but have not yet realized the perfection of *nirvana*. If they succeed in attaining versatility in the perfect fusion and interchangeable functioning of the six senses, they may speculate that the source of creation lies in (the) harmonious transformations (of the five elements that the senses reveal). They may then be tempted to worship the brilliance of fire, the purity of water, the freedom of wind, or the creativity of earth. They may take these elements as fundamental causes of creation and insist that they are the permanent reality (everlasting). For attributing creation to that which has no power to create, they become followers of the doctrine of Kasyapa and the Brahmins who devote themselves to diligently worshipping fire and water in their quest to escape the cycle of birth and death. Thus, they miss the true *bodhi* of the Buddha-nature and lose correct knowledge and understanding.

"This is called the fifth false condition of the skandha of consciousness, which sets up the worship of the elements, throwing away one's mind in the pursuit of external objects, and wrongly chases false causes and effects. In this way one strays far from enlightenment, turns one's back on *nirvana*, and sows the seeds of a distorted view of transformations.

[The practitioner is one who mistakenly thinks "the five elements are the ultimate cause of everything, including life and consciousness itself."]

6. "Continuing, as the disciples come to thoroughly perceive that the skandha of volition is empty, they are able to wipe out birth and death but have not yet realized the perfection of *nirvana*. In this state of perfect clarity, they may conclude that consciousness is itself emptiness and that all transformations end in annihilation (extinction). Therefore they may seek to take refuge in eternal extinction, and believing this to be the supreme state, these practitioners fall into taking as a refuge that which is not a refuge and become adherents of a samadhi of thoughtlessness. Thus, they miss the *bodhi* of the Buddha-nature and lose correct knowledge and understanding.

"This is called the sixth false condition of the skandha of consciousness, which posits a perfect empty consciousness of no thoughts whatsoever (a samadhi of nothingness), but leads to an empty fruition. In this way one strays far from enlightenment, turns one's back on *nirvana*, and sows the seeds of annihilationism.

[The practitioner is as one who thinks "the absolute nature is absent of thoughts so I will try to have no thoughts to become like it." Perhaps this is similar to the formless samadhi absorption of infinite nothingness. Some recognize that the perfect nature of consciousness, or pure consciousness, is absent of thoughts and so try to cultivate that state of nothingness or ignorance believing it is the highest state.]

7. "Continuing, as the disciples come to thoroughly perceive that the skandha of volition is empty, they are able to wipe out birth and death but have not yet realized the perfection of *nirvana*. In this state of perfect constancy (that seems to represent permanence), they may desire to attain physical immortality in order to share in that perfection through everlasting deathlessness. If they misinterpret this as the supreme state, they will fall into the error of desiring

something unattainable and become adherents of the immortality seekers. Thus, they will miss the *bodhi* of the Buddha-nature and lose correct knowledge and understanding.

"This is called the seventh false condition of the skandha of consciousness, which pursues the false cause of preservation or maintenance (immortality) in the search for a permanent fruition. In this way one strays far from enlightenment, turns one's back on *nirvana*, and sows the seeds of foolishly pursuing the prolongation (lengthening) of life.

[The practitioner is as if one who thinks "this pristine clear awareness (consciousness) is permanent so I will also try to become permanent."]

8. "Continuing, as the disciples come to thoroughly perceive that the skandha of volition is empty, they are able to wipe out birth and death but have not yet realized the perfection of *nirvana*. They may contemplate the fundamental unity that is the source of life and then fear that the material plane of worldly fruits will come to an end. Caught up in this idea, they may therefore use their mental powers to retire to a lotus palace, conjure an abundance of the seven treasures, surround themselves with beautiful women, and thus indulge their minds. They will fall into error for indulging in this fantasy, regarding as real what is not real, and become adherents of heavenly mara. Thus, they will miss the *bodhi* of the Buddha-nature and lose correct knowledge and understanding.

"This is called the eighth false condition of the skandha of consciousness, in which he decides to pursue the causes of phenomenal fruition (worldly enjoyments rather than *nirvana*) based on incorrect thinking. In this way one strays far from enlightenment, turns one's back on *nirvana*, and sows the seeds of becoming a deva mara.

[The practitioner is as if one who thinks "since the phenomenal realm is impermanent, I should create a situation where I enjoy myself until it ends."]

9. "Continuing, as the disciples come to thoroughly perceive that the skandha of volition is empty, they are able to wipe out birth and death but have not yet realized the perfection of *nirvana*. Practitioners at this stage of clear understanding of the source of life may begin to make distinctions about the subtle and coarse, true and false, and seeking results from the laws of cause and effect may turn their backs

on the path of purity. They may look into the causes of suffering, the severing of its causes, its destruction, and way (path or means) to do so. They will cultivate its cessation, take pride in this achievement, and make no further progress (won't strive to advance further). If they interpret this as the supreme state, they will follow those of the arrested *sravaka* stage (of cultivation progress) and become companions of ignorant monks (who fail to cultivate further) and the uneducable devas of the four dhyana heavens. Thus, they will miss the *bodhi* of the Buddha-nature and lose correct knowledge and understanding.

"This is called the ninth false condition of the skandha of consciousness, which takes the perfection (mastery) of consciousness as realization of the fruit of *nirvana* (mistakes it for *nirvanic* fruition). In this way one strays far from enlightenment, turns one's back on *nirvana*, and sows the seeds of obstructive emptiness (clings to an empty mental state as enlightenment).

[The practitioner does not penetrate through to realize the absolute nature root source of consciousness, but instead tries to master the functioning operations (transformations) of consciousness.]

10. "Continuing, as the disciples come to thoroughly perceive that the skandha of volition is empty, they are able to wipe out birth and death but have not yet realized the perfection of *nirvana*. As they contemplate the bright and pure essence of consciousness, if he looks deeper into its depth, they may take this as *nirvana* and will not strive to advance further. If they believe this to be the supreme state, they may become a *pratyeka-buddhahood* aspirant and go to live apart with others to seek self-enlightenment. Thus, they will miss the *bodhi* of the Buddha-nature and lose correct knowledge and understanding.

"This is called the tenth false condition of the skandha of consciousness, which is realizing a profound clarity based on the union of mind with pure consciousness (awareness). In this way one strays far from complete enlightenment, turns one's back on *nirvana*, and sows the seeds of incomplete enlightenment.

[Believing that clear consciousness is *nirvana*, the practitioner uses the causal chain of dependent origination as his cultivation guide (which is what *pratyeka-buddhas* do) to cultivate to reach the clearest possible substance of consciousness expecting that this will ultimately lead to perfect *nirvana* (whereas the attainment of enlightenment actually requires a detachment from consciousness and the realm of interdependent origination).]

"Ananda, these ten states of dhyana are due to foolish notions because the practitioner becomes deluded and thinks they have reached the ultimate goal (of perfect and complete enlightenment) when they have not. They are the result of the interaction between the skandha of consciousness and your meditative efforts (they are due to your cultivation efforts). Ignorant and deluded (confused) practitioners do not evaluate their own level of cultivation accomplishments. Encountering such experiences, their minds are deluded by infatuation and old habits, so they stop to rest in what they (errantly) take as the final refuge (the ultimate attainment). They will wrongly claim to have realized supreme *bodhi*, and thus violating the Buddha's prohibition against lying, become contaminated with the evil karma of heretics and maras which will send them to the relentless hells. As to those *sravakas* and *pratyeka-buddhas*, whose minds become arrested at their respective levels of attainment, they are not able to make further progress.

"After my *nirvana*, in the Dharma ending age, you must all proclaim and transmit these teachings so that living things awaken to them. Do not allow the maras (delusions) of false views to cause them self-inflicted calamities and fall. Teach all practitioners to be on their guard and wipe out heterodox views. Teach them how to discipline their bodies and minds so that they achieve the Buddha knowledge and understanding, and so that they never stray onto deviant paths from the beginning of their practice to the very end.

"It is by relying on this dharma-door that Tathagatas, as innumerable as particles of dust over kalpas as numberless as the sands of the Ganges, have enlightened their minds and attained the highest Tao.

"When the skandha of consciousness comes to an end, then all of your senses can intermingle uniformly, and you can enter the first stage of the indestructible wisdom of the bodhisattva. Your perfect, pure, clear mind (enlightened mind) will manifest like a pure crystal that contains a precious moon within. In this way you will transcend the ten stages of bodhisattva faith, the ten stages of Bodhisattva wisdom, the ten necessary practices, the ten commitments, the four stages of intensified effort, the ten stages (*bhumis*) of bodhisattva progress to Buddhahood, and the state of universal enlightenment to enter the Tathagata's majestic sea of perfect and complete *bodhi* (enlightenment), and thus return to where nothing can be attained (the state of non-attainment).

"These are the subtle mara states discerned by past Buddhas while practicing *samatha-vipasyana* (cessation-contemplation practice). If you are familiar with these mara-states then you will be able to avoid wrong views. In this way you will not fall into unorthodox views, the maras (delusions) of the five skandhas will vanish, the heavenly demons (Deva Mara) will be smashed, the powerful ghosts and spirits will lose their nerve and take flight, the spirits of the rivers and hills will not come to trouble you, and you will achieve complete *bodhi* without the slightest deficiency. You will thus be able to begin your practice from inferior states and progress to *nirvana* without suffering delusion or discouragement."

The Falseness of the Five Skandhas

After hearing the Buddha's instruction, Ananda rose from his seat and prostrated himself with his head at the master's feet. Then, without forgetting a single word, he recited the Buddha's message to the assembly. Then he addressed the Buddha, saying: "As the Buddha has said, the five kinds of falsehoods arising from the five skandhas are rooted in the thinking mind, but we have not yet heard your explanation in detail. Moreover, (on the path of cultivation) are the five skandhas wiped out simultaneously or separately one at a time (in sequence), and what are the boundaries between them? We only hope that, out of great compassion, you will explain this so that we can all purify our vision and thereby serve as guiding lights for all living things in the Dharma ending age ahead."

The Buddha said to Ananda: "The perfect purity of basic enlightenment contains no trace of birth and death, defilements, or even emptiness, for these all arise from delusive/delusory/false thinking. From the profound clear true essence of basic enlightenment arises the illusion of the material world in the same way that Yajnadatta deceived himself about his head when he saw his own reflection (he could not find his true head because he saw its reflection in a mirror and took that reflection as his head). Falsehood (Maya, the Great Illusion or *samsara*) fundamentally has no cause, but false cognition (false thoughts, deluded thinking, delusory thinking) sets it up. Those who are confused about the principle of causality consider it spontaneous. Since even emptiness is in truth an illusion, how much more so are causality and spontaneity. All of these are the products of discrimination arising in the unreal (false) minds of living things.

"Ananda, if you know from whence deluding cognition (differentiation or discernment) arises then you can speak of its causes (the prior causes and conditions behind it). However, if delusory cognition doesn't have a source, then you cannot speak of there being a source for its causality. How much more is this the case when you do not know its source and just regard it as being spontaneous? For this reason the Tathagata reveals to you that the root cause of all five skandhas is delusory (false) thinking.

[It is because of thoughts that we can establish the identities of cause and effect. The natural process of cause and effect is all a judgment in the minds of sentient beings. It is just a set of concepts contingent upon having a mind. Since Maya, Shakti or the Grand Illusion is fundamentally non-existent, when we speak of its original generational causes and conditions these are also entirely non-existent. You cannot explain the reality of an illusion that doesn't truly exist. There may be an appearance but it lacks true beingness, true reality.]

"The original cause of your body was your parent's thought to give birth (to a child), but if you had not entertained any thoughts in your mind, there would have been no chance for you to incarnate through their longing. As I have said before, if you think of the taste of vinegar in your mind, your mouth will begin to water; if you think of scaling great heights, your feet may begin to ache. However, neither the mountain cliff nor the vinegar actually exist. If your body were not of the same nature as false thoughts, how could saliva appear at the mention of vinegar? Therefore, you should know that your physical body is brought about by the first kind of delusory cognition, which is 'firm (solidified).'

"As I have mentioned, the mere thought of scaling great heights was sufficient to produce the sensation of aching in your body, and so emotions (the sensation skandha) were able to affect your body, which is moved by favorable or unfavorable (pleasant or unpleasant) feelings. These two types of emotion that compel you are brought about by the second kind of delusory cognition called 'illusory (empty) reflection (cognition).'

[**Editor:** The sensation skandha of feelings and emotions can affect the form skandha of the physical body, which is itself actually a form of solidified higher energy. Once through the form skandha then your mind will be clear, but feelings/emotions that arise in response to your situation will still affect your mind and body (subtle body). You can be drawn into clinging to or rejecting those feelings because you like or dislike them.

In other words, something arises and because of our relatedness to it, we derive notions of like or dislike (attachment or rejection) and attach to (crave) or reject these feeling states. We determine whether we like something or not in a reflexive manner of judgment, and this subjective response and the thoughts themselves are "illusory reflection." They only pertain to us because other people will think and judge differently. Thus they are conditional judgments rather than absolute realities and hence, illusory reflections/judgments.

Illusory thought therefore does not represent absolute reality because it contains false objective knowledge. It is only conditional knowledge within a being who has conditional/limited sense organs and thinking capabilities. It only represents what is true for us, but not necessarily for other sentient beings. We should use it, but not absolutely depend upon it.

If we can just let thoughts and sensations arise without attaching to them or rejecting them, we can eventually become free of the sensation skandha because that is the path of meditation that will lead to our Qi moving and generating an independent subtle body that can leave the physical shell at will. The sensation skandha of these emotions, which you feel in the subtle body and then physical body, arises from personal reflections/reactions to the circumstances that arise.

If you can extinguish any attachments to these types of responses then whatever arises in the mind will appear without any stickiness or clinging, like images that freely appear within a mirror. An example, for instance, is someone who doesn't hold grudges but just lets things come and go graciously.]

"Your thoughts are able to direct (control) your body (via will and intent); if your body was not the same (ultimate substance or composition) as your thoughts, how could your body (ever) follow the orders of your thoughts (mind)? From all our impressions of the external world, the mind generates thoughts and the body then reacts. In the waking state the thinking mind is active and during sleep you (also) dream. Thus, your thoughts are always stirring up your delusory feelings (sensations). This is the third kind of delusory cognition, which is 'comprehensive (pervasive).'

[**Editor:** The conception skandha is the source of the sensation skandha because conceptions stir up the reflective reactions of like or dislike, which in turn cause us to be drawn into feelings. We see something, our mind discriminates to determine what it is according to the comprehensively connected references in the memory, and then the relatedness of all those discriminations gives rise to feeling-emotional responses. In other words, emotions arise from thoughts.

The pervasive conception skandha interlinks countless thoughts and memories in a comprehensive whole and is thus another layer of ignorance screening the empty pure state of consciousness. Emotions screen the pure state of consciousness too. The screen or veil is created by countless interlinking thoughts.

The concept of being a self with a personal mind (the I-thought or I-am) is natural and rational, of course. However, people don't ordinarily recognize that their thoughts are a subjective creation of ideational consciousness. They appear naturally because the body has a brain that is a knowledge generating mechanism that interprets thoughts in a self-reflexive manner; knowledge simply talks to itself without any absolute basis to it. Thoughts are said to be delusory in the sense that they are subjective rather than objective (therefore their judgment is not absolute).

Another point made by religions is that we all cling to private self-notions not just because we normally cling to thoughts but because we don't understand correctly; *all I's actually refer to the one original nature that is the base substance of creation.* You are That, so when you say "I" the true meaning is what you ultimately are. That is the only *true I* whereas the conventional "I" of the personal self refers to your body you!

By clinging to thoughts, including the superfine thoughts of being an I, we screen a state of pure and clear consciousness, a state of pristine consciousness or ultra clear awareness. Anytime we say "pure" or "empty" consciousness in cultivation works we are identifying such a state and also insinuating that this mental purity resembles the purity of the uttermost absolute energy substance that is clear, formless, doesn't change and comprises the universe because while pure it also gives rise to everything. The analogy is pure consciousness that gives birth to thoughts (a pollution of consciousness) arising in the mind. Therefore, from this analogy of everything created being a pollution upon the original nature, thoughts are an unwanted delusion upon the true pure nature of the mind (that obscure its true nature).

Rather than recognizing that we are appearances or evolutionary manifestations that arise within the original nature out of its substance, to run our lives in the regular world we all cling to what is essentially delusory, delusive, illusory, false thinking – erroneous cognition or erroneous differentiation. It is conditional thinking composed of relative judgments that certainly works and we must have it, but from the aspect of the original nature this is all an impurity. From the aspect of the original nature nothing exists at all except itself, and to think there is such a thing as a "independent living being soul" when everything is all IT is ludicrous nonsense. What we define ourselves to be is not what we actually are.

This is the type of dialogue you usually encounter in cultivation texts, but they don't fill in the details as I have done. Its only purpose is to *help you let go of holding onto thoughts*. Its purpose is not to make you realize that you are just an evolute of the original nature therefore let go and through that detachment your Qi will begin to move and you will then be on your way to cultivating the subtle body. The purpose of such dialogues are to make analogies about how the original nature is empty and pure, and thus so should be your mind in order to get your Qi to move (so that you can generate a subtle body), therefore cultivate meditation without attachment to thoughts to be like it.]

"The process of transformation never ceases with subtle

(imperceptible) changes happening every moment. Nails grow and hair sprouts, vitality declines as you age, and wrinkles appear. These processes continue day and night without our noticing them. Ananda, if those changes are not yours then why does your body change; on the other hand if those changes are really part of you, why is it that you don't notice them? Thus your volition skandha continues moving in thought after thought unceasingly. This is the fourth kind of delusory cognition, which is 'subtle and hidden.'

[This subtle force, power or energy constantly stirs thoughts and other processes in the universe. That energy is ultimately responsible for birth and death.]

"Furthermore, if you say that your perfect, clear, still, and unmoving consciousness is permanent, why does it not extend beyond your seeing, hearing, feeling, and knowing (if it is permanent it should be infinite, so why is it limited and not omniscient)? If it is real (which means it is changeless), it should not be affected by your errant habits. But how is it that you may have seen some unusual object in the past and after many years completely forgotten about it, but when you suddenly see the same unusual object again you can vividly remember it as if you never forgot a single detail? This shows that the contamination of your perfect, profound, unmoving consciousness continues, instant after instant, in unbroken continuity. But how can you know this is true?

"Ananda, you must know that this mental stillness (you achieve) is not genuine. It is like flowing water that looks still at first glance, but is simply flowing too fast for us to perceive the movement. It is not that there is no flow. If this was not the source of delusory cognition, how otherwise could you be influenced by errant habits? If you are not able to (wipe out separateness and) unite the functioning of the six senses so that they operate interchangeably, your delusive cognition will never cease. Thus, behind your seeing, hearing, feeling, and knowing there is a subtle chain of old habits, and within your (apparently) empty (still) consciousness there is still something there that doesn't (openly) appear as existing but does exist. This fifth kind of confusion is 'very subtle thinking.'

"Ananda, the five skandhas develop from these five kinds of delusory thoughts. You also wanted to know the depth and boundaries of the skandhas. They are as follows: form and space are the boundaries of the skandha of form; contact and separation are the boundary of the skandha of sensation; remembering and forgetting are the boundaries of the skandha of conception; production and destruction (birth and death) are the boundaries of the skandha of volition; consciousness returning to unite with its substance are the (two) boundaries of the skandha of consciousness (mental clarity merges with its clear essence, meaning the clear awareness of consciousness enters into and merges with the absolute nature to produce a realm of profound clarity).

"These five skandhas arise by piling themselves upon one another. They originate with (the skandha of) consciousness, but their elimination must begin with the skandha of form. In principle they all vanish with sudden (supreme and complete) enlightenment (the moment one is instantly awakened they are abandoned), but in practice they are overcome gradually, one by one in sequential order.

"I have already shown you how to untie the six knots in a cloth. What is it that you do not understand that causes you to ask about it again? You should gain a thorough understanding of the origin of delusive cognition and issue a warning to practitioners (cultivators) in the Dharma ending age ahead so that they may come to understand their falsehood and learn to detest its arising, and so that they learn of *nirvana* and not become enamored of the three worlds of Desire, Form, and Formlessness.

"Ananda, suppose someone were to fill all of space in the ten directions with the seven treasures and then offer them to Buddhas as innumerable as particles of dust, and serve them devotedly with a faultless mind, what would you say of him? What would be the meritorious rewards of serving the Buddhas in this way?"

Ananda replied: "Space is limitless and the treasures that would fill it would be uncountable. Once in the past, a man offered only seven coins to seven Buddhas, and for this he was rewarded with rebirth as a heavenly king; how much more so would be the unlimited rewards derived from serving the Buddhas and offering unimaginable treasures that fill all space and the Buddha-lands."

The Buddha answered Ananda saying: "The words of the Buddhas and Tathagatas are without falseness (deceit). If there was another man, who though guilty of committing the four sins and ten offenses, and after falling into the eternal hells of suffering, can open (explain) this dharma-door for just the space of an instant in the Dharma ending age for the benefit of those who have not yet studied it, this man's sins would be eradicated and his hells of suffering would become like the peace and joy of heaven. The blessings he would obtain would surpass those of the other person who faithfully served the Buddhas, and could not even be reckoned as a hundredfold, thousandfold, or ten-thousandfold more than the former's. Indeed, his merit would surpass the other's by so many times that no calculations or analogies could express it.

"Ananda, those who read this sutra, uphold these vows, and practice my teachings will gain such merit that this whole kalpa will pass before his merits can be enumerated in full. If you rely on my teachings and practice accordingly, you will realize *bodhi* and not be disturbed by the maras."

After the Buddha had expounded this sutra, all the monks, nuns, male and female devotees, together with all the devas, men, bodhisattvas, *sravakas*, *pratyeka-buddhas*, *rsis*, and newly initiated ghosts and spirits were all filled with great joy, paid reverence to the Buddha, and withdrew.

ABOUT THE AUTHOR

William Bodri is a popular author of many spiritual cultivation books including:

- *Nyasa Yoga*
- *Visualization Power*
- *Move Forward: Powerful Strategies for Creating Better Outcomes in Life*
- *Look Younger, Live Longer*
- *The Little Book of Meditation*
- *The Little Book of Hercules*
- *Easy Meditation Lessons*
- *Internal Martial Arts Nei-gong*
- *What is Enlightenment?*

If you enjoyed this book you would probably enjoy his *Nyasa Yoga*, *The Little Book of Hercules* (which contains similar materials), *The Little Book of Meditation*, *Visualization Power*, *What is Enlightenment?* and *Move Forward*, all of which contain similar materials.

Nyasa Yoga is particularly recommended as this one book alone is enough to introduce all of the most powerful yoga and meditation methods required to attain enlightenment.

Made in the USA
Middletown, DE
11 September 2019